Feijoa

KATE EVANS

Feijoa

A story of obsession & belonging

MOA
PRESS

Published in New Zealand and Australia in 2024
by Moa Press
(an imprint of Hachette Aotearoa New Zealand Limited)
Level 2, 23 O'Connell Street, Auckland, New Zealand
www.moapress.co.nz
www.hachette.co.nz

Copyright © Kate Evans 2024

The moral right of Kate Evans to be identified as the author of this work has been asserted in accordance with the *Copyright, Designs and Patents Act 1988.*

All rights reserved. No part of this publication may be reproduced, stored in a retrieval system, or transmitted in any form or by any means, electronic, mechanical, photocopying, recording, or otherwise, without the prior permission of both the copyright owner and the above publisher of this book.

A catalogue record for this book is available from the National Library of New Zealand.

ISBN: 978 1 8697 1801 5 (paperback)

Written with the assistance of Creative New Zealand

Cover design by Megan van Staden
Cover images © André, Revue Horticole 1898 illustration and POM00007435
Typeset by Megan van Staden
Line art by Ruby Watson (rubywatson.com)
Author photo by Omar Quintero
Printed and bound in Australia by McPherson's Printing Group

The paper this book is printed on is certified against the Forest Stewardship Council® Standards. McPherson's Printing Group holds FSC® chain of custody certification SA-COC-005379. FSC® promotes environmentally responsible, socially beneficial and economically viable management of the world's forests.

*For the feijoa-lovers,
from 4000 years ago to today*

Contents

PROLOGUE   1
INTRODUCTION: *A Cultivated Obsession*   3

ORIGINS
Brazil
Chapter 1: In its Natural Habitat   14
Chapter 2: The First Feijoa Eaters   26
Chapter 3: At Least We Still Have the Feijoa   42
Chapter 4: The Primeval Feijoa Forest   51
Recipe: Elizabete's Feijoa Compote   59

NAMING
Germany & Uruguay
Chapter 5: The Plant Hunter   62
Chapter 6: The Specimen   77
Chapter 7: The Lost People   87
Chapter 8: The Reclamation   98
Chapter 9: What's in a Name?   107
Recipe: Laura's Feijoa Mousse   113

COLLECTING
France & Italy
Chapter 10: A New Fruiting Tree   116
Chapter 11: The Hunt for Villa Colombia   130
Chapter 12: Finding the Oldest Feijoa   141
*Recipe: Mirazur's Fish and Feijoa Tartare in
   Feijoa Kefir Vinaigrette*   151

TAMING
California

Chapter 13: The Fruit of the Century 154
Chapter 14: It's All About the Cultivar 167
Recipe: Phil's Great-grandmother's American-style Feijoa Pancakes . . . 179

CELEBRATING
Colombia

Chapter 15: The Tropical Feijoa 182
Chapter 16: The Festival of the Feijoa 195
Recipe: Jaiver's Feijoa Envueltos 213

CLAIMING
New Zealand

Chapter 17: This Remote Archipelago 216
Chapter 18: The People's Fruit 227
Chapter 19: The Feijoa of the Future 247
Chapter 20: The Taste of Home 264
Recipe: Joe's Wild Mushroom and Feijoa, Manawa Tāwari
    Honey and Foraged Greens Venison Pōneke in Pastry . . . 278

EPILOGUE: *Homecoming* 280

ENDNOTES 287
ACKNOWLEDGEMENTS 308

Prologue

Let me introduce you to this plant that has become my obsession, this fruit that feels like home for me. Here is the one in our garden: a straggling thing, just a few years old. When I am old, it will be a good-sized tree with a gnarled trunk wider than my waist, but for now, it is a compact bush the height of my head. In winter, it is unremarkable. Grey-brown branches. Shiny, dark green leaves flash silver underneath in the low sunlight. A pīwakawaka, the curious native fantail, pauses on a twig. She flicks her splayed tail-feathers side to side and darts away.

In early spring, the tree puts forth fresh leaves, paler green, as soft and faintly furry as my littlest girl's cheek. Not long after I hear the welcome cry of the pīpīwharauroa, or shining cuckoo, returning to these shores from its winter sojourn in the tropics, our tree bursts into flower. A bright spray of crimson stamens, each daubed with a dot of yellow pollen. Six cup-shaped petals, sugar-white on the outside, blush deepening to full-blown embarrassment on the inside. Scattered over the bush in profusion, the overall effect is of a star-spangled sky, or a Christmas tree covered in lights - just in time for the midsummer festivities here in the south of the world. Better still, these flowers are edible. Each white petal is fleshy, juicy and sweet, the flavour a gentle promise of the tangy fruit to come.

All through the summer the fruit ripen, beginning as tiny velvety orbs at the base of each flower and swelling into bright green ovals. Finally, just at the moment when summer slides into autumn – when the bar-tailed godwits leave the New Zealand mudflats and fly to Alaska via their refuelling grounds in North Korea, when the setting sun tracks back towards the Whāingaroa harbour mouth, and the dropping humidity sharpens the silhouette of Karioi, my local bush-clad volcano – the fruit begin to fall. Overnight, one or two stems gently release their hold on the branches. The first fruits thud to the ground. In the morning, they are waiting for me in the damp grass. I pick one up, cut it in half crossways with a knife, ready my spoon.

This tree has many names, including pineapple guava, kanakreĩn and guayabo del país, but I have always known it as feijoa: a strange-sounding word which we New Zealanders pronounce something like FEE-jo-ah.

INTRODUCTION:
A Cultivated Obsession

The scent comes first, when you sink your knife – or your teeth – into a feijoa's skin. It is zingy, heady, a burst of bright perfumed flavour unlike any other. In New Zealand, the traditional method is to scoop out the creamy-clear insides with a teaspoon and discard the skins, though in other parts of the world people simply eat them whole. In the centre, the flesh is translucent and jelly-like where the tiny seeds hang in spiralled suspension. Closer to the skin, it is opaque and slightly gritty. Some have compared the taste to a mixture of pineapples and strawberries, but really, the flavour is something all its own. In the United States, where feijoas are called pineapple guavas, a 1912 newspaper article declared, 'he who drinks beer, thinks beer. But he who eats pineapple guava thinks of pineapple, raspberries, and banana, all at once.'[1]

My love affair with feijoas began with the walk home from school on shortening April afternoons, the light as crisp as a Granny Smith apple. My sisters and I would cast off our schoolbags and sit under the feijoa tree on our rural gravel driveway, armed with a spoon and a knife – or sometimes just our teeth. We were only allowed one chocolate egg at Easter, but we could eat as many of these sweet green orbs as we wanted.

My Australian-born mother couldn't stand the taste, but she

would happily gather buckets of them for the rest of us when she went up to the orchard to feed the chickens. The plum, apple, lemon and guava trees were enclosed from the wind – and the cows – in a protective hedge of seedling feijoas. They produced fruit that was very variable in size, shape and quality, and most we just let rot into the grass. If you stood on one by accident, the liquified insides squirted out between your bare toes (we were always barefoot). Some New Zealanders, I was later told, call feijoas 'lawnmower fruit', because as kids mowing lawns for pocket money they would be instructed to simply run over the fallen feijoas, puréeing hundreds into a sticky, pungent mess.

At our place at Leigh, on the still-rural border of Auckland and Northland, the best fruit came from Dad's specimen tree on the driveway. By the time Monica and I were teenagers, and Tessa at primary school, it produced enough large, delicious feijoas to last most of the season. Usually, we could keep up with that tree just by eating them fresh, and my father and I shared a particular love of feijoas on our muesli. He experimented with making feijoa ice cream (delicious), and later, feijoa wine (not so much).

Feijoas reeled me in as a child, and I think they did it on purpose. The plant's whole strategy – honed over millions of years of evolution – is to attract animals to their juicy, tasty fruit, in the hope we will spread their seeds far and wide. Humans might think that in domesticating plants we have turned them to our own ends, but as Michael Pollan writes in *The Botany of Desire*, the reverse is also true: 'it makes just as much sense to think of agriculture as something the grasses did to people as a way to conquer the trees'.[2] By appealing to our desires, certain plants have inspired us to plant them, protect them, transport them across oceans, and even write books about them.

Feijoas haven't done this quite so triumphantly as the apple, potato, tulip and cannabis plants that Pollan profiles. But they have still been astoundingly successful: of the world's roughly

30,000 edible plant species, only around 150 are now cultivated for human consumption. Most of those were domesticated hundreds or thousands of years ago. Feijoas are one of the very few plants that have made this journey from the wild to the orchard in the last few generations – meaning they provide an unusual opportunity to watch, up close, how plants worm their way into our collective hearts.

From its homelands in Uruguay, southern Brazil, and a skerrick of Argentina, the feijoa induced humans to help it conquer the world – or a few far-flung, particular parts of it, anyway. First, the south of France, where feijoas were cultivated among date palms, eucalypts and New Zealand pōhutukawa in the exotic Riviera gardens of the European aristocracy. From there, we obligingly carried them to subtropical gardens in both hemispheres, from Azerbaijan to Egypt, Japan to Australia. Today, if you look, you can find feijoas growing on the Gaza Strip and at Disney World in Florida. You can order a feijoa cocktail in Tbilisi, the capital of Georgia. In just a few places, they took hold, entered into the hearts of the people, and became entwined with culture and cuisine, memory and celebration.

One of those places was my birthplace, New Zealand. Feijoa season here – extending roughly from March to the beginning of June – is a time of profligate generosity. Kids sell them for a pittance at roadside stalls. People take bagfuls of feijoas to the office and give them away to co-workers. Others leave laden wheelbarrows parked outside their houses, with handwritten signs reading 'help yourself' propped up among the bounty. Because of this gifting, they are sometimes called 'the people's fruit'. For me, and for many other New Zealanders, feijoas have become a kind of unofficial national emblem, a totemic symbol of home.

Every year, that first glistening mouthful evokes a powerful rush of something like nostalgia. There is no proper term in

English for this flavour-prompted feeling, but two words, one from the feijoa's native land (Brazil) and one from that of my distant Evans ancestors (Wales), come close: the Portuguese 'saudade' and the Welsh 'hiraeth': a bittersweet sort of homesickness, a wistful longing for a faraway land.

My preoccupation with this humble green fruit took me on a decade-long journey across four continents to discover its origins and its story. This book's pollination occurred when I was thirty, newly arrived home in New Zealand with my Australian partner Sam, after twelve years living overseas. It flowered through my thirties, growing up alongside our two little girls and the feijoa trees we planted on the land in Raglan we bought with my sister Monica and her partner Manu.[3] It's now bearing fruit as a published book, just after my fortieth birthday.

I spent my late teens and twenties exploring far from New Zealand. A high-school exchange in Italy; studying journalism, Spanish and history in Sydney, where I met Sam; internships at newspapers in Cambodia and Argentina; becoming a journalist at the ABC in Canberra; travelling alone to Guinea and Mali for a dance camp and a music festival; and moving with Sam to Indonesia where he worked on his PhD while I made videos and wrote articles about deforestation for a tropical forest research organisation. I went hang-gliding in Rio de Janeiro, journeyed on a boat with no toilet for two days up the Congo River, and survived dengue fever in Turkey. I didn't quite check off all the outlandish activities on the list my high-school friends made for me of 'Things to do before you turn 30', though I came pretty close.

But still, I felt the pull of home, especially on those occasions when I managed to find a single, expensive feijoa (I once paid $3 for one at a Canberra market). On my trips back to New Zealand,

I'd begun to feel that the place was moving on without me, and that the umbilical cord anchoring my heart to my homeland was beginning to stretch and slip. I worried that if I didn't return soon, I never would; I would create a life elsewhere, I would change too much. In the national online encyclopedia, Te Ara, I read a quote from New Zealand writer John Mulgan's *Report on Experience* (1947):

> They come from the most beautiful country in the world, but it is a small country and very remote. After a while this isolation oppresses them and they go abroad. They roam the world looking not for adventure but for satisfaction. They run service cars in Iraq, gold-mines in Nevada, or newspapers in Fleet Street. They are a queer, lost, eccentric, pervading people who will seldom admit to the deep desire that is in all of them to go home and live quietly in New Zealand again.[4]

That desire become increasingly insistent as I neared the end of my twenties. When a job came up at TVNZ as a current affairs producer, I applied and got it. Sam and I moved from Java to Auckland at the end of 2013, a couple of weeks before our thirtieth birthdays.

I wasn't sure what re-entry would be like. It was surprisingly seamless, though in some ways I still felt like something of a foreigner. But that first autumn, stuffing myself with unlimited fresh feijoas under a smog-free sky made me feel that I'd made the right decision to come back – that I really was home, if not yet fully rooted. And as I thought more about my favourite fruit and the outsized emotional effect it had on me, I had questions. Lots of questions.

Firstly, how did this alchemy happen? Why did this South American fruit become so loved in New Zealand, but not in

France or Australia? What can that tell us about the influence of botany on culture, and vice versa? Whether it's pumpkins in North America, grapes in France, tomatoes in Italy, potatoes in Ireland, oranges in Spain, maize in Central America, or rice in Asia, the plants we use to make food and drink become an integral part of custom and tradition. Often, though, the supposedly local plants we use to give us a kind of national or regional identity end up having deep historical roots that stretch across the globe. Tomatoes and potatoes are originally South American, grapes were domesticated in the South Caucasus (present-day Georgia and Azerbaijan, where feijoas now thrive), oranges originated in the Himalayan foothills – and the feijoa comes from the highlands of southern Brazil, the undulating valleys of Uruguay and a fragment of northern Argentina.

I wanted to know more of its origins than just geography. How did the feijoa evolve, and how did the tree's relationships with the plants and animals of the ecosystem around it shape it into the form it has today? I wondered about the first people to eat one, and what the fruit might have meant to them. I wanted to know what feijoas mean today in their ancestral home, and I visited both Uruguay and Brazil, years apart, to find out.

The more I discovered, the more questions I had. I wanted to learn about Friedrich Sellow, the nineteenth-century German naturalist honoured in the plant's Latin name (*Feijoa sellowiana*), who was responsible for sending the first dried-out feijoa specimens to Europe. I wanted to understand the stories behind the feijoa's various scientific, common and indigenous names, and why the feijoa never made it big in the United States, even though it was predicted to be 'the fruit of the century' there. And from the moment I heard about Colombia's *Festival de la Feijoa* in the tiny Andean town of Tibasosa, I knew that one day I had to go.

'When we try to pick out anything by itself, we find it hitched to everything else in the universe', wrote the North American 'father of conservation' John Muir, who in 1911 travelled in Brazil among the feijoa's ancestral forests – though it's not recorded whether he tasted one.[5] Researching this book, that's exactly what I found. As I tried to pick out the feijoa's story, I realised it was entangled in larger forces and ideas: evolution and exploration, domestication and gift-giving, nostalgia and neuroscience, slavery and colonisation, conflict and reconciliation, knowledge lost and knowledge reclaimed.

In following the feijoa from South America to New Zealand – via German museums, the French Riviera, California's Central Valley and a small town in the Colombian Andes – I discovered a gamut of ways that humans relate to plants, and the different kinds of meaning we derive from them: as food, as medicine, as spoils of empire, as livelihood, as purpose, as resistance, as objects of desire, as symbols of identity. And as a Pākehā New Zealander, with British ancestors who first settled here in the early twentieth century, I began to question what it meant for both me and the feijoa to belong to this place.

These explorations happened in the margins, whenever I could carve out a fragment of space from parenting and my paid writing work, as my thirties unfolded and I began to make a home as an adult in New Zealand. A few years into my research for this book, my sister Monica had a dream that we would raise our kids together. It seemed prophetic, and it was. A month later – thanks to the banks of various mums and dads, a rushed sale and a poorly attended winter auction – we were the joint owners, with our partners, of nearly a hectare of southwest-sloping land in central Raglan, complete with a couple of small houses and a tiny, century-old rimu cabin.[6] A few months after that, we both fell pregnant in the same week.

While Sam and I stayed in Auckland, Monica and Manu moved onto the land and began to care for it. There was a lot to do – weeding, tree-felling, planting natives, making the cabin liveable, turning a vine-choked ditch into lawn. Manu had lots of ideas and the skills to execute them. Monica got excited about alpacas, and soon afterwards a trio of living lawnmowers arrived in the bottom paddock. But after more than a decade of renting, my priority was some feijoas of my own. I went to a North Shore garden centre and bought cultivars: Kaiteri and Unique, Mammoth and Apollo, and one little Kakapo – I loved imagining the round green fruit as a fat green parrot.

The next time we made the trip to Raglan for a working bee, the feijoas came with us, their tips brushing the roof of our old van's boot. Planting these spindly seedlings with my family that weekend felt like a kind of commitment to place, a conjuring of an imagined future when we would live here and eat their fruit year after year. It was a gamble. I wasn't sure if I could really transform myself from the 'anywhere person' I'd been through my twenties to a 'somewhere person' – but the feijoas were a way of sinking literal roots into the land and community where we'd chosen to make our home.[7]

This book is about the feijoa, but it's also about how people create culture, and how we weave certain plants into our sense of who we are. For millennia, plants have been one strand from which humans have constructed their sense of belonging and of place. It's no accident that the root of the word 'culture' is 'cultivation'. The philosopher Edward S. Casey wrote: 'The very word *culture* meant "place tilled" in Middle English, and the same word goes back to [the] Latin *colere*, "to inhabit, care for, till, worship." To be cultural, to have a culture, is to inhabit a place sufficiently intensely to cultivate it – to be responsible for it, to respond to it, to attend to it caringly. Where else but in particular places can culture take root?'[8]

In my travels in search of the feijoa, that intensity of attention is exactly what I found: people with a strong love of plants and of place, whose obsession with this one particular fruit was an expression of their care for the land they walked on and their love for the people around them. Plants change us, even as we change them – and in the feijoa's case, it revealed more to me than I ever could have expected.

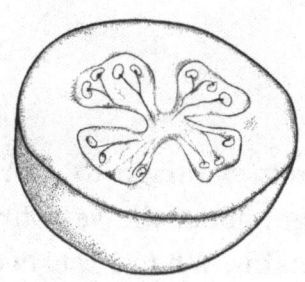

ORIGINS
Brazil

CHAPTER 1

In its Natural Habitat

As the plane from Santiago to Florianópolis crossed the Andes, I thought about the very first time I'd seen those glacier-slung mountains. When I was twenty-three, I'd lived in Argentina, perfecting my Spanish, reporting for an English-language newspaper, and travelling overland through Brazil, Bolivia and Paraguay. One weekend, I took a twenty-four-hour bus ride over the mountains from Buenos Aires to Valparaíso, Chile, to meet Monica for a drumming festival – she was studying at the university there. A picture of us dancing half-naked in the street wearing not much more than body paint had made the front page of a local tabloid. (The headline was '¡De exportación!' – translating, roughly, as 'export quality'.)

Now, it was March 2019, and I was squeezing jets of breastmilk into the cramped airplane toilet sink. Exploring South America alone again was a familiar and exciting prospect, but this time, I felt as though I'd left part of me behind as ballast – Sam, our two little girls, and our home in Raglan, where we'd moved six months earlier. Before leaving, I'd breastfed seventeen-month-old Indigo for what I thought might be the last time. I had never been away from her for more than a night, and expected my milk might dry up during the eight days I would be away.

I often feel torn between two great tidal forces I've come to call 'the hearth' and 'the wild'. The hearth stands for the desire for stability, family, childhood and home – a kind of rootedness in place. The wild is the call to adventure, faraway places, risk-taking, challenge and growth. At certain times I feel the pull of one impulse more than the other; sometimes I'm drawn to both at once. Feijoas, I realised as the plane began its descent, represented both hearth and wild – a deeply local symbol of home, a fruit I liked to eat on the deck after kindy with my kids, and yet a plant whose story stretches across oceans. A story that started right here, in the unfamiliar landscape unfolding beneath me.

We were flying over a vast plateau of forested valleys, farmland, plantations and riverside settlements. Somewhere in those hills were feijoas, growing in their ancestral home. I looked at the bundle of typewritten pages in front of me. In 1988, thirty-one years ago – to the day! – New Zealand botanist Grant Thorp had embarked on his own feijoa mission to southern Brazil. He'd given me the report he'd prepared on his journey for New Zealand's Department of Scientific and Industrial Research (DSIR), which explained that the highlands in this part of South America were formed from a vast ancient lava flow. Its basalt soils were high in aluminium and acidity, and had very low natural fertility.

Feijoas, Grant wrote, appeared to be survivors – persevering and resilient even in the most adverse growing conditions. I looked up. The landscape below suddenly dropped away in a series of sharp escarpments, and I peered out of the tiny plane window with mounting excitement. Up ahead, just beyond the curving coastline, was the island city of Florianópolis – the capital of Santa Catarina, Brazil's second-most-southern state. Its skyscrapers shone in the stormy evening light, and herons prodded the mangrove-edged mudflats as the plane crossed over the narrow ocean channel and approached the airport.

Twenty-four hours later, I'd fully embraced my traveller wild side – finding myself glitter-painted, beer-drenched and dancing enthusiastically in the middle of the road alongside Colombian feijoa researcher Juan Manuel Otálora Villamil and a group of his friends at a Carnaval street party.

My Brazilian contact, plant geneticist Rubens Nodari from the Federal University of Santa Catarina, had sent Juan – one of his doctoral students – to collect me from my accommodation on Sunday morning. Juan was in his early forties, with curly black hair and dark, mischievous eyes. We chatted in Spanish as he drove me around to Professor Nodari's place, a comfortable, spacious house in a quiet neighbourhood, with a feijoa planted in pride of place out the front.

Nodari – no-one except his wife seemed to use his first name – has now been studying the feijoa for thirty years. At the time of my visit, he was in his sixties, clean-shaven, with short grey hair and blue eyes. I soon learned he was a bit of a joker, and a lover of fine food and wine (preferably organic). We had been corresponding by email for a few years about his team's research, and he'd invited me on a road-trip through the feijoa's heartland to show me what they had learned.

But first, in honour of my visit, he organised a lunchtime barbecue and invited half a dozen of his students, who were all researching aspects of the feijoa's history, biology, genetics, evolution, domestication, management techniques and traditional uses. While they explained some of their findings, Nodari wore an apron, cooked six different kinds of meat on a special barbecue built into the wall of his garage, and brandished chicken hearts impaled on a skewer at me until I tried one. (It was chewy and gamey, but quite tasty.)

That evening, Juan offered to take me to a Carnaval party

in the historic neighbourhood of Santo Antônio de Lisboa. Obviously, I said yes. Samba music blared from loudspeakers set up in the square beneath the illuminated eighteenth-century church. Thousands of revellers from all walks of life sang and drank and danced through the streets, dressed as angels, or devils, or footballers, or in drag.

We ran into a group of Juan's friends from work; in addition to his PhD studies in feijoa genetics, he worked at a night-school for adult workers, he told me, teaching a course about the history of the spice trade that's really about the origins of capitalism and the oppression of the working class. 'They basically pay me to politicise the people,' he said, passing me a can of beer.

Someone's teenage daughter striped my cheeks with glitter and put colour in my hair, and soon Juan and I were gleefully jumping up and down with everyone else. When the floats of the samba parade finally reached us around midnight, the frenzy peaked in a whirlwind of shimmying and sequins and out-of-tune singing. The feijoa might have been embraced by New Zealand, but Brazil is where it really comes from.

———

Where *does* the feijoa come from? Asking that seemingly simple question led me down a surprising number of bifurcating pathways. There are many ways of telling the feijoa's origin story. Botanically speaking, however, it begins somewhere near here, in this part of southeastern South America, at the very end of what scientists call the Oligocene Epoch. The deep history of this time is an ever-evolving science, and there are still many uncertainties, but new research is offering glimpses into how, where and when the feijoa might have begun.

The latest genetic analysis suggests that the feijoa diverged from its closest living relatives around 23.7 million years ago, just before the Oligocene gave way to the Miocene, and that this probably happened in southern South America.[9] Those ancestral feijoas flowered in a world that was much warmer than ours; average global temperatures were around three to four degrees Celsius higher than in the twentieth century. The South American continent had detached itself from Antarctica and was gradually drifting northwards, but it was still an island: the isthmus of Central America didn't yet exist. South America's isolation led to the evolution of a wide range of unique species that would have shared the feijoa's early world. There were primitive ground sloths, and many kinds of strange-looking hoofed herbivores with tusks and stumpy trunks. Monkeys had arrived from Africa around 13 million years earlier, having floated across the Atlantic on rafts of storm-tossed vegetation, and were evolving into distinct New World forms. And the apex predators in South American ecosystems at that time were giant 'terror birds'.

All birds are descended from dinosaurs, but with these carnivorous, flightless hunters, the family resemblance was particularly noticeable. Around twenty species of terror bird have been identified from fossils across the continent, and in 1977 the almost-complete skeleton of *Paraphysornis brasiliensis* was unearthed in Brazil's São Paulo state, just north of the feijoa's homeland. *Paraphysornis* weighed up to 180 kilograms, stood 140 centimetres high at the back, and reached 240 centimetres with its head outstretched – not quite as big as the largest of the moa, but much more vicious. The South American bird's massive beak was designed for killing: a sharp, solid meat-cleaver more than half a metre long.[10]

The São Paulo fossil was dated to around 23 million years ago, so it's likely that this terror bird, or one of its relatives, was a part of the ecosystem in which the first feijoas were evolving. I like to picture fur and fruit flying as a munching mammal is snatched from under a feijoa tree by this avian monster. However, my mental picture probably isn't quite accurate: the feijoa may have looked (and tasted) quite different back then, as its current form has been shaped over millions of years by the animals with which it shared the forest.

Researchers from Kew Gardens in London recently mapped out the feijoa's family tree. Its Latin name is *Feijoa sellowiana*, and it is the only species in the genus *Feijoa*.[11] It belongs to the Myrtaceae family of plants, which includes Australian eucalyptus, European myrtles, American allspice and New Zealand pōhutukawa, a spreading coastal tree that coats itself in crimson flowers at Christmastime. Millions of years before there was a feijoa – around 40 million years ago – some of the ancestral plants of the Myrtaceae family came up with a successful new way of spreading their seeds around: juicy, delicious fruit.[12]

Botanically speaking, fruit can be fleshy – what we tend to think of as fruit – or dry, a category which includes legumes, cereal grains and nuts. Fleshy fruit has evolved many times in Earth's history. Though our contemporary fruit bowls tend to hold just a few examples – bananas, oranges, apples – evolution has produced a tremendous variety of fruit colours, shapes, aromas and textures. It can develop on ground-hugging runners (strawberries), on palms (açai), on vines (passionfruit) and on huge forest trees (kahikatea and Brazil nuts). There are stinking durians, hairy rambutans and giant jackfruits that weigh as much as a child. In West Africa, there is even a 'miracle fruit' (*Synsepalum dulcificum*) which makes sour foods eaten afterwards taste sweet.

I wanted to know how the feijoa fruit got the way it is: egg-sized, firm green skin, small seeds, tangy taste, fragrant scent, thrown to the ground when ripe. How did it end up with the particular constellation of traits that make it so unique? I called Omer Nevo, an expert in fruit evolution at the German Centre for Integrative Biodiversity Research. Generally speaking, he told me, fruits have evolved to be attractive to animals because plants need help to spread their seeds around. 'Plants are stuck in their place. If they released all their seeds under the mother tree, they would be in big trouble.' The young plants would all compete with each other – and their mother – for sunlight and water, and they'd be an easy target for predators and pathogens: 'They've found your entire family tree in one spot.' To solve this problem, plants have evolved a wide range of strategies for dispersing their seeds. Some use the wind, others the water, and others wrap their seeds in a delicious, attractive package full of sugars, water, vitamins and fats, and get animals to do the work for them.

It's not necessarily a loving relationship, Omer cautions. 'They're all selfish; the plants want the dispersal, and they want to invest as little as possible – and the animals want to feed on as much pulp as they can.' Since Charles Darwin, scientists have debated whether that tug-of-war has shaped the incredible diversity of fruits we see today, or whether other factors influence fruit evolution, and animals just come along and feed on what they like. But recent studies, including some of Omer's, have shown that there is a link. Not far from the feijoa's native range, in Brazil's Atlantic Forest, researchers showed that palm fruits dramatically decreased in size in just a few decades after the local extinction of the large birds, like toucans, that used to feed on them.[13]

There's also the fact that certain collections of traits tend to be observed together. Fruits that are dispersed by birds tend to be relatively small, as birds don't have hands: they can't pluck large fruits off a tree or rip them open with opposing fingers, as primates can. Bird-preferred fruits tend to have small seeds, too, with a hard coating that makes them more likely to survive long-distance transit inside an avian gut. Birds have good colour vision, and prefer fruits that change to a bright red, purple or pink when ripe and contrast with the leaves around them.

Mammals, on the other hand, have a well-developed sense of smell. Fruits that have evolved for distribution by mammals – particularly primates and bats – tend to be larger, with bigger seeds. Their smell often changes as they ripen, and they are more likely to turn a dull colour like yellow or brown when they mature.

What of the feijoa, then? It's a bit of an odd case: medium-sized, with small, hard-coated seeds. And yet the fruit develops a strong fragrance when ripe, remains green, and the tree drops them on the ground when they are perfectly ready to eat. The animals involved in the dispersal of feijoas in their native environment were unknown until recently. But between 2015 and 2016, some of Nodari's colleagues from the Federal University of Santa Catarina set up camera traps trained on twenty-eight feijoa plants at four sites in Brazil's subtropical highlands.[14]

The cameras recorded twenty different species munching on the feijoa's fruit in the autumn, including both mammals and birds. The fruits were eaten by tayra, a kind of large weasel, and coati, an adorable racoon relative with a fluffy banded tail and a long snout. Also caught on camera were cattle, small rodents, the big-eared opossum and the crab-eating fox.

Birds ate them, too. By far the most common bird disperser was the pūkeko-like *Aramides saracura*, the slaty-breasted wood rail, but feijoas were also enjoyed by a paintbox of bright, beautiful birds: the maroon-bellied parakeet, the rufous-bellied thrush, the dusky-legged guan and the azure jay.

Omer says that, based on the feijoa's characteristics and what he knows about fruit evolution in general, he expects that the feijoa we have today – its size, colour, scent, firmness, nutritional content and habit of falling when ripe – is the result of millions of years of interaction with, mainly, the mammals that ate the fruits. Birds might eat them today, but the feijoa has most likely shaped its fruits to appeal to ground-dwelling mammals, he said. 'Birds are so vision-oriented that it's very rare that they feed on fruits that are green. Green and odorous . . . that sounds like a mammal-dispersed fruit, though there is always some overlap.'

To make fruit at all, a flower must be pollinated, and this dance between plant and pollinator is another important driver of evolution. The particular shape and sweet taste of the feijoa's flowers is the result of an extremely unusual relationship with the animals that carry its bright yellow pollen from one upturned flower to the next.

One day in 1886, a five-year-old boy sat in a garden in Blumenau, Santa Catarina, his eyes pinned to a feijoa bush. His grandfather – the German settler, atheist and naturalist Fritz Müller, who was a regular correspondent of Charles Darwin – had set the boy the scientific task of observing which animals visited the flowers, their 'dazzling white' petals 'rolled together like omelettes, ready for a bite', according to the 1906 book where I found an English translation of Müller's findings. (It also claims the feijoa petals taste like 'orange-sugar'.)[15]

The diligent grandson, Hans Lorenz, apparently sat at his post for several days. Eventually, he called out: 'Come quickly, grandfather! A black bird is eating the flowers!'[16] Müller came, and watched the bird sit on an adjacent branch to devour the petals, brushing against the stigma and covering itself in powdery pollen in the process. Later, Müller saw a similar brown bird doing the same thing. These weren't the European blackbirds that pollinate my feijoas; Müller suspected the birds were the black males and brown females of a species of *Thamnophilus*, a genus of birds commonly called antshrikes.

Even today, 130 years after Müller's grandson's observations, the exact native pollinators of the feijoa are unknown. It seems Müller was probably right: there are recent reports of *Thamnophilus* species eating the petals and brushing off pollen in both Brazil and Uruguay. But in Brazil, various pastel-hued species of tanagers have also been observed with feijoa pollen on their heads, while colourful toucans have been spotted visiting the flowering trees.

In New Zealand, blackbirds, mynas and silvereyes are thought to contribute to pollination. In Florida, mockingbirds and fox squirrels have been observed nibbling on the petals. In Colombia, the main pollinators are thought to be mockingbirds and the blackbird-like great thrush (*Turdus fuscater*) – except in urban areas. In 2022, researchers trained binoculars on twenty-two feijoa trees growing in the city of Duitama, Boyacá – a study technique basically unchanged since Müller's day. Over sixty hours of observation, the vast majority of the animals they recorded visiting the flowers were brown rats. Just like the birds, they were nibbling on the petals, suggesting rats, too, could be acting as pollinators.[17]

The fact that so many different creatures can fulfil this role is one explanation for the feijoa's global success: many other edible plants have much more specific requirements, and can be pollinated by just a handful of species that may not be found outside their home ranges. Brazil nuts, for instance, are pollinated mainly by female euglossine bees, which are big enough to get into the lidded flowers in search of nectar. Male euglossine bees visit orchid flowers instead, to gather fragrant chemicals that make them attractive to females and are crucial to mating success. This means Brazil nuts are generally collected from intact rainforest that supports both bees and orchids; they do not thrive in plantations.[18]

A few studies suggest pollen-seeking bees and other insects may play a role in feijoa pollination, too, though others argue they are too small to actually transfer pollen to the feijoa flower's large spiky stigma when they land.[19] Müller's backyard study was the first-ever observation of flowers being pollinated by fruit-eating – not nectar-sucking – birds. The discovery was newsworthy enough to get a mention in a Melbourne newspaper, *The Australasian*, in 1886: 'that indefatigable naturalist, Professor Fritz Müller, has just published a description of certain flowers which are habitually cross-fertilised by birds. They are the white flowers of a Brazilian tree, allied to your Australian Eugenia, known as Feijoa ... The flowers are seldom visited by bees, and they contain no honey.'[20]

Later studies confirmed that feijoa flowers have no nectar at all.[21] The strategy of using edible petals 'as bait' remains extremely rare among flowering plants, only shared in South America by a handful of the feijoa's close relatives in *Acca* and *Myrrhinium* and one other genus.[22] That suggests the feijoa flowers' particular beauty – their array of scarlet stamens, magenta stigma, and sugary white-and-crimson petals – evolved to attract frugivorous, or fruit-eating, birds.

Feijoas, then, developed relationships with the plants and animals around them, some of which, like the terror birds, have gone extinct over the intervening millions of years. The feijoas provided sweet, nutritional food in both their fruits and flowers, and in turn, fruit-loving animals helped the trees to spread across subtropical South America. The feijoa we see today is the result of this meeting between plant and pollinator, fruit and frugivore, again and again through evolutionary time.

The wild species now occupies two east-west swathes of southeast South America: one through the Brazilian states of Paraná, Santa Catarina and the north of Rio Grande do Sul, and another, genetically distinct, stretching from the south of Rio

Grande do Sul into Uruguay. For years, I had longed to see those feral trees for myself, to visit the feijoa in its native forests – and now, at last, the day had arrived. The morning after the Carnaval party, tired and hungover, I waited outside my Airbnb at 6.30 am for Nodari to pick me up.

CHAPTER 2

The First Feijoa Eaters

When I climbed into the four-wheel drive, Juan was already slumped in the back seat, looking a little less exuberant than he had the night before. Another of Nodari's students, Lido Borsuk, was in the front passenger seat. I'd met Lido at the barbecue – a slender, quiet Brazilian of Polish descent, the same age as Juan, with whom he immediately began a friendly piss-taking banter that would last for the entire trip. They had known each other for decades, and played soccer together in a casual, hyper-diverse team alongside refugees and immigrants from Africa, the Caribbean and the Middle East (my geeky globalist soul loved that they named the team 'Pangaea', after the all-encompassing supercontinent that broke up 135 million years ago). I spoke to Juan in Spanish, and to Nodari mostly in English, while Lido's Portuguese was so rapid that I often needed translation help from the other two.

As the morning brightened, Nodari drove us across the long, traffic-ridden bridge that connects Florianópolis to the mainland. Soon, the road began climbing from the sweaty coast onto the escarpment, nearly 1000 metres up. The temperature dropped, and dramatic cliffs sliced into lush, steep valleys. Then the first araucarias appeared.

Araucaria angustifolia is a tall, spiky, mushroom-shaped

conifer. It is the keystone species and totemic lynchpin of an entire ecosystem that once carpeted southern Brazil, hugging this high plateau that slopes from the Atlantic Ocean towards Paraguay, nearly a thousand kilometres to the west. Brazilians often talk about saudade – a beautiful sadness, a melancholic yearning for someone or something that is loved but absent. It approaches the feeling I often get when I eat a feijoa. But I also felt a kind of saudade as we drove across the plateau, past rows of Gala apples and grapevines, fields of cattle and glyphosate-drenched transgenic soy. There were pockets of the unmistakable araucaria, with fragments of morning mist wrapped around their sparse, horizontal branches. But they were just a shadow of what once was.[23]

At Nodari's house, I'd talked to his wife, Eunice, a professor of environmental history at the same university, who has specialised in the araucaria's tragic story. *Araucaria angustifolia* is one of two *Araucaria* species in South America, she told me. The other, *Araucaria araucana*, known as the 'monkey puzzle tree', is native to Chile. They belong to an ancient family, the Araucariaceae, which includes the Norfolk pine and New Zealand's kauri and has existed for more than 200 million years.[24] Brazil's araucarias have remained basically unchanged since the time of the dinosaurs – and in fact, some evidence suggests the energy-rich, slow-fermenting leaves were a key food source for sauropods. These giant, brontosaurus-type herbivores, measuring up to 40 metres long and weighing 70 tonnes, would have been able to graze on the tops of the 40-metre-high araucaria like a rabbit nibbling on broccoli.[25]

The trees' spherical cones are up to 25 centimetres across, with around a hundred large and tasty pinhão, or pine nuts, packaged inside. In April and May, the cones ripen and fall, distributing the starchy seeds – an event eagerly awaited by a variety of birds and mammals. Indigenous peoples prized the nuts for food, and used araucaria wood in funerals and other rituals.

For centuries, araucarias have beguiled travellers, too. John Muir, the American conservationist famous for advocating for the establishment of Yosemite, visited this part of Brazil in 1911. He was seventy-three, and for half a century he had dreamed of seeing the araucarias of South America in the flesh. 'Rainy morning,' he wrote in his diary. 'Araucarias in hundreds and thousands. Wondrous sight.' This was the man who had campaigned to protect North America's giant redwood forests – and yet Brazil's araucarias, he wrote, were the most interesting forests he had seen in his life.[26]

Brazil's forests are legendary. The Amazon, the Atlantic Forest and the Cerrado are all among the most important biodiversity hotspots in the world. More than 55,000 plant species have been identified in the country, making up fully 22 per cent of the world's flora. The araucaria forests form the southern part of the endangered Atlantic Forest, and until relatively recently they stretched 200,000 square kilometres across Brazil's three southern states – Rio Grande do Sul, Santa Catarina and Paraná – as well as Argentina's Misiones province.[27]

Botanists call the ecosystem 'mixed Ombrophilous forest', as it is made up of a wide range of leafy flowering species that grow beneath the araucaria canopy. They include the feijoa, dozens of its relatives in the Myrtaceae family, other fruits and palms, and the shrub *Ilex paraguariensis*, or yerba mate, the leaves of which are used across southern Brazil, Uruguay, Paraguay and Argentina to make the ubiquitous hot or cold drink known as mate (Spanish) or chimarrão (Portuguese).

But even as Muir visited in the early twentieth century, those wondrous forests – the feijoa's original home – were being decimated. In less than a century, Eunice told me, from the late 1800s to the mid-1900s, between 95 and 98 per cent of the araucaria forest was toppled, both for timber and to clear land for farming and pine plantations. By the 1970s, araucarias were protected. Now, it's illegal to fell a single tree, or even cut up a fallen one for firewood. But the forests still teeter on the edge of extinction. New research suggests that climate change may hasten their decline, with models predicting the total disappearance of the araucarias' most suitable habitat by 2070.[28]

The sun climbed overhead as we continued across the plateau. Nodari stopped the car in São José do Cerrito, a tiny town with one main street and a lot of religious competition. There was an Assembly of God, a Kingdom Hall of Jehovah's Witnesses, and signs everywhere advertising upcoming 'missions': visits by travelling Catholic priests. After lunch, Lido and Nodari went into one of the shops to ask for permission from a landowner to visit a nearby archaeological site, a place where Lido had done some research a few years ago. It was siesta hour. The street was hot and silent. Juan and I sat on a bench to wait. Visiting was a bit sensitive, Juan said, because some members of the owner's family feared that any interest in the site's human past could kick off a land claim. But Nodari and Lido kept the conversation focused on feijoas, and emerged with a thumbs up.

Back in Nodari's four-wheel drive, Juan poured hot water into a mate gourd, soaking the dried leaves inside: top-quality organic chimarrão, certified by the Forest Stewardship Council (FSC) and pesticide-free. The tradition originated with the Guaraní and Tupí peoples of Paraguay, but many contemporary South Americans now consume the caffeinated drink throughout the day instead of coffee or tea. It's a powerful cultural symbol and social bonding ritual; typically, a group of friends, colleagues or neighbours share the same gourd, passing it hand to hand and mouth to mouth.[29]

Juan, Lido and I took turns sucking the hot, bitter liquid

through the steel straw, while Nodari turned onto a potholed gravel road. He pulled up at a small, remote community with a handful of houses and a church. Across the road were four stately araucarias with white words spray-painted onto their knobbly trunks. Translated from Portuguese, they read 'Faith', 'Missions', 'Peace' and 'Love'. One of the landowners, a shy cowboy in a straw hat, led us to the site on horseback, his three or four mutt dogs running behind. We crossed a small stream and followed a rough track uphill, araucarias looming on either side. At the top of the hill, the path levelled off and opened out into a wide meadow where cattle were grazing, and there they were: what I'd come thousands of kilometres to see.

Feijoas, in their natural habitat: old, gnarled trees, draped in moss and lichen, their bright leaves catching the afternoon sun. They were just beginning to fruit, and here and there the grey-green globes hung among the branches. Everywhere I looked, I saw more: some growing directly underneath an araucaria, others forming curiously straight lines, almost as though they had been planted in a row. Well, maybe they were: right there, in that glade, was some of the earliest evidence of a relationship between people and feijoas. The dogs followed the landowner and his horse back down the path, and when they were gone, Lido led the way to an area of denser forest on the edge of the meadow. 'There's something else I want to show you,' he said, and started to talk more freely about the real reason he had brought me here.

Among the trees were a series of large pits, several metres deep and 4 or 5 metres across – the remnants of underground houses, Lido said. They had been made many hundreds of years ago by the pre-Columbian people archaeologists call the Southern Proto-Jê: Southern, to distinguish them from related groups speaking similar languages in the north of Brazil, and Proto to show the culture differed from that of their surviving modern descendants, the Kaingang and the Xokleng. (The Southern Proto-Jê surely had a much lovelier name for themselves, but it – along with so much else – has been lost to history.)

At 1000 metres above sea level, winter nights here are cold, so the people dug their dwellings into the earth for protection and warmth. Back then, these pits would have been covered by a low, conical, wooden roof, and there would have been a cosy fire inside. Archaeologists found the remains of 107 houses here and have used the charcoal unearthed in the pits to radiocarbon-date the site. The earliest record of habitation is the sixth century AD, but it is not yet clear whether the site was permanently occupied, or if it was a seasonal camp the Southern Proto-Jê returned to again and again, in the season of abundance: the autumn, when the araucaria nuts were ripe, the feijoas were falling and the forests were full of game.

When they arrived in the southern highlands around 4000 years ago, the ancestors of the Southern Proto-Jê had carried the seeds or tubers of manioc, sweet potato, squash, beans, yams, peanuts and five varieties of maize in their pockets (or their luggage). They cultivated those crops, fished and hunted, collected honey and local fruits, and – most importantly – harvested protein-rich pine nuts from the araucaria trees. The new arrivals wove the forest into their culture, involving araucaria wood and pine nuts in ritual practices. But they also cut down some trees for timber, and gathered firewood. They made a particular kind of thin-walled pottery, and inscribed geometric shapes, people, animals and mask-wearing human faces on rock walls. The Southern Proto-Jê also built enormous ceremonial mounds and enclosures – flat-topped platforms involving considerable earthworks – where they feasted, initiated their young men, held funerals and cremated the dead on funeral pyres stoked with araucaria wood.[30]

Archaeological and anthropological evidence also suggests that their culture – like almost all of the Jê societies in Brazil – was rooted in a dualistic understanding of nature and of people. Their modern descendants, the Kaingang, told anthropologists that the world began when two brothers emerged from a mountain after a cataclysmic flood. The pair began creating plants and animals, Kamé working during the day, Kairu at night. Everything in the cosmos thus traces its lineage back to one of the two brothers: Kamé is associated with the sun, the day, the west, permanence and stripes, while Kairu represents the moon, the night, the east, transformation and circles. It was a complementary but asymmetric relationship. Kamé is seen as the stronger, dominant brother, while Kairu is perceived as weaker and less tenacious: when Kamé created the powerful jaguar, Kairu responded with the bumbling anteater. For the Kaingang, all plants and animals are divided into categories representing one brother or the other, and humans are, too: people are born into one of two clans anthropologists call 'moieties' and can only marry someone from the opposite group. Plants with thin or spiky leaves – like the araucaria and jacaranda – were Kamé, while those with rounded leaves – like the feijoa – tended to be Kairu.[31]

The use of plants reinforced those identities: in certain festivals, community members belonging to the Kamé moiety would use charcoal from burned araucaria chips to paint their bodies with black stripes and open shapes, while Kairu members would draw red circles and closed shapes with a pigment derived from the roots and rounded leaves of the Kairu plant sete sangrias (*Symplocos uniflora*), a medicinal shrub with citrus-like white flowers.[32]

Archaeologists think it's likely the Southern Proto-Jê shared this world view. When they excavated earth ovens in ceremonial funerary mounds and analysed the charcoal fragments, they found the Southern Proto-Jê preferentially used certain plant species – fragrant jacaranda trees in some sites, araucaria in others – as fuel wood for rituals and feasts, implying those plants were especially meaningful.[33]

Lido called me over to one of the pits. Surrounding it were fruiting trees, native to this area. 'These trees could be 200 years old,' he said. He pointed out the guabiroba, a feijoa-cousin with small, orange, guava-like fruit. The araticum has large yellow fruit covered in dragon-like scales, while the bizarre jaboticaba doesn't hold its fruit at the tips of its branches like other trees, but instead wears it as an all-over suit, the glossy black globules protruding directly from the trunk.[34]

Sadly, it wasn't the right season to taste any of these. But then Lido and Juan took turns giving a tall, smooth-barked tree a shake, and dozens of soft, bright yellow fruits came bouncing to the ground. 'Uvaia,' Lido said, handing me one to try. It exploded in my mouth, juicy and tart and delicious. Spitting out the big seeds – uvaias are dispersed by mammals – I asked Lido if he thinks these species were planted deliberately by the ancient people who lived here. 'Com certeza,' he said. Definitely. 'It's a kind of orchard,' added Nodari. 'They would eat the araucaria seeds for the carbohydrates and then the sweet fruits for dessert.'

So, can we confidently say the Southern Proto-Jê ate feijoas? The evidence is circumstantial. The huge number of feijoa trees in the meadow is very unusual, Nodari told me. 'You would not find this in the wild.' As part of his research, Lido analysed the genetic diversity of the plants here, compared with those in contemporary traditional communities and national parks. The feijoas here were highly diverse, which Lido thinks implies people brought seeds back from far and wide: either to deliberately plant, or because they were eating fruit from a favourite faraway tree, then returning home and depositing the remnants in whatever they used for a toilet. Either way, the old idea of Brazil's first peoples as hunter-gatherers with minimal impact on their environment is rapidly being overturned by a wealth of new evidence showing the extent to which Amerindians managed their forests – and that has implications for the feijoa's early contact with its first human fans.

Further north, in the Amazon, it's been shown that the forest's first inhabitants significantly changed its composition over thousands of years. Across the vast basin, economic or edible plant species are much more abundant around archaeological sites. The archaeological and botanical evidence strongly suggests Amazonian peoples farmed the forest without felling much of it, planting their crops under the canopy while enriching it with edible natives.[35] And it seems that the araucaria forests, too, were dramatically shaped by humans, long before Europeans arrived and cut them down. Mark Robinson, an archaeologist at the University of Exeter in the UK, has spent fifteen years getting South American mud in his hair while trying to find out more about the continent's first peoples, including the Southern Proto-Jê.

One day, Mark was digitally scrolling around the highlands area on Google Earth (a common pastime for archaeologists, apparently) when he noticed that in the more remote areas without much of a human presence, there was a distinct pattern to the araucaria forests: they only seemed to be found on the southern slopes of the hills. 'It was one of those eureka moments,' he told me over a video call. Pollen samples taken from a bog had already shown that, around 1000 AD, the araucaria forests had begun to spread dramatically, taking over the grasslands across the plateau. Layers laid down in a speleothem – a stalagmite –

from a cave in the region showed that the climate had gotten wetter around the same time.

Previously, it was assumed that was the reason for the forests' expansion. But the archaeological record also showed an intense cultural flowering at around the same time: developments in architecture and spiritual practices, population increase, and more sites over a wider area. It was the kind of chicken-and-egg question that's faced frequently in archaeology. Did the human presence intensify because the growing forest gave them more opportunities and resources, or did an expanding population take their prized forest with them?

Mark's eureka moment gave the Exeter team an opportunity to answer this question. In Santa Catarina, just a few hours' drive from the area I visited with Nodari, they dug holes near archaeological sites and in places with little human impact, on both south- and north-facing slopes. Conveniently, grasslands and forests store a different carbon isotope in the soil as they decompose. That meant the archaeologists could date each soil sample, then use isotopic analysis to find out what was growing there at a particular point in time.

The results were evocative: in spite of climate fluctuations, in the 'wild' areas, forests remained consistently limited to the south-facing slopes, where they would receive less direct sunlight and retain more moisture. But around 1000 AD, in areas with a human presence, forests replaced grasslands. In just a few generations, the araucaria spread from the southern slopes to cover the majority of the plateau – and presumably, the feijoa went with them. When he talked about this, Mark was careful. Araucaria are listed as 'Critically Endangered' on the International Union for Conservation of Nature's Red List of Threatened Species, but the forests are unpopular with local farmers who would prefer to use the land for grazing. 'We don't want to give people an excuse to just cut the whole thing down.' And yet the data is conclusive, he said: 'The modern distribution of araucaria is human-driven.'[36]

People created this landscape. How they did so isn't yet clear. 'Are they going out and planting; are they watering it every day? Maybe not,' Mark said. He thinks it's more likely that as the Southern Proto-Jê managed the landscape – burning, clearing, and planting crops – they changed the soils, potentially in ways that benefitted the araucaria. Alternatively, or perhaps as well, they cut down other trees while leaving the culturally and culinarily important araucaria standing. 'It's still a choice,' Mark said. 'You have to choose to let those trees grow.'

What does it all mean for feijoas? There's no direct archaeological evidence, yet, that the Southern Proto-Jê were eating or planting them, Mark said. 'But we know they were actively managing plants on the landscape. They were introducing other edible species, maize and manioc, and we know they were actively engaged on their landscape to increase their food security.'

There is one more tantalising hint that suggests feijoas might have been valued by the Southern Proto-Jê. As we walked among the pit houses, Nodari told me he was recently invited by a team of Brazilian archaeologists to a site they were excavating – an altar mound not far from here. They had unearthed a funerary urn around 800 years old. It contained charred human remains, araucaria nuts, and some tiny, rounded seeds. Nodari examined them, but because they had been burned, he couldn't be sure if they came from a feijoa or one of the other Myrtaceae relatives that have similar-sized seeds. 'The fact that there were araucaria seeds in the urn suggests the burial took place during the pinhão season, which overlaps with when the feijoa is fruiting, so ... it is possible.'

It's all rather shadowy and suggestive. But people lived in this very place, right where I was standing, for more than a thousand years, until European colonists drove them away from their lands. I found it hard to believe that, over dozens of generations, there weren't some individuals, at least, who devoured feijoas with as much gusto as I do – and changed them in the process. 'If you're in the forest and you see a small fruit and a big fruit, which one do you choose to eat?' Lido asked me, waving at the feijoa trees in the meadow. 'That's surely what they did. They carried the bigger fruit back to their house, and they did this for thousands of years. It's very improbable that they didn't manage these trees in some way.' The same process that made the apple larger and sweeter over generations – human selection – means we might have the Southern Proto-Jê to thank for some of the feijoa's deliciousness.

Standing in this beautiful, human forest, with the light shafting in, I felt a rush of emotion. It was easy to imagine that these people had a feijoa connection, one much stronger and deeper than mine: the first feijoa connection, forged over millennia. I pictured an autumn morning a thousand years ago, in this very spot. Someone walked out of their underground house, just over there, and walked among the trees, stretching. They slurped a fresh uvaia, then helped themselves to a fallen feijoa.

The vision made me wonder when the first human met the first feijoa. There's good evidence people had made it all the way to the tip of Chile by 16,000 years ago, so someone might have wandered past and plucked one way back then. But 4000 years ago – before the fall of Troy, before the Roman Empire, long before New Zealand was settled by Māori – there's a surge of charcoal in the archaeological record in southern Brazil. According to Mark Robinson, that's the first strong signal that the Southern Proto-Jê people had settled here, burning and shaping the land, gardening the forest, sowing their crops, and beginning to form a relationship with the unique plants and animals of this environment. These people are remote from me in almost every way. We're separated by centuries, geography, language, culture. And yet we share this specific, earthy pleasure – foraging on an autumn morning beneath a feijoa tree for the fruits that have fallen in the night.

As Nodari, Lido, Juan and I made our way back down the hill in the late afternoon, there was a rustling in the leaves, and a russet-brown shape glowed in the evening light. 'It's a veado,' Juan said, a kind of native deer – sought-after game for the Southern Proto-Jê, and for modern hunters, too. 'We're really lucky to see one.' Now, like their araucaria forest home, they are increasingly rare. Elegant and nimble, the veado threaded its way up the slope, between the araucarias and the feijoa trees, and disappeared.

———

I couldn't stop thinking about that first feijoa culture. What happened to the Southern Proto-Jê? In pre-colonial times, their descendants, the Kaingang and the Xokleng, each relied on the araucaria pine nuts as a mainstay of their diet – but the arrival of Europeans inevitably altered their way of life.

Brazil's brutal colonisation began when the Portuguese explorer Pedro Álvares Cabral came ashore in present-day Bahia in 1500. One of the first things his sailors did was cut down a tree. They shaped the trunk into a crucifix and held a Catholic Mass beneath it, and claimed the whole vast territory for their country's far-flung global empire, one of the largest and longest-lived in world history. For the next few decades, preoccupied by their Asian possessions in India, the East Indies and Macau, the Portuguese didn't pay too much attention to developing their South American colony, apart from fighting off rival European colonisers and harvesting 'brazilwood' – the plant that gave the country its name. *Paubrasilia echinata*, a yellow-flowering tree endemic to the Atlantic Forest, was prized for its red sap (used in dyes) and its scarlet heartwood (still considered the only proper wood for high-quality violin bows).[37]

In the eighteenth century, Portuguese roads began to penetrate into Brazil's southern highlands, scoring conflict through the Kaingang's traditional territories. As troops, workers, cattle drovers and colonists began to course along these arteries, their camps were repeatedly sacked by Kaingang warriors. During the second half of the 1700s, the Kaingang fought off numerous colonial expeditions that were attempting to open up parts of the region for European settlement, and occasionally attacked farmers and their African slaves.

At the end of 1807, Napoleon's army invaded Lisbon, and the entire Portuguese royal family and court – around 15,000 people – fled to Rio de Janeiro. It was the first time a European monarch had set foot on American soil. The whole of the Portuguese Empire, including Portugal itself, would be ruled from Brazil for the next thirteen years. In charge was the Prince Regent Dom João VI, who was ruling on behalf of his mother, nicknamed 'Maria the Mad' on account of her advanced dementia. On arrival in 1808, he took an interest in the colonisation project in the south of the country. It wasn't proceeding as quickly as he had hoped, perhaps because it was 'infested with Indians ... who cruelly kill the farmers and landowners', as he wrote in a royal decree in November that year. The decree ordered colonists to 'suspend the effects of humanity' when dealing with the Indigenous peoples, and instructed: 'That from the moment you receive this, you should consider that the war against these Indian barbarians has begun.' He called it a 'just war', but it was essentially genocide, authorised by the prince.[38]

Thus emboldened, a new expedition entered Kaingang territory in 1809. After three months of bloody battles, this time the colonists prevailed. Over the following century, to free up the land for settlers, groups of the Kaingang and the neighbouring

Xokleng were moved into reserves too small to allow them to live their traditional way of life. They were forced into agricultural labour in exchange for clothing and one meal a day. At the same time, the so-called 'indigenous protection service' installed sawmills to topple the araucaria forests across the highlands. In one reserve, 60,000 araucaria trees were felled.[39] Presumably, the ancient feijoas growing underneath were lost too, crushed into the slash.

As Nodari drove us to the nearby town of Campos Novos to spend the night, Lido explained that despite all of the dislocation and discrimination, the original peoples of the southern highlands do maintain traditions of feijoa use. For his research, Lido visited dozens of Kaingang and Xokleng communities across the three southern states, interviewing more than 200 people about their traditional knowledge of the feijoa – a plant they call kanekreĩn.

In the Kaingang reserves, the fruits were extremely popular, especially among children. 'We leave the fruits for our grandchildren, so they can eat them and know them,' one elder told Lido. In another community in Rio Grande do Sul, children said they seek out the white flower petals in the spring, because 'they are sweet and good to eat'. In several villages, Lido wasn't able to find a single fruit to take for his analysis, because every last one had been eaten by local children before it even had a chance to fall.

The feijoa is also used in traditional medicine. Some communities mixed ground feijoa leaves with the mate in their chimarrão gourds, to make it tastier and provide health benefits. Older people told Lido they still use a tea of feijoa leaves to treat diarrhoea, stomach pain and the flu. In two Kaingang communities, one in Paraná state and one in Rio Grande do Sul, feijoa tea is used by women in labour to assist with the dilation of the cervix, and after birth as well, to help bring back the appetite.⁴⁰

Nodari and Lido were not able to arrange for me to visit a contemporary Indigenous community. But there are other traditional Brazilian communities that have developed a deep relationship with the feijoa over generations. The following day, we went to visit one.

CHAPTER 3

At Least We Still Have the Feijoa

It took us a while to find Invernada dos Negros. The gravel roads wound among the rolling hills, and the place we were going wasn't marked on Google Maps. We asked for directions three times, and got contradictory answers. A guy cranking upbeat music from his truck stereo pointed the way with the leafy homemade broom he was using to sweep the tray. A farmer in a straw hat chewed on a piece of grass as he pointed us in the opposite direction.

Eventually, we pulled up outside a modest weatherboard house, painted a pale turquoise. Three men, two women and a couple of boys with a soccer ball had been waiting for us for some time. We sat down together on a collection of wooden chairs, tree stumps and benches, arranged in a circle in the shade near the house. An aluminium kettle hung from one of the trees. Across the yard, I could see a couple of feijoa bushes along the edge of a fenced paddock.

One of the women, in her late thirties, poured the first chimarrão into a gourd encrusted with fake pearls. Her name was Elizabete Aparecida de Lima, and she was wearing a leopard-print top and sleeveless denim jacket with 'Girl Power' scrawled on the back. An African-print headband held her long brown hair off her face. Lido introduced Nodari, Juan and me, then opened a small laptop and began to share the results of the feijoa research he had conducted here and in other communities across the region. 'Traditional communities like yourselves have been using the fruit for a long time,' he began.⁴¹ Elizabete nodded, and started taking notes in a little diary.

Invernada dos Negros is a quilombo, a semi-autonomous settlement of Afro-Brazilians founded by escaped or freed slaves.

———

No country in the Americas was as wedded to slavery as Brazil. For 350 years, the institution was at the heart of the country's economy, and it wasn't abolished until 1888, making Brazil the last nation in the Western hemisphere to free its slaves.

Of the 10 million Africans stolen from their homelands and brought across the Atlantic to toil in the soil of the New World, 40 per cent ended up in Brazil. In 2011, as workers carried out a multi-billion-dollar renovation of Rio de Janeiro's docks in preparation for the 2016 Olympics, they stumbled on the remains of the Valongo Wharf: the place where an estimated 600,000 Africans staggered ashore from slave ships after long, brutal voyages. Many did not survive the journey, and were thrown overboard or buried in mass graves in the hills above the city.⁴²

Slavery fuelled Brazil's sugar boom and then a gold rush. But during the long centuries of abuse, slaves resisted. They developed capoeira – a martial art disguised as a dance – as a form of physical and psychological resistance to oppression.⁴³ And they escaped, forming self-governing outlaw communities in remote parts of Brazil.

The most famous and long-lived of these by far was Palmares, founded in around 1605 in the northern state of Alagoas, near Recife. Hidden among rugged, forested mountains, Palmares was home to as many as 30,000 runaway slaves, who defended it against dozens of colonial attempts to destroy the kingdom. The last siege finally ended in 1694, and Palmares' revered king and military leader Zumbi was publicly decapitated.[44]

The authorities likewise demolished many of these communities of ex-slaves – quilombos – over the centuries, and their inhabitants – quilombolas – dispersed. But some Afro-Brazilian communities have continued to communally occupy the same lands for generations. In 2019, government estimates indicated there were almost 6000 quilombos in Brazil, each with their own origin story.

Invernada's is a little atypical. One of the men sitting in the circle, Edson Luiz de Souza, explained what happened. In his forties, with a round clean-shaven brown face and close-cropped greying hair hidden under a handwoven straw hat, he spoke softly but passionately about the history of his people. 'Our ancestors were kidnapped in Africa – the same story as all the quilombolas in Brazil – and they were brought here to work near the coast at Florianópolis and other ports,' he said. At some point in the mid-1800s, a colonist with a mouthful of a name, Matheus José de Souza e Oliveira, bought eleven slaves and took them to work on his station, up on the Santa Catarina plateau.

In 1877, Oliveira realised he was dying. He had no children, and fearing his wife would be left alone and defenceless, he made a will. In it, he promised to liberate his slaves and leave a third of his land to them and their descendants in perpetuity, if they would take care of him and his wife until their deaths. It sounds like a generous act, but Edson doesn't think it was made out of respect, just desperation. 'I don't think he had a good relationship with the slaves. My speculation is that he saw that his days were short, and he needed someone to look after himself and his wife – either that or the land would have ended up back with the government.' Most importantly, he said, 'it wasn't a gift. They had already paid for it with their slave labour.'

Oliveira and his wife did die shortly afterwards, and descendants of the four slaves that had children have lived there ever since. Today, Invernada dos Negros is about 25 kilometres across and covers 8000 hectares. The end of slavery did not mean the end of discrimination. All over Brazil, and particularly in the white-majority south, Afro-Brazilians continue to be marginalised. Oliveira's will specified that the land must remain communally owned, and it could not be sold or subdivided. But in the late 1920s, during the height of the araucaria boom, an unscrupulous lawyer apparently persuaded some residents to (illegally) sell off nearly half of the original land to logging companies, Edson said. ('Lawyers will always benefit the elite,' Nodari chimed in, ever the cynical socialist.) After that, many quilombolas left, dispersing to the cities and the suburbs, taking their stories with them.[45]

In their relative isolation, over 150 years, the quilombolas that remained at Invernada dos Negros developed a deep sense of place and connection with their land, including an intimate knowledge of the area's plants.

Around the back of the house, in a wooden pen, a fat sow and her piglets were rooting around in the soil beneath a pair of large feijoa trees. As the fruits fall, they eat them up. This is a common management technique across various communities, Lido said. His research found that those who used it had a much lower occurrence of a common pest, the *Anastrepha* fruit fly.[46] With no fruits rotting on the ground, its life cycle is disrupted – and his informants reckoned the practice produced tastier pork, too. Other Invernada residents told Lido they had used young feijoa leaves as a deodorant or perfume. They crushed them repeatedly with a hammer and rubbed the mixture on their bodies.

Elizabete's mother and father grew up in Invernada. 'My father never took medicine from the pharmacy, he used medicinal plants,' she told the group. 'His kettle was always full of herbs and leaves.' Quite often, it held feijoa leaves. (Like other Brazilians, the quilombolas call the plant goiabeira, but I've translated it here as feijoa.) 'When we were little and had a sore tummy, my father would make a tea from feijoa leaves for us,' Elizabete said. 'It has a lot of significance medicinally for us.' Lido said later that he thinks the commonalities between Indigenous and quilombola feijoa use suggest the two peoples exchanged knowledge about medicinal uses of plants in the past, even if memories of those interactions haven't been passed down.

An older man, Afonso Pedroso, pointed to his ankle. I couldn't fully understand his rapid Portuguese, so Nodari explained: 'He says he used to pour feijoa tea over cuts and wounds to help them heal. What he says actually has scientific backing: it's been proven that feijoa has antibacterial properties.' (It's true: more on that in Chapter 19.) Elizabete's mother used feijoa medicine as well. She had diabetes, and used a feijoa-leaf tea to control her blood sugar, Elizabete said. 'She made a tea and put it in the fridge, and drank it like water – eventually she stopped getting diabetes, and her vision improved as well.' Nodari was unsurprised. 'In the United States there's a company that has taken out a patent for the use of feijoa against type 2 diabetes,' he said.

Later, I looked into this patent, and discovered that it was part-owned by a New Zealand research institute, Callaghan Innovation. They had patented the use of feijoa fruit extract to treat and prevent rheumatoid arthritis and type 2 diabetes.[47] The Kiwi researchers had chemically analysed feijoa skins (a waste product from the juice industry) and discovered they had high concentrations of two kinds of polyphenols: micronutrients that can act as antioxidants and are thought to reduce inflammation.

The patent has now been licensed to a New Zealand nutraceutical company, which is selling feijoa extract as a powdered health supplement called Feiolix, and is marketing the product at diabetics and pre-diabetics as a way to improve blood-glucose management. As of 2023, clinical trials of the feijoa powder's ability to boost the benefits of weight loss and reverse pre-diabetes were underway at the University of Auckland.

Worldwide, as researchers and companies race to commercialise genetic resources, the patent system has at times been used to appropriate traditional forms of plant knowledge. While the patent-holders reap the profits, Indigenous peoples and rural communities – who in many cases have safeguarded these healing plants and their habitats – are rarely compensated.[48]

In the 1990s, the use of turmeric for treating wounds and ulcers was patented by two US-based researchers, although this was later overturned on the grounds that this knowledge was hardly new: Indians had been applying turmeric to their wounds for thousands of years. Part of the problem is that intellectual property regimes weren't designed to give benefits to communities, just individuals. Indigenous peoples around the world are now demanding equivalent protection for traditional knowledge systems, where ideas often belong to the collective. In 2020, Queensland revised its laws on 'biodiscovery' to require researchers and product developers working with native plants, animals, fungi and micro-organisms to gain prior informed consent from Aboriginal and Torres Strait Islander communities and equitably share any commercial benefit with them.[49]

In feijoa's case, I'm not convinced the New Zealand researchers were cutlass-waving bio-pirates. The feijoa had already been in New Zealand a century. Yeap Foo, the retired New Zealand chemist who first identified the polyphenol compounds in the feijoa skin, told me he had no idea the quilombolas used feijoa tea to treat diabetes. He was just looking for something useful in a waste product that would otherwise be thrown away.

The patent protects a very specific method for creating the feijoa extract, and doesn't prevent the quilombolas from using the plant in their traditional ways. Still, for Edson, the patent's very existence was confirmation of his community's marginalisation. 'This shows that the traditional knowledge of our old people was so advanced ... and yet, we are invisible.'

While Afonso took Nodari off to show him his heritage maize plot, Elizabete poured another chimarrão. She and Edson are part of a project of cultural revival at Invernada. Both returned to live on the land three years back, after spending their adult lives in nearby towns. In 2003, Brazil's leftist then-president Luiz Inácio Lula da Silva (widely known as Lula, and returned to power in 2022) issued a decree affirming the rights of Indigenous peoples and quilombo communities under the constitution. That laid the foundation for the Invernada descendants to be awarded formal land title to the remaining area in 2013 - and gave those returning more security.

'Before, I lived to work. I didn't have any time,' said Edson. 'Now, in the quilombo, I have rediscovered the luxury of talking to my neighbour.' He's trying to become self-sufficient: raising pigs, chickens and cows, keeping bees, and growing his own maize, manioc, beans, chillies and feijoas. Around a hundred families - all descendants of the original enslaved people - are now living in the community, each farming their own small block.

Elizabete is a trained teacher, working remotely on a Master's degree in education through the Federal University of Santa

Catarina, and is the vice-president of the quilombo leadership committee. 'To live here within the community is a realisation of a dream – of the history of my parents, of the meaning that Invernada has for us. Living outside, you need to struggle each day to affirm yourself as a human being. Here, people feel valued.'

The quilombolas are still fighting to get back the land that was taken from them in the 1920s and '30s. They want to establish their own culturally specific schools, and pass on the wisdom of their elders before it is lost. 'We're rescuing our culture,' Edson said. 'Our traditional form of education is more verbal than written. We believe we learn from each other, by talking as we are now, in a roda.' (A roda is the human circle within which Afro-Brazilians sing and dance samba, play capoeira, and hold meetings.)

Alongside music and other traditional practices, Elizabete added, making feijoa tea is a part of the quilombolas' cultural response to hardship and discrimination: one source of the self-reliance that has helped to make them who they are. 'In times of pain and suffering, our ancestors didn't cry. They sang, in a roda de capoeira. It's what gave them the strength to fight and continue to survive.' Just like the feijoa itself, the quilombolas are persevering and resilient, survivors against the odds.

Elizabete asked about our own interest in feijoas. Juan told a story about the day he first met Nodari, at his office at the university. Nodari had showed him a picture of the fruit. 'I said, I know that plant, it's a Colombian plant, I've been eating those fruits since I was a kid,' Juan said, laughing. When it was my turn, I explained that the feijoa is beloved in my homeland, too: that it's become such a national symbol that some New Zealanders also think it's a native plant, even though it does not grow wild.

In the streets of the Colombian capital Bogotá, here in the quilombo, and in my own corner of rural New Zealand, Juan, Elizabete and I had each grown up loving feijoas, believing they belonged to us. For a moment, I felt a bit sheepish – I adore feijoas, but for me they're not a matter of life and death, of cultural survival. But sitting there in the roda, sharing stories about this plant we all loved, I felt a connection form between us, too – something of the fellowship I had come to Brazil to find.

'Feijoas are at the core of the history of the quilombo,' Elizabete continued. 'Something that was ours,' – 'is ours,' interjected Edson – 'is ours,' she agreed, 'but which was valued, seen and improved by other countries.' She was on a roll now, impassioned and articulate, and speaking so clearly even I could understand every word of her deliberate Portuguese. 'This is not just about the feijoa, but part of how our culture, and our history, has been stolen from us. There were many other fruits, other customs, other traditions that belonged to us. But with the passing of time, and the massacres that we suffered, that was taken away.'

'We lost that knowledge,' she said. 'But we still have the feijoa.'

CHAPTER 4
The Primeval Feijoa Forest

The next morning, Nodari, Juan, Lido and I woke ourselves up at a roadside restaurant with coffee and pão de queijo – springy, salty balls of tapioca flour and cheese – and drove for a few more hours to a place called Bom Jardim da Serra. The name translates as 'Good Garden of the Mountains', and it was indeed lovely. The village was perched among stony peaks dotted with araucarias, and was so quiet that dogs lay sleeping in the middle of the hexagon-paved streets.

A way outside town we arrived at the home of Aristeu Rodrigues, a fifth-generation farmer of Portuguese descent running cattle and semi-wild pigs on 180 hectares of tumbling, forested hills. When we knocked on the door, Aristeu's wife informed us he was in the bath. She was distinctly unimpressed by our feijoa mission, and pulled a disgusted face when I asked her if she liked eating them. But when Aristeu emerged, wearing gumboots and a torn red cardigan, and sporting a few days' worth of grey stubble, it was soon clear he was one of us. 'I collect lots of wild fruit up in the forest,' he said. 'But feijoas are the best.'

Up in the hills above his home, we followed him in the car along a muddy, rough four-wheel-drive track. When the feijoa season started in earnest, Aristeu said, he would come up here on his horse. He's got a favourite prolific tree where he can reliably fill a 20-kilo sack with fruit. 'I just collect them to make juice, and eat myself,' he told me. 'My wife and children don't like them much.' He was teaching his grandchildren about them, though, and they had seen the light. He also used feijoa tea to treat diarrhoea, he said: plant lore learned from his grandmother.

Nodari stopped the car, and Aristeu led us off the track and into the trees. I soon found myself standing in a forest of feijoas. Draped in beardy lichen, their outlines blurred by mosses and the dim light, they were some of the tallest feijoa trees I'd ever seen, stretching perhaps 8 or 10 metres towards the dripping, vine-draped araucaria canopy.

Epiphytes and ferns perched between the feijoas' wavering trunks and straggly branches. The feijoas' leaves were much bigger and darker than I was used to at home. These were not the mannered garden plants I thought I knew, offering their flowers to the suburbs. These gnarled, ancient trees felt wise – and wild.

It was only the very beginning of the season, but in one massive, mossy tree Juan found some almost-ripe fruit. He climbed up into the branches and shook them, laughing. Nodari and I ducked, and feijoas fell like hailstones at our feet. Finally, I could taste one in its ancestral home! I picked one up, broke it open, and sucked out the tangy flesh. It was acid and slightly unripe, with an unusual touch of pink to the insides, but the sharp, fragrant smell was deeply familiar. As always, I felt the faint tug of a flashback to childhood.

This fruit, though, had thicker skin than any feijoa I'd seen before, and the seeds were bigger, the size of a peppercorn rather than a poppy seed. That's typical of the 'Brazil-type' of feijoa, Juan explained. Grant Thorp – the Kiwi botanist who'd given me his 1988 report to read on the plane – was the first to identify two main populations of feijoa, the 'Brazil' and 'Uruguay' types. In fact, he came to this very spot, and collected seed from here to take back to New Zealand.[50]

Juan has since mapped the feijoa's range in detail, as part of his doctorate in Nodari's programme. He aimed to identify the influence of the landscape on feijoa diversity and domestication, and spent three summers travelling around Brazil's southern states, Uruguay, and into the north of Argentina, collecting more than a thousand feijoa specimens for DNA analysis. He searched herbaria records to identify likely locations, then went door-to-door, armed with photos of the plant's flowers and fruit.

He envisioned himself as a modern-day Alexander von Humboldt: the famous Prussian naturalist who explored what's now Colombia and Venezuela at the dawn of the nineteenth century. Instead, some of the locals thought he was a Jehovah's Witness, scouting for converts. 'I had to say, "No, no, I'm not religious, I'm here looking for feijoas."' He walked for days through fields and forests, and slept in a hammock outside or on people's verandahs. A few times, his car broke down. In one place, locals said they had problems with armadillos carrying away the fruits.

The feijoa's current range stretches from Paraná state in the north to Uruguay in the south, but there's a 100-kilometre gap in the middle of Rio Grande do Sul. In the southern population, in Uruguay and the very south of Brazil, feijoa trees tend to be smaller, the leaves grey-green, and the fruits thin-skinned with small seeds. They grow at lower altitudes, from 100-500m above sea level. Almost all feijoas grown internationally descend from this 'Uruguay-type' population, but it represents perhaps 10 per cent of the species' genetic diversity, Juan said.

The 'Brazil-type' is much more varied. The trees can grow much taller, and some have much darker leaves. The fruits have a wider range of size and shape, from round to elongated. Some are smooth, while others have thick, knobbly skin. A few have a distinctive yellow hue. Many have the large, peppercorn-sized seeds. To Nodari and Juan, the diversity suggests that Brazil might be the evolutionary centre of origin of the feijoa. Perhaps right here, in these Santa Catarina mountains, the first feijoas came into being.

In the end, Juan visited 80 municipalities, and found feijoas in 67 of them. He analysed the genetic make-up of 21 of those populations, and compared the genetic diversity of feijoa plants between forested and farmed areas, using satellite photographs dating back to 1985 to check how land-use was changing.

He discovered that the feijoa retains a huge amount of genetic diversity in its ancestral home. In general, the highest diversity occurred in relatively untouched forests. But when Juan examined the samples Lido had collected in Kaingang and quilombola communities, he found that those feijoas were also highly diverse. And one other location stood out, Juan said: an entirely feijoa-dominated true feijoa forest in a remote part of the pampa – a vast, grassy, mostly treeless plain – in southern Rio Grande do Sul, near the border with Uruguay. There, the local gaúchos (cowboys) tended to keep their fields free of trees, but they had allowed an expanse of feijoas to thrive. Every year during the Holy Week at the end of Lent, people would collect a few feijoas for their own enjoyment – and then leave their cows among the trees to gorge on the fallen fruit.[51]

'If it were any other kind of tree, they would cut it down – but the fact that the feijoa has a direct use allows it to survive,' Juan said. It's an example of what he calls 'conservation through use'. Governments locking up land in national parks is only one way to protect biodiversity; people also take care of the plants that mean something to them. 'People conserve these trees because they use them.'

Safeguarding that rich genetic diversity is also a passion of Nodari's, a bulwark against what he sees as the takeover of agriculture by a flawed system – monoculture. During our long drives across the plateau, he pointed out the rows of identical Gala apples (a variety bred in New Zealand) and the acres of patented soy. At one point, he pulled over next to a field, wanting to take a photograph to use in one of his lectures. I couldn't figure out what I was meant to be looking at.

'That's the point,' Nodari said. The soy was completely dwarfed by giant weeds, taller than a person. But Roundup-resistant genetically modified soy isn't supposed to have a weed problem – in theory, you apply small amounts of herbicide, and everything except the soy is killed. In practice, evolution is getting in the way, Nodari explained. Most of the weeds *are* killed, except for the few that naturally have some resistance to the herbicide. They breed with each other, adapt, and over generations, become more resistant. Then you need to apply another herbicide, and so on.

It's not just about the overuse of toxins. Monocultures flatten out the flavours of food, and can increase the burden of pests and diseases. 'When you go into the forest, how often do you see a whole lot of plants that have been killed by a disease or insect? You don't see it!' Nodari continued as he drove on. 'You will have plants that are more affected, some that are less, and others not affected at all. Genetic diversity is like a barrier against insect plagues and disease.' In mainstream agriculture, though, we don't replicate the structure of a forest, Nodari said. Worldwide, an enormous amount of genetic diversity has been lost as farmers turn from multiple local varieties to high-yielding clones. And where every plant is identical, every plant is at risk.

Nodari doesn't want any of this for feijoas. In the neighbouring state of Rio Grande do Sul, he's working with smallholder farmers to breed their own feijoa varieties. Each one chooses a handful of wild individuals from their own property to cross and select from, so that the plants of each farmer are genetically different from their neighbour's – maintaining richness and spreading risk. 'We don't have another option – it's central to the sustainability of global food production, and it needs to be at the centre of our concerns as scientists and as societies.'

———

On our last night in feijoa land, before we headed back down the winding escarpment to the city and the coast, Nodari, Lido, Juan and I went to a restaurant in São Joaquim, a small city in the highlands where it gets cold enough to snow in winter. We ate a lot of local meat, drank a regional (organic) wine meticulously chosen by Nodari, and shared a bottle of Lothlorien liqueur I had brought over from New Zealand: feijoa and mānuka honey flavoured, of course.

We got talking about why all this matters. Why had they each spent so many years dedicated to the study of this one, not particularly profitable, fruit? Partly, it's the scientific challenge of the new, Nodari said. 'The feijoa is still an enigma for us. We still don't know exactly what climatic conditions it requires to flower and fruit.' The feijoa growing outside his house in Florianópolis flowers but rarely fruits, and it's not clear whether that's because the summers are too hot, or the winters insufficiently cold.

For Juan, though, studying feijoas is a kind of political resistance. 'Normally, agronomists work on just a handful of key species – beans, corn, soy, wheat, grapes, apples. That reduces the possibilities for workers, and it means city people eat less fruit – not everyone here can afford to eat fruit every day,' he said. 'Talking about this fruit is a way to help people to value their own resources, and value the plants that are around us.'

Juan was also interested in the contradictions. 'In New Zealand you love the feijoa, and we do in Colombia, too – but here, where it's native, and where there's the vast majority of the genetic diversity, it's been difficult for it to become part of the culture.' Forget Rio de Janeiro and São Paulo – most people I spoke to in Florianópolis, the city closest to the feijoa's heartland, hadn't even heard of them. But even in the towns of the cooler highlands, at the heart of their native range, feijoas aren't widely eaten or well known, except in a handful of Indigenous, rural and quilombola communities.

Near São Joaquim, we had visited the apple-and-feijoa orchard of Sabrina Dutra de Lis Costa, a friendly, joyful woman around my age, with perfect eyebrows and dyed auburn hair in a low ponytail. She and her husband are among just a handful of people growing feijoas commercially in Brazil, and they proudly showed us their 750 trees, set in a wide green valley beneath araucaria-clad hills. Sabrina said she collects the fruit together with her dark-eyed six-year-old daughter and displays boxes of them in her beauty salon in town – often selling them to clients who have never tried one before. 'People come to have their hair done and leave with feijoas,' she said.

Another of Nodari's PhD students, Morgana Lopes – who is studying a fungal disease that affects feijoas and is so committed to the plant that she named her dog Acca sellowiana, the former Latin name – seemed aggrieved by its lack of popularity in Brazil. 'It's not right that it comes from here, and yet hardly anyone knows about it,' she told me. 'I want to be part of its story.'

But as Lido discovered, cultural traditions inspired by this native fruit do still exist, even if they're a faint echo of what once was. Hanging on to those connections between people and plants is crucial, Nodari said now, brandishing his fork. 'Without traditional food, there's no culture, no identity. If that family on the quilombo stopped using the feijoa, they would lose another piece of their culture.' Food is more than a physical and biological necessity, he added. 'Food is seduction, food is commemoration, food is politics.'

'Correction!' Lido raised his glass. 'Food *and* drink!'

Nodari, Lido and Juan are scientists, but their work is not detached or emotionless. There's now very little money available for studying feijoas in Brazil. But for these scientists, feijoa research is a political act, claiming ground from powerful agribusinesses and a president – then Jair Bolsonaro – openly hostile to Indigenous and Afro-Brazilian culture. It's about valuing the grassroots, and the marginalised. In a world of monocultures and homogenisation, studying the feijoa is a return to the specific, the diverse and the local.

I found my companions' intensity thrilling. Feijoas in Brazil, I realised, had a completely different meaning than they do in New Zealand, where they are almost apolitical. It seemed both ironic and fitting that our ordinary, backyard fruit had come from such a vibrant and passionate place. After all, feijoas had managed to inspire a kind of fervent infatuation in me.

That infatuation was only deepening. My travels in Brazil were helping me to see the plant differently, to understand how its story was embedded within this particular place, this history, this ecosystem, these people. The connection I'd felt with almost everyone I'd met – the scientists, the students, the quilombolas and the farmers – had added to my sense that there existed a latent worldwide community of feijoa obsessives, people who, despite all our differences and distance, shared this one point of commonality: we understood how special this plant could be. In making these pilgrimages, writing this book, I was beginning to weave the fellowship of the feijoa into being.

Now I knew where feijoas came from. What I didn't yet know was how they got their name, or how they got from Brazil to New Zealand in the first place. The answers to those questions weren't to be found in either my homeland or theirs. For that, I had to go to Europe.

RECIPE
Elizabete's Feijoa Compote
Contributed by Elizabete Aparecida de Lima, Brazil

INGREDIENTS:
2 kg whole feijoas (weigh them with the skin on)
1 kg sugar
1 litre water
juice of one lemon

INSTRUCTIONS:
Peel the feijoas and mash them to a pulp.
Mix the sugar, water and lemon juice in a pan.
Stir for 3 minutes, then add the feijoas.
After 10 minutes of boiling, tip into sterilised jars and cool.

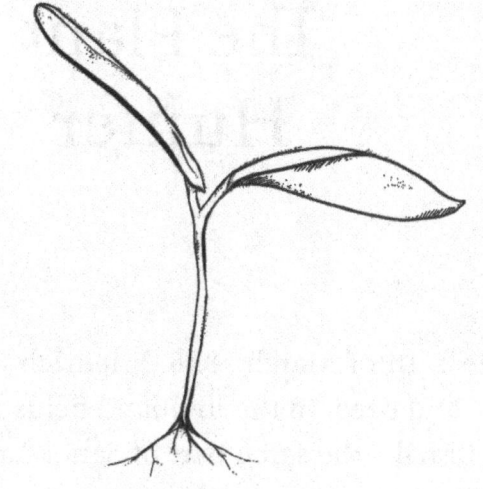

NAMING

Germany & Uruguay

CHAPTER 5

The Plant Hunter

On the 24th of March 1828, Friedrich Sellow's mules were lame and tired. In the highland fields near Curitibanos in southern Brazil – the same part of Santa Catarina that I visited nearly 200 years later – the German naturalist rested for a few days, his animals grazing on the rich pasture. While Sellow waited, he made notes about the soil (black in the fields, red-brown clay in the valleys), the geology ('dense green stone with very few impurities') and the agricultural possibilities ('wheat should also thrive here in this black soil and at this altitude').

Although the fields were abandoned – an old wall indicated they had been inhabited long ago – Sellow must have found someone to tell him stories of the place. 'This area is reputed to be inhabited by aggressive tigers,' he wrote, most likely referring to jaguars, frequently called tigres in South America. 'At our camp, a cross marks the grave of a servant, who was attacked by a tiger and bitten in the knee while guarding the fire at night. When his companions started shouting, the tiger let him go, but he died of the wound.' From the higher ground, Sellow could see mountains. Surrounding the fields were forests, mainly araucaria, but not solely. 'There are a lot of leafy trees among them.' Were some of them feijoas? Sellow doesn't give enough detail to say.[52]

Sellow was one of the first European scientific explorers of this part of South America, and rampaging 'tigers' were just one of the many dangers he faced during seventeen years spent traipsing through the backcountry of southern Brazil and Uruguay on the back of a mule. There were injuries, illnesses, warnings of 'murderous savages' and altercations with slave-owners. Shipwrecks sent some of his hard-won specimens to the bottom of the sea. In the end, Sellow faced one danger too many. He drowned in mysterious circumstances in Brazil's Rio Doce when he was just forty-two.

Perhaps because of that untimely end – preventing him from returning to Europe, telling his traveller's tales and taking credit for his discoveries – Sellow is barely remembered outside of Brazil and his native Germany. But some of his drawings and diaries survive, as do his vast collections of plants, rocks, birds, lizards, frogs, insects and mammals. And his name lives on in hundreds of the plant species he introduced to science.[53]

Although he was a relative latecomer to the feijoa's domain, Sellow is the first named individual whose life entwined with the plant. He was one of the European 'species seekers' – a group of eighteenth- and nineteenth-century adventurers and naturalists that fanned out around the world, seeking to describe and discover, to notice and name, and to make connections between living things. Though South Americans had of course known of the feijoa for millennia, Sellow was the first person to send samples of feijoa leaves and flowers to Europe. There, they would eventually be entered into the 'book of life' of scientific taxonomy and assigned a Latin species name: *Feijoa sellowiana*.

Who was Sellow? What can be gleaned about his encounter with the plant that would bear his name? What happened to the feijoa samples he sent home? I went to Germany to find out.

Four months after visiting Brazil, I landed in Berlin – part of a larger three-week feijoa trip that also included Colombia and France. It was a summer afternoon, and I went straight out to dinner with two German friends from different parts of my previous globetrotting life. We jumped on ride-share electric scooters and hooned past the Brandenburg Gate and a remnant of the Berlin Wall to get to a Georgian restaurant – which served the food of the Eastern European country, not the American state.

I knew that the Georgians loved feijoas, and was thrilled to see 'feijoa kompot' on the menu, though I had no idea what kompot meant. We ordered it, obviously, and it turned out to be a refreshing sweet drink served in a jug with whole preserved feijoas floating in it, which the waiter carefully ladled into our glasses.

The following morning, I got up early and caught the train to the Museum für Naturkunde, the Berlin Natural History Museum. Sabine Hackethal – easily the world expert on Friedrich Sellow – was waiting for me. The curator was petite and blue-eyed, immaculately dressed in a navy jacket, pearl earrings and an elegant hat, and she greeted me quite formally. Now I was out of my language comfort zone, speaking no German at all. Sabine, too, was worried about her English, but we agreed to take our time, and that she could switch into German if needed, and I'd get friends to help translate the tape.

The museum was not yet open to the public. Sabine opened a staff door and set off through the vast building's echoey corridors, moving so quickly and purposefully I had to trot to keep up. Her keys jangled as she strode. The lights were dim, and out of the gloom loomed something toothed and terrifying. It was Tristan, a complete *Tyrannosaurus rex* skeleton here on loan. Sabine barely looked up; she walks past Tristan every day on her way to her office. As we power-walked on, I caught a glimpse of another dinosaur, a Brachiosaurus so huge its head reached the roof of the vast display hall, while its tail wove out the door. In another room, hundreds of taxidermied animals mounted in floor-to-ceiling glass cabinets represented the web of life in a rainbow of feathers, scales and fur.

Sabine stopped briefly to point out a new exhibit, the 'wet collections'. Stacked on layer upon layer of shelving inside a brilliant glass cube, the museum's one million fish and amphibian specimens were preserved in a mixture of alcohol and water in 276,000 glass jars of all shapes and sizes. The liquids' array of colours reminded me of craft beer – blonde and lager, golden and amber – but each jar had an unappetising, contorted creature inside: wrinkled eels, spotted rays, small hammerhead sharks and bizarre deep-sea monsters.

Then we were off again, across a courtyard, into another building, up several flights of stairs. Sabine unlocked a creaking door and led the way into a small office with a large table in the middle. The room smelled of coffee. There was a potted plant in the corner, and on one wall hung a scientific drawing of an echidna, the spiky Australian marsupial. Unlocking another room nearby, Sabine took down a stack of grey cardboard boxes from a shelf, and, groaning with the weight, carried them into the office.

She opened them to reveal the legacy of Friedrich Sellow: letters, sheaves of paper containing twenty-six excursion reports, and seventy-two palm-sized handwritten journals, each tied up in a green ribbon. Sabine was six months away from retiring (she planned to spend more time gardening and flamenco dancing) and had spent a large part of her curating career studying these writings, ever since they were rediscovered in the 1970s after being filed in the museum's mineralogy department.

The excursion reports are fluent descriptions of side-trips or particular portions of Sellow's expeditions, she explained, while the journals are harder to decipher. There are mysterious lists of numbers, and the tiny, cramped handwriting is nearly illegible in some places. Not only is nineteenth-century German handwriting particularly idiosyncratic, Sabine said, 'You have to remember that he made these notes while riding on a mule!'

Sellow wrote with a pencil as he rode along, and in some of the diaries it's clear that he later wrote over the text in ink. Not that that makes them any easier to read, Sabine said, sighing. Still, by poring over the 200-year-old documents and painstakingly digitising them, she and her colleagues had gradually begun to build up a picture of Sellow - where he came from, what drove him and what he left us.

Sellow was born Friedrich Sello in Potsdam in 1789, adding the 'w' as a young man (it's not clear why). His ancestors didn't pass on wealth or status, but they did bequeath a love of plants.[54] His father, uncle and grandfather were gardeners at the court of Sanssouci, the summer palace of the Prussian kings. Prussia, which included the city of Berlin, was a powerful independent kingdom prior to the unification of Germany.

Sellow's father died when Friedrich was just seven, and young Friedrich was sent to a strict Protestant boarding school, where he spent hours in the library, poring over missionaries' accounts of their travels. According to one of his patrons, even in high school Sellow was 'inspired by an insurmountable zeal for the natural sciences, constantly carrying around the idea of one day becoming useful through long journeys around the world'.[55] Dreaming of adventure, but under no illusions about the hardships he might face, he began to train himself: sleeping on the bare earth, washing outside in winter, and eating raw fish and freshly slaughtered poultry.

After finishing school in Potsdam, he learned the science

and art of gardening from his uncle, then got a job at the Berlin-Schöneberg Botanical Garden. There he got his big break: the garden's director noticed him and introduced him both to the science of botany and to Alexander von Humboldt, the nineteenth century's most famous naturalist.

From 1799 to 1804, the great Prussian polymath Humboldt had journeyed through northern South America (today's Venezuela, Colombia, Ecuador and Peru) as well as Mexico and Cuba. With Aimé Bonpland, his French sidekick, Humboldt had paddled a canoe up the crocodile-infested Orinoco River, experimented with electric eels in the Venezuelan Llanos, walked at night through dense forests lit with fireflies, crossed the Andes under soaring condors, and climbed the 6263-metre-high Ecuadorian volcano Chimborazo, then believed to be the highest mountain in the world.

He returned to Europe a celebrity, and spent the rest of his life writing prolifically – public lectures, books and essays about his travels, and thousands of letters to correspondents around the world. More species and landmarks are named after Humboldt than anyone else: towns, lakes, rivers, waterfalls, a penguin, a squid, a lily, a glacier, a geyser, a current, mountain ranges from New Zealand to China, even part of the moon. His great insight – a vision that came to him atop Chimborazo – was that nature is an interconnected web of relationships, and that the distribution of plants is influenced by climate, latitude and altitude. Though it seems obvious today, this was a completely new conception of the natural world.

Before Humboldt, botanists had focused on classification: imposing order on nature using the classification system devised by the Swedish botanist Carl Linnaeus, still the basis for the naming of plants and animals today. But in his illustrated books and lectures, Humboldt emphasised the connections between things, and in doing so 'unpeeled a previously invisible web of life', writes Andrea Wulf in her recent biography of Humboldt, *The Invention of Nature*. Although he was a disciplined scientist, he also emphasised the importance of the imagination and emotion. For Humboldt, 'nature had to be experienced through feelings', Wulf writes.[56]

Back in Europe, Humboldt settled in Paris, which considered itself the global centre of scientific inquiry in the early nineteenth century. There, he took aspiring naturalists under his wing, encouraging them to get out into the world and begin exploring. ('The most dangerous worldviews are the worldviews of those who have never viewed the world,' he wrote.) One of those young disciples was Friedrich Sellow.

———

Sellow arrived in Paris in the spring of 1810, and soon landed a meeting with Humboldt. It must have gone well, as Humboldt began giving Sellow contacts and supporting him financially. The mentorship would continue throughout Sellow's life. Sellow studied botany at the Jardin des Plantes, and attended lectures at the University of Paris given by some of the leading minds of French biology.

The following year, Humboldt paid for him to travel to London, where he met with English botanists including Joseph Banks, famous for his voyages forty years earlier with James Cook to Australia and New Zealand. In January 1813, Sellow was introduced to the Baron Georg Heinrich von Langsdorff, a self-taught German naturalist who was passing through London on his way to Brazil, to represent Russia as the Consul-General.

Until just five years before, information about the flora, fauna and resources of the Portuguese colony had been treated as a state secret, and foreign naturalists were not permitted to travel there. With the arrival of the entire Portuguese court in Rio de Janeiro in 1808, the ports were opened, and for the first time in generations, the country – with its rich forests, rivers, fields and mines – was open for outsiders to explore. You should come, Baron Langsdorff told Sellow. Finally, here was a chance for a real adventure, and Sellow took it.

He spent the next year preparing his expedition and securing funding from Banks and other botanists. In the spring of 1814, aged twenty-five, Sellow set off from London. To keep himself busy during the long sea journey, he taught himself Portuguese. He stepped ashore in Rio de Janeiro in August, just a few months before Brazil ceased to be a colony and became part of the 'United Kingdom of Portugal, Brazil and the Algarves'. True to his word, the baron welcomed Sellow at his country house, and introduced him to Rio's growing international scene of intellectuals and naturalists. Keen to make a good impression on his illustrious funders, Sellow immediately began collecting specimens in the area around the town.

Because he was on the road until the last day of his life, Sellow never sat down and wrote a full account of his travels intended for a wide audience. But many of his contemporaries did. One of those was Prince Maximilian of Wied-Neuwied, another Prussian, who arrived in Rio nearly a year after Sellow. Wied was a decorated soldier and had served in the Prussian Army against Napolean, marching with the victorious allied forces into Paris in 1814.[57] Wied, too, was inspired, encouraged and assisted by Humboldt. But unlike Sellow, he was an aristocrat with money, and as the eighth of ten children, he also had the freedom to follow his interests: natural history and ethnology.[58] His *Travels in Brazil, in the years 1815, 1816, and 1817* gives some idea of the city Sellow would have encountered: 'A European, on first landing in these tropical regions is astonished at the beauty of the natural scenery and the luxuriance of the vegetation,' Wied wrote.

The gardens are everywhere shaded by gigantic mango trees, cocoa trees, banana trees, green orange trees loaded with golden fruit, melon trees ... Groves of these trees form delightful promenades in the vicinity of the city, and present to the admiration of the stranger multitudes of curious birds and butterflies. In Brazil nature has hitherto done more than man ... The abundance of fruits and vegetation of every kind which this fertile climate produces is almost inconceivable.[59]

Wied mentions oranges, mangos, figs, grapes, guayavas and pineapples, all growing 'in singular perfection' – but feijoas don't appear in his list of fruits.[60] The guayava he speaks of is *Psidium guajava*, the round, green common guava, and feijoas don't grow naturally as far north as Rio. But Wied does say that araucaria nuts were for sale on the streets, and those must have been brought up from the south.

Soon after Wied arrived, he met Sellow, likely through their mutual contact, Baron Langsdorff. The two naturalists realised they both planned to make a similar journey – north along the coast from Rio to Salvador de Bahia, a distance of 1500 kilometres – and they agreed to undertake the expedition together. On 4 August 1815, Wied and Sellow set off, accompanied by another naturalist, Georg Freyreiss, as well as ten local servants. There were also sixteen mules, each one weighed down by two leather-bound wooden boxes full of equipment.[61] While Humboldt had been outspoken against slavery, believing it was 'the greatest evil', Wied appears to have had no such qualms. In Porto Seguro, he purchased an Indigenous man, Joachim Quäck, who became his property as well as his guide. (When Wied returned to Europe in 1817 he took Quäck with him. Dressed in European clothes, and with his traditional lip-plugs removed, he lived in Neuwied until 1833, when he died from liver cirrhosis due to alcohol abuse).[62]

The expedition travelled north from Rio, crossing rivers and a mountain range draped in lush Atlantic forest. Wied's travelogue captures some of the wonder the explorers must have felt in this strange new world. 'Leaving Inuá, we found in the shade of an ancient wild forest, many objects totally unknown to us. On the ground appeared the hairy bush-spider . . . the bite of which is said to produce a painful swelling; it makes holes and lives in the earth. We also met with a variety of large broad toads, though not so numerous as in the *Serra* which we had just left; for there, when the evening came on, the ground was entirely spread with them.'[63]

Sellow makes small appearances in Wied's narrative, and is usually described shooting birds or gathering plants: he collected 1800 specimens during the journey. Wied is also responsible for the only known images of Friedrich Sellow - which unfortunately don't give much sense of what he looked like. One of Wied's hand-drawn watercolours from December 1815 shows the explorers paddling a canoe through lush jungle along the Rio Doce: the same river that would end Sellow's life years later. The three naturalists - Wied, Freyreiss and Sellow - appear to have their rifles aimed at the canopy, ready to shoot down any interesting birds and turn them into specimens, while their servants - or perhaps their slaves - paddle the canoe and hack at the vegetation with machetes.

Some of the native plants are labelled, including several kinds of mimosa (wattle) and heliconia, with its bright red, parrot-like flowers. No feijoas, though: the Rio Doce is too far north. Geologist Carsten Eckert from the Museum of Nature in Gotha, who collaborated with Sabine on the Sellow project, told me he 'never solved the enigma' of which one of the three Europeans pictured is Sellow. He sent me one more image, though, a sketch Wied made in black pen.

It shows the expedition returning from a visit to a Purí community in 1815, in Paraíba. Sellow leads the way, with his herbarium of preserved plant specimens strapped on behind him. Freyreiss is on the next horse, with a Purí man sitting behind him, and a Portuguese soldier and another Purí bring up the rear. (Wied didn't show himself in this picture.)

Sellow has short curly hair and is clean-shaven. He's wearing a nice coat, a top hat and buttoned-up riding gaiters. I can't help wondering if he maintained that impractical-looking standard of dress for the next sixteen years of his adventures, but there's no way of knowing. Those two drawings are the only glimpses we have.

Meanwhile, back in Paris, Humboldt was urging the Prussian government to give Sellow ongoing financial backing, saying he was 'quite qualified to do his best'. In 1817, Sellow got the good news that the Prussian state would support him from then on, with the condition that he send his specimens to Berlin. He also received instructions from the director of Berlin's Zoological Museum and Botanical Garden for how the various collections should be packed and sent.

'Amphibians, snakes, frogs, lizards, and turtles of all kinds are particularly welcome to us', reads one instruction. 'Mr. S. should carry one or more barrels of strong wood bound by iron hoops with him ... Snakes and lizards with a smooth surface can be sent in it, but if there are delicate, protruding scales and fragile toes, it is necessary to sew them into a bag of old canvas beforehand.'[64]

In 1818, Sellow set off on another expedition through the provinces of Minas Gerais and São Paulo, this time with the man who would become a lifelong friend, Ignaz Franz Maria von Olfers. Sellow would be in charge of the plants, birds and mammals, while Olfers focused on insects, fish, reptiles and geology. The pair spent considerable time in a Coroado village, where Sellow produced a series of remarkable sketches of the people he met there. Sellow and Olfers made a commitment to each other that they would one day work on their specimens together, and that if one died in the course of their adventures, the other would take care of his collection.

Together, they planned to head to Brazil's far south, where the feijoa waited, as yet 'undiscovered' by Europeans. But Olfers, like many foreigners in Brazil, was required to return to Europe with the Portuguese king when the court went back to Lisbon in 1821. Not Sellow. For the next ten years he would travel largely alone – with just his mules and the occasional local guide or bodyguard for company – collecting, describing, drawing and measuring, while constantly having to justify himself to those who held the purse strings in Berlin.

In November 1821, Sellow travelled to Montevideo, and spent nearly a year exploring the territory now known as Uruguay. (The area had been invaded by Brazil five years earlier and was, briefly, a Brazilian province.) In his first Uruguayan expedition, he followed the Rio Cebollatí into the northeast of the country. The river runs close to Quebrada de los Cuervos, a place known today for its abundance of feijoas. This was his first expedition in feijoa territory, so in all probability, that year – or the following one, when he explored further inland, around Salto and Tacuarembó – must have been when Sellow first encountered the feijoa. With its bright flowers and juicy fruit, along with the fact that it would have been new to him, the feijoa must have drawn Sellow's attention.

At the end of September 1822, he sent a shipment from Montevideo to the Berlin Natural History Museum. Alongside 2300 insect specimens, 116 species of birds, 20 species of fish, several snakes and a sample of intestinal worms, he also sent a box containing fragments of 700 species of plants.[65] Was the feijoa among them? It must have been, but where did Sellow collect his specimen? What details did he record about the plant? Did he, as Humboldt encouraged, note the relationship between the feijoa and its surrounding ecosystem? Did he notice – or shoot – any of the birds that pollinated its flowers? Sadly, we don't know, because of two pieces of astoundingly poor decision-making a century apart: one a misguided attempt to appeal to the masses, the other the result of the fog of war.

Taxidermied birds stared with sightless eyes from the glass cabinets as I followed Sabine Hackethal into the Berlin Natural History Museum's ornithology department. The lights were off, and it was all a bit unnerving, those feathered faces staring at us from all sides as we strode down the row. There were pelicans, bitterns, eagles, storks, even a kiwi; some of them had been dead for more than 200 years.

'Herr Eckhoff?' Sabine called. 'Ja!' echoed from a back room, and Pascal Eckhoff emerged. 'So, you're interested in tanagers and antbirds?' he asked me after the introductions. I didn't know much about them, I said, but Sabine had asked which of Sellow's thousands of bird specimens I might like to see, so I picked the families thought to be among the feijoa's natural pollinators: *Thamnophilidae*, the antbirds Fritz Müller and his grandson watched eating the sweet petals, and *Thraupidae*, the tanagers that have been observed doing the same today. Pascal led the way to one of the glass cabinets. He swept his arm across a 2-metre stretch of the shelves, crowded with stuffed and mounted birds. 'These are all tanagers. It's a huge, very uniform group, and there are many specimens from Sellow,' he said. 'Antbirds are from here to there. Now, this is the one I want to present to you.'

He opened the glass door and took out the largest, most impressive of the birds. Around the size of a magpie, it had a grey body, a red-brown crest and a hooked beak. The bird's wings and tail were striped black-and-tan. Its long claws were wrapped around a branch, and it was mounted on a small piece of wood. Today, this bird is called *Batara cinerea*, the giant antshrike, and it's found in roughly the same area of southern Brazil as the feijoa. The looping handwriting on the label affirmed it was one of Sellow's birds, included a now-defunct Latin name, and indicated that this was a female bird. But that was all: for the collecting location, the label said only 'S. Paulo'.

Sellow would have recorded exactly where and when he shot this specimen from the sky, Pascal said, and probably other information as well. But all that data was destroyed in the 1830s, by the then-director of the museum, Hinrich Lichtenstein. Lichtenstein directed his students to remove the original, detailed labels, and replace them with simplified ones. For Sellow's birds, the only locations given are 'Brazil', 'Bahia' or 'Montevideo', which could also apply to southern Brazil. 'Why would a man of science do such a thing?' I asked. Pascal shrugged. Priorities were different back then, he said. Now, museums display a tiny proportion of their collections to the public, keeping the majority behind the scenes for use in scientific research. In Lichtenstein's time, absolutely everything was on display – and they probably wanted their labels to look tidy and match.

'For them, Brazil was so far away and so exotic that it was enough to know it was from Brazil,' Pascal said. Information about exactly where and when a specimen was collected was erased. 'They knew at the time that some birds migrate, so sometimes the month is documented, so you get an idea if it's a resident bird or a bird on migration. But that means for some specimens we have the stupid situation where we have the exact date, 27th of March, and then I have to put, "between 1860 and 1880", because that's all we know.'

Lichtenstein's order to destroy the labels was a tragic piece of deliberate vandalism, Pascal said. 'It killed the big part of the value of these birds for many studies.' Advanced genetic tools are allowing scientists to return to museum collections and glean new information from old specimens. But for almost all the questions they want to answer – about evolution, say, or how population distributions have varied over time in response to environmental changes – they need more specific information about where and when an animal or plant was collected.

Pascal put the antshrike back on its shelf. Most of the other antbirds and tanagers in the cabinet were smaller, blackbird- or sparrow-sized – and some of them were downright scruffy. 'Is that a result of their long sea journey from South America?' I asked, thinking of storms and shipwrecks. Pascal shook his head. The damage was caused by a much more recent cataclysm, he said: World War II. When Berlin was bombed by the British and Americans, the Natural History Museum wasn't completely destroyed, as were other buildings nearby. Still, in February 1945, the museum's East Wing was hit by a 500-kilogram bomb and collapsed to its foundations. Some people hiding in an air-raid shelter in the museum's basement were killed in the attack.

The bird collection wasn't directly hit, but the shock wave was so strong that the windows and many of the glass cabinets were smashed. Sellow's long-dead birds took to the air one last time. The explosion flung their small, still bodies out of the shattered windows, and they landed with soft thuds in the wintry courtyard below. Afterwards, when the air-raid sirens had stopped wailing, museum staff found them there and gathered them up, riddled with glass splinters. Some have since been restored, but others are still bent and straggly from the ordeal.

That wasn't the only impact Allied bombs had on Sellow's collections. Berlin's 'type specimen' of the feijoa – an original sample of leaves and flowers that represented the plant for science – was utterly destroyed in a fiery inferno.

CHAPTER 6
The Specimen

A few years before my Berlin visit, I had called up Hans Walter Lack on Skype. He was a professor at the Free University of Berlin, a former director of the Botanic Garden and Botanical Museum Berlin-Dahlem (BGBM) and a globally recognised expert on the history of botany. He had also just written a book chapter (in German) all about Sellow and the feijoa.[66]

'I have no personal feelings about feijoa or the juice and so on,' he told me. 'But I always find it outstanding if a field botanist finds a plant which has an economic potential. Considering the masses of plants we know, only a tiny fraction is really directly valuable for man. Most of these – like maize or wheat – have been known for millennia. But few were added to this list of new economic plants as late as the nineteenth century, and one of those was the feijoa.' Lack doesn't think Sellow had any idea of the plant's potential, but said he wouldn't be surprised if the naturalist had tasted the fruit.

Unfortunately, when I travelled to Berlin in July 2019, Professor Lack was in hospital. He arranged for me to meet his colleague instead. Leaving Sabine, Pascal and the Natural History Museum behind, I took three trains to the south of Berlin and turned up at the wrong entrance of the BGBM. I hurried through the gardens, and on the path near a large glasshouse I bumped into Peter Hein, the botanist I was looking for. We walked to the herbarium: thirty rooms stuffed full of dried plants.

Peter led the way down a stairwell and along a series of dark corridors lit with neon lights. There were no windows, and it felt like we were underground. Eventually, he opened the door of a small room lined with shelves. This was the home of the Myrtaceae specimens, the plant family comprising 6000 species including the European myrtle, Australian eucalyptus, New Zealand's pōhutukawa and South America's feijoa. Peter turned a handle and the metal shelves separated, and he walked in between them. 'D, E, F ... Feijoa!' he said, pulling out a blue manila folder.

Inside was a stack of folded papers. Peter gently opened the first one, and there it was: the pressed, dried remains of two feijoa twigs. One had a faded flower, the other a tiny immature fruit. Almost all their natural colour was gone, and they had become a dull dark brown. 'Can I sniff them?' I asked. Peter laughed, and nodded. I bent my head to the herbaria. 'And what could you smell?' he asked. 'Not much,' I said. There was no trace of the fruity feijoa aroma, just the faint scent of old books and tobacco. The sample smelled ancient, and it was: 200 years old. A label, written in cursive ink pen, showed they were collected by 'Sello' in 'Brasilia' (meaning not the area of today's capital city, far from feijoa land, but Brazil in general, which also included parts of Uruguay at that time).

Walter Lack had already told me the little leaves' full story. This was one of perhaps half a dozen pairs of feijoa twigs that Sellow collected on his travels, he had said. 'You have to imagine the fascination in the places where all this material arrived. In England, France, in what's now Germany, every month they got packets of material. Often it was 90 per cent dead, but perhaps 10 per cent was living, and no-one knew what these plants would look like, how they would flower. These were courageous people who, on the basis of fragmentary facts, produced solid information, and described new taxa. The funny thing is, in this period you would often find a description of a new species, with the annotation: "sprang up in the soil of a plant sent from Brazil". It was a seed hidden in the soil – not even one they meant to send.'

The volume of material was so great that the feijoa samples were ignored, at first. The plant wasn't a stinky *Rafflesia* or a mysterious giant moa, and no-one was going to get famous publishing a paper about an obscure South American shrub. For at least thirty years, the twigs stayed in storage, enclosed in paper. In 1840, a group of German and Austrian botanists began work on an ambitious new book, *Flora Brasiliensis*, which wouldn't be completed for another sixty-five years. Its fifteen volumes included 22,767 species, of which around a quarter were new to science.[67] Finally, in 1855, Otto Karl Berg, a professor of pharmaceutical botany at the Friedrich Wilhelm University in Berlin, got to work categorising the South American myrtle plants for *Flora Brasiliensis*. It took him six years, and he named more than 1400 new species. One of those was the feijoa.[68]

Sellow might have done the hard yards on the back of a mule, but 'it was Berg who really understood [the feijoa] was something new', Lack told me. 'It's a step-by-step process. Often someone collects something and doesn't realise that it is new to science, because you need a huge collection to compare with.' Berg got Sellow's feijoa specimens out of their folder, compared them with the other Myrtaceae he had access to, and, in 1857, he officially named the plant *Orthostemon sellowiana*, after Sellow. However, he soon discovered the generic name *Orthostemon* (meaning 'erect stamens' or 'straight threads' in ancient Greek) had already been used for another plant group, and so he changed it to *Feijoa sellowiana*, in honour of a Brazilian naturalist, João da Silva Feijó.

When a biologist describes a new species, they are free to call it whatever they want, Lack explained, as long as it's completely original and refers only to one organism. 'You can name it after your girlfriend if you like. You can name it after your favourite politician, your dog – or the collector, and many people choose that.' Berg picked Sellow rather than his girlfriend, and that is how the feijoa became *Feijoa sellowiana*. To officially become a species, each of a plant's parts – seed, fruit, leaf, flower – must be intricately described. Berg's description was in Latin, but a later (supposedly) English-language description of the feijoa, by Joseph Hooker in the 1898 *Curtis's Botanical Magazine*, is no more accessible:

> An erect shrub or small tree, with brown bark, and leaves clothed beneath with snow-white appressed tomentum. *Leaves* two to three inches long, opposite, shortly petioled, oblong, obtuse, smooth, deep green and shining above. *Flowers* solitary, axillary, stoutly pedicelled, drooping, about two inches broad across the petals. *Calyx* white-tomentose, tube elongate, sub-clavate, bibracteolate at the base, not produced beyond the ovary, lobes orbicular, reflexed. *Petals* orbicular, spreading, externally white-tomentose, internally blood-red, with white margins. *Stamens* very many, filaments erect in bud, at length spreading, longer than the petals, blood-red, anthers small, yellow, pubescent. *Ovary* four-celled, cells many-ovuled; style stout, narrowed below the capitellate stigma. *Berry* two inches long, by one and three-quarters in diameter, oblong, crowned with the calyx-lobes, many-seeded, pericarp thin, green, sarcocarp fleshy, aromatic. *Seeds* reniformly orbicular, compressed, testa coriaceous. *Embryo* spirally coiled.[69]

It's almost completely unintelligible to the non-botanist, but even though I can barely understand any of it, I love the sound of the words: *stoutly pedicelled, testa coriaceous*. It's like a kind of mysterious poetry, or a magic spell conjuring the feijoa into being. 'Leaves clothed beneath with snow-white appressed tomentum.' The plant had existed for 23 million years, and it had been eaten by humans for perhaps four thousand. Now, the feijoa was claimed for science – pinned, like a butterfly to a board, to the great system of taxonomy devised a century earlier by the Swedish physician and botanist Carl Linnaeus.

In 1861, one of the Sellow feijoa specimens was donated to the herbarium of the French National Museum of Natural History, and a handful of others were sent to other institutions around Europe. At least one remained in Berlin. These half-dozen sets of pressed leaves were the type specimens, the material evidence of the new species that had been described and named.[70] A type specimen is a kind of anchor, a link between the real and the symbolic, Lack explained – the same way that a platinum stick in a safe in Paris defines the metre. (Linnaeus himself is now considered the type of *Homo sapiens*.) 'The type specimen is forever the point of reference for *Feijoa sellowiana*,' he said. Or it would have been, if World War II hadn't put an end to that.

Peter Hein carefully turned the pages of the folio. Inside were a dozen more pressed feijoa specimens: one from Rio Grande do Sul, collected in 1886, one from Santa Catarina in the 1960s, another that Peter collected himself from a garden in New Zealand. As we examined them, he told me about the war: 'a very dark age, as you know'.

'In 1943, the British government decided to bomb Germany. They bombed town by town, as the Germans did themselves, of course.' (The Germans had, in fact, already bombed the Natural

History Museum in London, causing some damage to the herbarium there.) Fearful of counter-attack, the botanists at the Berlin Herbarium began removing important specimens and storing them for safekeeping in a mine. But they were too late. They had only moved a small portion of the collection when the bombs starting falling on the night of 1 March 1943. The building that housed the herbarium was hit directly, the library caught fire, and by the morning of 2 March, about 80 per cent of the collection was lost.

Berlin had been the second-most-important herbarium in the world, after that at Kew Gardens in London. It's estimated it held between four and six million specimens. It has taken more than seventy-five years to painstakingly build the collection back up to four million objects, and it now pales in comparison to those at Kew, Paris and elsewhere. There's very little published information in English about what happened. The only reference I could find was an article in the American journal *Science*, dated December 1943. After a (false) wartime dig at the Germans – 'there is no evidence that any attempt was made, in Berlin, to safeguard its especially important botanical material . . . and types borrowed from foreign institutions' – the author lamented:

> The loss of the Berlin herbarium is a catastrophe of major proportions to world botany. This herbarium, one of the largest and most important in the world, built up over a period of at least 175 years, contained the basic historical collections of Germany outside of those at Munich. Scores of thousands of type specimens from all parts of the world were thus destroyed.[71]

The bombs reduced all the Myrtaceae specimens, including the feijoa, to ash.

They obliterated written records too, including, probably, Sellow's botanical notes. The existing diaries and expedition reports contain surprisingly little about plants for a botanist. Sabine and Lack believe Sellow made separate notes about the plants he found, and – if they weren't lost earlier – that these would have been kept in the herbarium library, going up in smoke along with everything else. Sadly, without them, there's no chance of finding out what Sellow thought of the feijoa, or where exactly he collected his specimen.

How was I looking at one now, then? Thanks to what Lack called the 'green network', the Berlin herbarium did get one of its feijoa specimens back. In the late 1940s – though their countries had so recently been bitter enemies – French and German botanists began corresponding again and exchanging plants. The Natural History Museum in Paris sent back one of the original Sellow feijoa type specimens that Berlin had given them in 1861. A stamped label on the bottom corner of the feijoa herbaria tells the story: 'Donné par the Musée d'Histoire Naturelle de Paris.' These informal networks of exchange help to ensure the continued existence of museum collections, Lack said. 'Because what happened in Berlin could easily happen somewhere else.'[72]

Peter packed the specimens away and replaced the folder on the shelf under F. I followed him to his office on one of the herbarium's upper floors, and my mouth fell open. It was beautiful, a museum exhibit all of its own, a room that could only have belonged to a botanist. Plants sprouted from almost every surface. A palm tree in a pot brushed the ceiling, echoing three palms depicted in a botanical drawing leaning against the central desk. A dried ginkgo frond adorned a wall. Next to Peter's landline phone on the windowsill there was a sky-blue enamel watering can. A climbing vine tumbled over his computer monitor, and on the shelf above, three pine cones sat alongside a stapler. Floor-to-ceiling shelves held books, papers and specimens of all kinds.

Peter pointed out a huge pyramid-shaped seed – it was actually the dried fruit of *Barringtonia asiatica*, the fish poison tree, he said: 'a mangrove from New Guinea. It's very light, it can float on the sea.' There were dozens of mysterious jars holding terracotta and rose-pink crystals, their ancient labels reading 'Resina Dammarae' and 'Colophonium'. These resins are derived from different kinds of plants, including *Agathis australis*, New Zealand's kauri, Peter explained. There was even a bottle of Humboldt Gin. 'Ah, that's our new invention,' he said. To mark the 250th anniversary of Alexander von Humboldt's birth, the herbarium's botanists had collaborated with some gin distillers to make a drink inspired by the naturalist. They provided the distillery with a list of botanicals Humboldt collected on his South American journeys, and seven of them were added to the gin. The label showed Humboldt and his travelling companions approaching Mount Chimborazo. (I loved this idea so much I spent the following morning tracking down a few bottles for myself – then accidentally locked them in my friend's apartment as I raced to the airport.)

On the other side of the desk was a workspace laid out with scissors, glue, pencils, paperclips, and a wooden stamp and inkpad. 'My work is quite a practical one,' said Peter. 'We have a lot of new collections coming in – 30 to 40,000 every year – from nature or from old collections forgotten somewhere.' He opened a yellowed sheet of newspaper. There was a dried plant inside. 'This is what a Mr Ludwig collected in 1950. You can see he made a quite good label.' The herbarium bought this collection in 1958, and it had sat in storage for sixty years until Peter had taken it out. When he had assembled all the parts, it would be sent to the preparation office to get mounted on special paper and become an official herbarium specimen.

'Have *you* ever named a species?' I asked.

'Yes, but I was collecting in the field,' Peter said. He had once roamed the deserts and woodlands of the Arabian Peninsula looking for new plants. 'Our eye is trained for green, for newness, and you are going to areas where nobody else is looking.' On a cape in Yemen in 2001, he spotted a plant with a little purple flower. He thought he'd never seen it before in any of his books, and he was right. It turned out to be something completely new to science. He named the plant *Campylanthus hubaishanii* after his friend Mohamed Ali Hubaishan, a Yemeni botanist. Did he like the process of describing and naming? 'I did not like to make the writing. You have to be very detailed.'

'You're more of a Sellow than a Berg?' I asked.

'Maybe! Sellow was a gardener – me, too. That was my job before I became a botanist, just like him. A lot of botanists started professional life as gardeners.'

I realised I'd been thinking of Sellow as belonging to a bygone age. But talking to Peter, it suddenly dawned on me that the work of botanists hasn't really changed all that much since Sellow went to South America, or Berg sat in Berlin poring over specimens. You can look things up on the internet now, and you need to provide more information about the plant's form, but discovery and description is still the core job of botanists. We still need Sellows, and we need Bergs: both the hardcore adventurers and the meticulous desk jockeys.

And there is still much to discover. Even though scientists have already named nearly 400,000 species of plants, around 2000 new ones are identified every year. In 2016, for instance, those included a new kind of bougainvillea from Ethiopia, a new parsnip from Turkey, a caper from the Philippines, and five endangered species of rosewood from Gabon.[73] Botanists waited ten years for a newly discovered Madagascan bamboo species to flower so that they could fully describe the plant. There might be another 100,000 species of higher plants out there waiting to be identified, Peter said. 'And in the other groups – mosses, lichens, fungi – I think the number of not-known species is much higher. We might know 10 to 20 per cent. Of course, nobody knows for sure, and a lot of them will be extinct before they're found.'

I love finding out about people's obscure worlds, and I found this world of taxonomic botany very strange and very beautiful. I wasn't sure, though, that I totally understood the point of it all – all this careful labelling, these dried plants hidden away in dark rooms, the hair-splitting over whether a plant is more closely related to this or that. 'These collections are documentations of the whole planet's vegetation,' Peter explained. Not just in space, but in time, too. 'Some of the collections are 400 years old, so we know what was where 400 years ago.' At a time when the climate is changing at an unprecedented pace, and in places like Brazil or New Zealand where massive deforestation and landscape change has occurred over the past century, this kind of information can help to answer vital questions. Learning how a plant's distribution has altered over time, for example, can illuminate environmental changes that happened before climate instruments were invented.

But more fundamentally, before you ask *any* other question about a species, you need to know what it is, Peter said. Imagine if all anyone knew about plants was whether they were a 'tree', a 'shrub' or 'grass', he said. 'This incredibly rich world could not be understood. We would not know what we see when we look out the window.' We wouldn't know which plants could heal us or fuel us, or how each interacts with the ecosystem around it and the animals that depend on it.

And we might not lift a finger to save any teetering on the edge of extinction.

CHAPTER 7

The Lost People

Friedrich Sellow wasn't only interested in the plants, birds, insects and rocks of the lands he was exploring. He was curious about the people, too. In Berlin, Sabine Hackethal had showed me Sellow's sketchbooks and folios, full of beautiful drawings of various peoples of Brazil and Uruguay, as well as their tools, weapons, houses and some words of their languages.

However, Sellow was a European man of his time. Reading his expedition reports, among all the sober commentary on the natural world, I found glimpses of ingrained prejudice and bigotry. While staying on an estancia (a large farm) in Rio Grande do Sul in 1826, for instance, Sellow was impressed with the horse-riding and cattle-slaughtering abilities of the Guaraní men working there. But he also wrote that they were 'only created to obey' and 'must always be under strict supervision'. As for the Guaraní women, Sellow had only racist and sexist things to say about them: 'These Indian women who surrender themselves with the greatest ease, have on the other hand a very negative influence on the customs of the settlers themselves and their families.'[74]

At one farm, Sellow described seeing a 'negro woman' chained up to a wooden block in the communal hall in the middle of the house 'because she had run away a few times'.

He himself relied on slaves' labour during his expeditions. In another report, he recounted a 'small quarrel' he got into with another slave-owner: 'A negro who was working here in the fields had stolen a hat and a portion of coffee off my negro and was caught hiding the coffee. The hat could not be found; to get him to confess, I had his hands tied, and some canes cut, just to scare him; alas, before he confessed, he managed to run away.'[75]

When the slave's owner arrived – she was a 'rich and very well-dressed woman' – she berated Sellow for not being more brutal with the slave. It's not clear what Sellow thought about this incident: whether he had any regret for raising the owner's ire, or sympathy for the enslaved man and the possibly dire consequences awaiting him. And although both Humboldt and Darwin consistently condemned slavery, Sellow offered no opinion about the cruelties he witnessed. I couldn't help thinking of Elizabete and Edson, the quilombolas I'd met in Brazil. Sellow could have been talking about their ancestors.

I shouldn't have been surprised to uncover these uncomfortable overtones in the feijoa's story. The history of plants contains many troubling 'unburyings' of this kind, writes Eleanor Byrne in an essay about the work of the post-colonial Caribbean writer and gardener Jamaica Kincaid. 'It appears that the historian of plants cannot fail to unearth stories of colonial devastation and appropriation that intrude onto the illusory peacefulness of the flower garden. It produces a double vision, looking with two eyes ... where the garden is at once raw, alive and corporeal, timeless and also where all is a sign, a code that leads to a vertiginous dizzying set of unfolding and unending narratives of conquest, exploitation and disaster.'[76]

Sometimes my research felt like that too – giving me a sense of vertigo as I looked deeper and deeper into the feijoa's history. I'd thought I was writing a sunny book, a story of joy and connection between humans and plants – and I am – but it felt dishonest to ignore some of these darker, more unsettling aspects of the feijoa's story, the parts that reveal what Byrne calls the 'complicity between Imperialism and Botany'.[77] Kincaid, who was born on Antigua in the Caribbean but grew up in New York City, writes that the 'plant hunters are the descendants of people and ideas that used to hunt people like me'.[78] Likewise, the land-grabbing, massive European immigration, deforestation, and repression of Indigenous culture that happened in Uruguay and Brazil in the nineteenth and twentieth centuries has close parallels with the British colonisation of New Zealand during the same period – a legacy we are still reckoning with in my own country.

Had I been naive to think that the international travels of my beloved feijoa were 'the good kind' of globalisation – an innocent sharing of a yummy fruit among people of different nations – and not just as entangled with capitalism and colonisation as everything else? My questions had led me to this precipice, and now I had to look over the edge.

―――

Like most naturalists of the early nineteenth century, Sellow did things that he would have considered just part of the job, but that today would be unthinkable: collecting the skulls of people, shooting rare birds, and sending both across the sea to decorate the museum collections of Europe. His casual assumptions about the Guaraní, and his dispassionate descriptions of the terrible conditions under which Afro-Brazilian slaves lived, are a stark reminder of the racist attitudes that underpinned the naturalist project.

Colonial powers sent botanists into the world not only to document new species, but to identify and extract plants that could be grown elsewhere to enrich the empires. Forests were cleared so that monoculture plantations of those crops – rubber, sugar, cotton, indigo – could be harvested by slaves and exploited labourers, with the profits going to the empires. Fruits were part of this nexus, too. The English naturalist Joseph Banks sent William Bligh to Tahiti on the *Bounty* to collect breadfruit, a nutritious, fast-growing plant the British Empire hoped to use to feed slaves toiling in the sugar plantations of the West Indies. (The mission was torpedoed by the famous 1789 mutiny, but four years later Bligh succeeded, delivering 678 breadfruit specimens to the Caribbean.)

At the time, many of the species-seekers themselves were quite aware of that complicity, and some seemed to view it as a good thing: the feijoa's disciple in California, Frederick Wilson Popenoe – who we will meet in Chapter 13 – wrote admiringly that 'the march of empire had gone hand in hand with the transplantation of crop plants from one part of the world to another'.[79]

Like Sellow, many beloved figures in the history of science and conservation held abhorrent views. John Muir – the US environmentalist who walked among Brazil's araucarias – described Native Americans as 'dirty' and used racial slurs.[80] Charles Darwin might have been outspoken against the slavery he witnessed in Brazil, but he also labelled the Indigenous peoples of Tierra del Fuego 'savages', called 'their voices discordant, and their gestures violent', and described their 'filthy and greasy' skins. 'Viewing such men, one can hardly make oneself believe that they are fellow-creatures, and inhabitants of the same world,' he wrote in his bestselling *The Voyage of the Beagle*. 'I believe, in this extreme part of South America, man exists in a lower state of improvement than in any other part of the world.'[81]

That sweeping dehumanisation from such a well-regarded scientist may have been used as a justification for the genocide that followed: in the late nineteenth century, white settlers in Tierra del Fuego – many of them actually New Zealanders who had come across the Pacific to run sheep stations – formed militias that hunted and killed the Selk'nam people. In just a few decades, their numbers were reduced from 4000 to a few hundred, in what a visiting missionary described as 'systematic extermination'.[82]

None of this means we have to disregard the discoveries of people like Darwin, Muir and Sellow; but we shouldn't tolerate or ignore their bigotry, either. As Agustín Fuentes wrote recently in Science: 'Today, students are taught Darwin as the "father of evolutionary theory," a genius scientist. They should also be taught Darwin as an English man with injurious and unfounded prejudices that warped his view of data and experience ... We can acknowledge Darwin for key insights but must push against his unfounded and harmful assertions.'[83]

Botanical and scientific institutions have begun to recognise the shameful parts of the plant-hunting history. In 2020, London's Kew Gardens announced they would begin 'decolonising' their plant collections, and addressing 'exploitative and racist legacies'. 'Scientists continue to report how new species are "discovered" every year, species that are often already known and used by people in the region – and have been for thousands of years,' wrote Kew's Director of Science, Alexandre Antonelli, who is Brazilian. 'The first inhabitants of Brazil and the first users of plants in Australia often remained unnamed, unrecognised, and uncompensated. They are quite literally invisible in history. This needs to change.'[84]

In the United States, there are moves to alter the common names of birds that remember enslavers, murderers and other unsavoury characters; others are trying to replace racist plant names like 'Kaffir lime' and 'wandering Jew'. It has also been argued that in giving plants Latin names, botanists simultaneously extracted and erased Indigenous knowledge: 'By supplanting the local name, the world in which the plant existed also disappeared.'[85] Some New Zealand researchers have proposed that where there is one long-held, commonly used Indigenous name for a plant species, the scientific name should be changed to reflect that: for example, the massive, iconic conifer *Agathis australis* would become *Agathis kauri*, reflecting its Māori name and the name by which most New Zealanders know the tree.

The idea is not without its critics – other taxonomists argue that it could destabilise the scientific naming system and make it hard for researchers to keep track of all the information about a given species.[86] Still, perhaps the feijoa might become *Feijoa kanakreĩn* one day; remembering and honouring the Kaingang people of its ancestral home, and forgetting Sellow the plant hunter.

But kanakreĩn is not the feijoa's only Indigenous name. What was it called in Uruguay? Of the many painful tales I unearthed while tracing the feijoa's history, the story of how that name was lost was the most shocking of all.

―――

On the 12th of March 1823, Sellow spent a day visiting a group of nomadic Charrúa in the northwest of Uruguay. They were camped by a stream with their horses, which Sellow said were mostly 'miserable and skinny'. There were about twenty huts: simple portable tents with frames made of sticks, covered with mats woven from horsehair rope and sedge leaves. The floors were lined with thick furs made from the skins of monkeys, deer and peccaries (a relative of the wild boar), and the whole thing could be quickly packed up when the group moved on.[87]

Sellow was introduced to the leader, Coronel Bondieu, a reserved man in his fifties with fine facial features. He was sitting on a jaguar skin and wearing a blue braided jacket 'like a Portuguese colonel wears'. Everyone else was naked apart from a small, decorated poncho. Sellow gave Bondieu a hunting knife and some tobacco, telling him through an interpreter he wanted to learn about the Charrúa and their language. Bondieu did not appear particularly enthusiastic about the request.

Colonisation had already been brutal for the Charrúa. Like other Indigenous peoples across the Americas, their numbers had been decimated by European diseases, conflict, outright murder and the loss of their traditional territories. Sellow was told there were just '200 men' left in the province holding out against an organised state campaign to drive them from their homelands. (No mention of how many women and children; it is not clear whether Sellow considered them worth counting or not.)

Sellow was very interested in the Charrúa weaponry – they apparently refused to use guns – and he sketched their axes, spears and arrows in great detail. He noted that a lance was made of a 'pale brown flexible wood, probably from a Myrtle species': the family of plants that includes the feijoa. Bondieu's bow was shaped from the wood of the guaviyú tree, a close feijoa-relative with small, dark purple, guava-like fruits. The arrows were struck from the straight, wand-like stems of the sarandí shrub, another native species that would later be named after Sellow: *Phyllanthus sellowianus*. Sellow didn't mention anything that sounds like the feijoa, but the Charrúa surely knew it well.

Next, Sellow visited a Charrúa man he called 'the captain'. The captain was also uninterested in conversation, as he was busy making bolas – a hunting weapon made of weights attached to connected cords, used to bring down running animals from horseback. Beside him lay a large pack of playing cards that had recently been used. Each card was made of oxhide, scraped clean and smooth, with the designs painted in earthy colours 'in imitation of old Spanish maps'. (The Charrúa made these paints from coloured earth and charcoal mixed with monkey blood, Sellow reported.) The cards were so big – around 6 inches by 3 and weighing more than 3 pounds (over a kilo) – that they had to be shuffled in the arms rather than the hands. Sellow tried to buy them, but the man refused to sell, saying cattle hides were hard to come by due to a shortage of feral cattle for hunting. (Perhaps they had a gaming rivalry going on, too, just like I have with members of my own family, and wanted to play again soon.)

The captain's wife, meanwhile, was frying the shoots of a kind of vine in horse fat, though she did not seem pleased with the recipe, and kept asking Sellow what he thought of it. The rest of the Charrúa women had been out collecting berries from the riverbank; Sellow saw them returning with bunches of onions in their hands. Describing the children, he unfortunately couldn't resist using a common racial slur of the time: 'they were happily jumping around, most of them very dark in colour. From a distance, one could have mistaken them for goats.'[88]

For the next eight years, Sellow criss-crossed Uruguay and southern Brazil, still collecting, still sketching, still making notes in shaky pencil in his little books from the back of a mule. In March 1831, he embarked from Ouro Preto on a last great journey, north into the Amazon Basin. But on the 4th of October 1831, in the upper reaches of the Rio Doce, Friedrich Sellow drowned, aged forty-two. Though his local guides advised him against it, Sellow had gone alone to the riverside near a set of rapids. When he didn't return, his companions went looking for him. On the riverbank, they found his clothes and one of his scientific instruments. There was no trace of Sellow.

Two days later, after a long search, they found his body downstream and buried it there on the shore. A month later, the news reached the King of Prussia, with the official report from the Brazilian authorities describing the death as a 'sad accident'. Others still speculate whether it was suicide, as Sellow had mysteriously made a will before leaving Ouro Preto.[89] It was a tragic end to an adventurous life; but what happened to the Charrúa that same year was far, far worse.

In 1831, Uruguay had just won its independence from Brazil, and the new republic's first president was Fructuoso Rivera, a military leader with dramatic eyebrows and a sweeping side part (his first name, believe it or not, translates as 'Fruitful'). On the 11th of April 1831, Rivera invited all the remaining Charrúa - several hundred people, including women and children - to a meeting in a narrow ravine by the Salsipuedes stream.

It was a trick. When they arrived, the Charrúa were ambushed by heavily armed government troops. In the massacre that followed, forty people were killed, and more than 300 were taken prisoner along with their families and livestock. It was an explicit and deliberate genocide. According to Rivera's own report on the massacre, penned the following day, it was designed to free up 'the most beautiful portion of the territory' for white settlers to farm, and to subjugate the 'savage and degraded hordes'. A few managed to flee the trap, but Rivera sent soldiers after them: 'the forces of the army continue to pursue them until their ... total extermination'.[90] The stream's name was eerily prescient: 'Salsipuedes' is Spanish for 'escape if you can'.

The surviving Charrúa - mostly elderly, women and children - were forced to march to the capital, Montevideo, where they were handed out as slaves to farmers or city elites who agreed to 'Christianise' them.[91] Some resorted to self-harm; mothers who had been separated from their children 'cried for hours on end ... and sometimes pulled out their own hair'.[92] In an even more grotesque twist, a French schoolmaster in Montevideo took four of the Salsipuedes captives to Paris where he exhibited them to the public as ethnographic curiosities. The group included two elderly warriors, Senaqué and Vaimaca Pirú, and a young couple expecting a child, Laureano Tacuabé and María Micaëla Guyunusa.[93]

Tacuabé brought with him a deck of leather playing cards that sound very similar to the ones Sellow tried to buy from the Charrúa he visited in 1823. Tacuabé's original cards went missing in Europe, but a copy made of them in the 1830s remains. Scholars believe they are modelled on the Spanish and French decks, but feature Charrúa designs – lines and circles, triangles and crosses – in a blend of local and colonial culture.[94]

As for the four Charrúa, they all died in France, as did the baby girl Guyunusa gave birth to shortly after they arrived. In 1938, the Uruguayan government erected a sculpture of them in Montevideo and called it 'the last Charrúas'. The national football team was named after them, too: it is known as the Garra Charrúa to this day, supposedly representing an underdog fighting spirit.

In the history books and the public narrative, the Charrúa people and their culture were extinct. With them, apparently, went their language and their knowledge of the useful and tasty native plants of their once-vast territories. Tragically, the feijoa's original Charrúa name was extinguished in the years following Salsipuedes, along with many other aspects of Charrúa culture.

The settlers flooding into the country from Europe brought with them the familiar plants of their own homelands, with seemingly little interest in what was already growing in the Uruguayan monte (woods). By 1867, a Scottish traveller reported that although a great variety of fruits and vegetables were cultivated in the fields of the country, 'the stranger will look in vain for much that is new or peculiar to America. Nearly everything is familiar, and of European origin'.[95] Oranges and peaches were already growing rampant and wild in the countryside, but the feijoas and other native trees went unnoticed among them.

By the time I went to Uruguay, few people knew what a feijoa was. The reason, I was told, was the ongoing process of colonisation – including an almost total rejection of anything Indigenous or native – that had been happening since Salsipuedes. But, incredibly, all was not lost. In Uruguay today, there is a dual re-emergence and rediscovery, both of the Charrúa themselves, and alongside them, the feijoa.

CHAPTER 8

The Reclamation

I visited Uruguay in November 2014, four days after a heavy blue line on a plastic stick told me I was pregnant for the first time, when the idea for this book was at the same embryonic stage as my daughter. Having a kid wouldn't change me, I was sure (ha!), and so it seemed natural to continue with my travel plans – I'd tacked a week in Uruguay on to a job reporting on a conference in Peru.

I went looking for wild feijoas in the north of the country, and found only a few. The countryside in general felt overly familiar, superficially similar to many parts of New Zealand: irrigated green fields, eucalyptus plantations, cows, hay bales, olives, apricots and roadside farm-equipment stores selling tractors in bright primary colours.

But in the Valle del Lunarejo, I saw tarantulas crouched among the stones, and ñandú – the grey, ostrich-like rhea – running over the hills. One night at dusk, I walked home to my posada along the gravel lane, while fireflies threaded through the fenceline and glittered in the grasslands, and thousands of white egrets wheeled across the thin crescent moon to settle squabbling in the nearby wetland. I felt I was at the very beginning of something important but as yet unformed.

A friend sent me to stay with the Uruguayan chef Laura Rosano, her husband Alejandro Arcauz and their three boys, on the family's small farm, or chacra, outside Montevideo.[96]

Alejandro was balding and bespectacled, brimming with ideas and opinions, and Laura was warm and passionate, her loose dark hair flowing over her shoulders. The little wooden house they had built together was painted red, blue, yellow and white, and strung about with hammocks, staircases and verandahs. In the garden was a duck pond and a flying fox for the kids.

The first golden, summery evening, Laura took me for a walk around the chacra, her four dogs tumbling around her. Stretching across the open field were rows and rows of small bushes the family had planted a few years earlier: all native Uruguayan fruit trees, including hundreds of seedling feijoas. Laura called them guayabos, short for guayabo del país, and pronounced in her Uruguayan accent as gwa-jah-boh.

I recognised one of the other plants, the arazá (*Psidium cattleianum*): my parents had one growing in the orchard at home, right next to the feijoas. As a child, I once ate too many of the maroon, sour-sweet fruit we called guavas, leaving me with a sore, clenched tummy. (That never seems to happen with feijoas: I can still eat dozens at a time and feel perfectly fine.) Laura's feijoas weren't ripe yet, and neither were the guaviyú - the tree the Charrúa had made their bows from - but she handed me a pitanga (*Eugenia uniflora*) to try instead. This was a gorgeous little jewel of a fruit, glistening and ruby-scarlet in colour, with scalloped edges like a miniature pattypan squash. It popped in my mouth in a burst of juice.[97]

The next morning over breakfast, Alejandro lectured me about Uruguayan history and the multinational corporations planting up the countryside with transgenic soy, while Laura made me a tea with pieces of dried feijoa in it, and ripped me off a piece of a dark, quince-like paste she had made by boiling down feijoas with sugar. In 2006, the couple returned to Uruguay after eleven years living abroad in Sweden and the Netherlands. In Europe, Laura had worked as a chef, making desserts and sauces from local berries and forest fruits. Coming home, she wanted to do the same with the native fruits of her homeland. 'We don't really have a national cuisine like Peru or Mexico,' she said. 'My idea was to work with local plants to create a kind of identity for Uruguayan cuisine.'

Her Guaraní grandmother, she remembered, had had a special feijoa tree growing in the garden when Laura's father was young, and had preserved the fruit in syrup. In the countryside, she knew, it was common to flavour rum with pitanga berries. But that was about it. Like most Uruguayans, Laura knew almost nothing about her country's native fruits. So, she began investigating what fruits existed, and where they could be bought or gathered or grown. She looked for any traditional recipes involving them, but couldn't find any. She and Alejandro planted their first native fruit trees, and in her kitchen she started to experiment. In 2012, Laura published her first recipe book, featuring arazá pancakes, pumpkin flowers stuffed with pitangas, guaviyú pannacotta, and rabbit-and-feijoa kebabs with eggplant and zucchini.[98]

In the book's foreword, fellow Uruguayan chef Francisco Neves writes that Indigenous cultures have been submerged and hidden for many years in a kind of cultural colonisation. But despite the official silence, 'it is impossible to hide the tempting sweetness of the pitangas, guaviyú, butiá, and arazá from the many Creole children who grew up on the banks of the rivers, streams and lagoons of the country ... Sooner or later the truth emerges.' Gastronomy generates culture, he writes. 'For beginners, I must warn them to prepare their senses to receive a broad-spectrum, persistent, long-lasting impact. Whoever tastes these little gems will not forget them.'

I'd let Laura know by email before arriving about my pregnancy, but at first she didn't mention it at all. I wondered if it was a social faux pas to talk about bodies to a stranger, or to reveal news of a pregnancy so early. At the end of the week, though, when I was starting to feel the first stirrings of morning sickness and exhaustion, we visited the orchard of one of her friends, Lucía de Castro.

Lucía was a feijoa fanatic from childhood, and got inspired to grow them commercially after seeing Grant Thorp speak at Uruguay's Encuentro de Frutos Nativos (a native fruit meeting). She and her husband had even visited New Zealand on the way to Bali for a surfing holiday, and Grant had given them a tour of Kiwi feijoa orchards. Now, in 2014, she was in her late forties and had two teenage boys.

That morning, as I sat with Laura and Lucía under one of her feijoa bushes, drinking mate and eating Lucía's homemade feijoa dulce, the women gave me sisterly advice about motherhood and relationships and what to expect from the tiny creature now growing inside me. It was around the size of a blueberry, the app on my phone told me. But Lucía had a better idea. The baby was my guayabito, she said – my little feijoa.

Seven years later, in 2021, I caught up with Laura in a video chat. My guayabito was now a sassy schoolgirl, and she had a little sister, too. Laura's three boys were grown men, and she was on her own – Alejandro died of cancer not long after my visit. But she had continued their joint project, and things had changed in the years since: the native-fruit revival she hoped for is underway.

'Now, when summer comes, all the chefs want to have frozen feijoas to use in their restaurants,' she said. You can buy feijoa kombucha, and feijoa features as a flavour in all the ice-cream shops. Lucía is now selling freeze-dried feijoas. Laura and another friend make feijoa beer from the fruit growing in her chacra – a dream of Alejandro's. They made it first the year after he died, in remembrance, but it was such a success they now make it every year. Laura hosts schoolchildren at the farm, teaching them about native plants, sustainability and cooking. Ultimately, she wants to see native fruits given out in public schools as a free snack. The feijoa would be perfect, she says: nutritious, delicious and loved by children.

A group of scientists at the National Agriculture Research Institute (INIA) are also working to promote native fruits, and have developed half a dozen Uruguayan feijoa varieties, which are being planted in a growing number of commercial orchards.[99] (Laura still prefers her 'hippy' seedlings: 'uniformity in food or flavour is not what I'm looking for'.) As a member of the Slow Food movement, hers is not primarily a commercial operation: instead, she's an evangelist for eating the local, the forgotten and the weird.

The plant hunters might have transported hundreds of new plants across the world, but ironically, the human diet has diminished in the centuries since. In 2019, the Food and Agriculture Organization reported that of the 6000 plant species historically cultivated for food, fewer than 200 make a significant contribution to human diets today. Only three – maize, rice and wheat – account for more than half of the plant-derived calories consumed worldwide.

Wild food species are disappearing everywhere, and Latin America is seeing the biggest declines. While you can find avocados, quinoa and kiwifruit in high-end supermarkets everywhere, in general, national diets are becoming more similar to each other – converging on a Western diet dominated by cereals, sugar and oil.[100]

'Everything has the same taste, everything is full of salt and sugar,' Laura said. 'We are losing the original flavour of our foods, and we are losing thousands of species that humans used to eat. We're losing richness. We're losing health.' For Uruguayans, eating feijoa and pitanga, arazá and guaviyú can be a form of reclamation, Laura believes. Native fruits simultaneously provide new flavours, nutrition, and a sense of identity and belonging. For Indigenous Uruguayans, that reclamation is even more profound.

When Mónica Michelena was a child, everyone said that Uruguay was un país sin índios – a country without Indigenous peoples. But at age six, an elderly relative called her negrita, and when Mónica looked in the mirror, she wondered at her dark skin and wavy black hair. She knew her Basque ancestry, three generations back on her pale-skinned father's side, but nothing about her mother's family. 'Why are we so dark?' she asked. 'Oh, there are many skin colours in the world,' her mother replied vaguely.

It was only when Mónica turned eighteen, in 1981, that she learned the truth. One of her aunts took her aside and told her that her mother's grandfather was Charrúa – at that time considered a shameful secret. 'It was like something just clicked inside me,' she told me over Zoom, standing in a field at dusk under a spreading canelón – a native tree that gives its name to the Uruguayan department and city of Canelones. 'I felt like somehow I had always known inside.' The discovery gave her a strong sense of meaning and responsibility, and set her life on a whole new path.[101]

Her mother's parents had already passed away, so she started by grilling her great-aunts and great-uncles for information. When Uruguay's military dictatorship ended in 1984, she began to meet up with other Charrúa. In 1989, they formed the Association of the Descendants of the Charrúa Nation, and began to campaign for recognition – calling themselves 'descendants' because they didn't yet dare to call themselves Charrúa. 'But now we do.'

The group began to reclaim what they could about their ancestors' culture, language and traditions by scouring colonial accounts of the Charrúa, reading past the contemptuous language to recover useful knowledge. Eventually, Charrúa elders began to open up about the ceremonies and customs that had been continued behind closed doors down the decades.

Mónica discovered that many families had kept up a Charrúa tradition of showing their newborn babies to the full moon. They would wrap the naked child in a cloth and hold them up at the window or out in the yard so that the moonlight would endow them with strength and good health. Others had learned from their grandmothers the practice of keeping the baby's umbilical cord as an heirloom, dried out and treasured in a little bag. When the children were grown, their mothers sometimes gave them back the cord and told them to bury it under a tree, with the idea that they would always remain connected to that place (a custom strikingly similar to the Māori tradition of burying the whenua – a word that means both land and placenta, earth and afterbirth – and planting a tree on top).[102]

There are no more speakers of the Charrúa language; it is considered extinct.[103] But Mónica learned of a glossary of seventy Charrúa words that had been compiled by a Uruguayan doctor and historian in the nineteenth century: guidaí, moon; hué, water; bilu, beautiful; ilabum, sleep. These seventy words are all that is left of the language. Still, Mónica and the others began using the limited vocabulary to write poems and songs and to make theatre.[104] 'For us, art was a political tool to say here we are, we were not exterminated, not everything ended in Salsipuedes,' Mónica said.

One of those cultural remnants concerned the moon, Guidaí. The Charrúa considered Guidaí an intimate friend and confidant. One of the women Mónica interviewed told a story her mother used to tell her. When she was a girl, her white father wouldn't allow the children to visit their Charrúa grandmother. One summer evening, she snuck around to the house anyway, and happened upon her grandmother sitting beneath a tree in the garden, praying to the incandescent full moon.[105]

That tree she prayed under? It was a feijoa tree.

———

Did the feijoa have a special meaning for the Charrúa, too? Sadly, the only plant word the Charrúa glossary contains is lajau, for the iconic ombú tree (*Phytolacca dioica*), a massive evergreen with a sheltering canopy that has become a cultural symbol of Uruguay. And while the woman praying in the garden might well have known the Charrúa word for the feijoa, it has long since been forgotten.

As a child, Mónica knew nothing of the feijoa, though she immediately loved the fruit when she encountered it as an adult. 'For me, it was a great discovery when I first tasted it.' When I reached out to her, she said she felt a little ashamed to learn that this native Uruguayan fruit was beloved in New Zealand, and yet went so unappreciated in its homeland.

Plant knowledge is one of the elements of Charrúa culture that has almost entirely been lost, and Mónica's own family story gives some idea of how that happened. Mónica's mother grew up in poverty in the 1920s and '30s. When there was nothing to eat, she was sent out into the forest to look for edible roots. Decades later, Mónica tried to convince her mother to go into the woods with her and show her which plants she used to collect. But every time, the conversation made her mother cry, Mónica said. 'To her it was something shameful to have to eat the roots of the forest.'

Now, in her old age, Mónica's mother is starting to remember things about her childhood, and for the first time she is sharing those memories with her daughter. Having watched Mónica's thirty-year effort to rediscover her culture, Mónica's mother has begun to identify as Charrúa herself. 'Today, she is ninety-three years old and is proud to be a Charrúa,' Mónica said.

The Charrúa are still fighting to be recognised by the Uruguayan government, academia and the public, as a legitimate Indigenous community and culture. Mónica spends part of her time with a group occupying three hectares of remote ancestral land in an attempt to regenerate their connection to place. Seven mature feijoa trees were already growing there when they arrived. She is also working alongside Laura Rosano, and some other Indigenous women, in a new project that aims to re-create a Charrúa cuisine using native fruits and aromatic plants.

Like southern Brazilians and Argentinians, Uruguayans are rarely seen without a thermos full of hot water for pouring into their mate gourds. When the coronavirus pandemic arrived in Uruguay, Mónica and her friends read online that feijoa leaves had antioxidant properties, and started putting them into their thermoses in the hope of increasing their immunity. Mónica even made a tea from the feijoa leaves, like the quilombolas do, and gave some to her husband who suffers from diabetes.

When her daughter was little, Mónica planted a feijoa tree in her garden in Montevideo. Now, both tree and child are grown. Every autumn, when the fruit falls, the two women make it into dulces, or preserves, and they eat some fresh, too. 'It is very, very important to us.'

The feijoa's Charrúa name might have been lost, but both people and plant persist.

CHAPTER 9

What's in a Name?

Names matter, says the Native American botanist and writer Robin Wall Kimmerer. Many Indigenous cultures recognise plants as living beings, and to call a being by its name is a sign of respect: 'Words and names are the way we humans build relationship,' she writes, 'not only with each other, but also with plants.'[106]

We don't know what the feijoa's first name was. In the Santa Catarina highlands, the Southern Proto-Jê must have had a name for the tree-with-green-fruit that grew under the araucarias, but it is lost to history. Their contemporary descendants, the Kaingang, call it kanakreĩn or kanekreĩn, so perhaps that most ancient name sounded something like that. In another community in Paraná, Lido told me, they call it okré. And the Charrúa name has faded away.

Today, most Brazilians call the feijoa goiabeira da serra or goiaba-serrana – mountain guava. Others call it goiaba do mato – forest guava. (Feijoa is too easily confused with feijão, a hearty stew of pork and beans.) In Uruguay it is guayabo del país (national guava, perhaps, or guava-of-our-country). Some Guaraní speakers there call it nyandua-pishá, others arazá-yaquá or arrayán. In the small pocket of northern Argentina where it's thought to grow naturally, locals call it guayaba verde, green guava.[107] In the United States, the fruit is sometimes called pineapple guava.

Nearly everywhere else, it's a variant of feijoa. To Anglophone ears, the word sounds Hispanic, but it's actually more Latin than Latino. The name sounds so odd to Colombians that they sometimes add an r – freijoa – to give it a more natural ring in Spanish. In Georgia, in far Eastern Europe, feijoa is written ფეიხოა and pronounced fay-HOY-yah. In Russia, it's фейхоа or feykhoa.

The plant's Latin species name comes from the explorer Friedrich Sellow, of course, but what of the genus name, the first part of *Feijoa sellowiana*? As we've seen, the German botanist Otto Berg named the plant *Orthostemon sellowiana* at first, but when he realised that name had been used for another plant genus, he thought of the Brazilian scientist João da Silva Feijó, latinised his name, and came up with *Feijoa*. (For a few decades, the plant was temporarily reclassified into the genus *Acca*, but recent genetic work indicates it is so unique it deserves a genus all of its own, so the genus *Feijoa* was restored.)[108]

Feijó was a travelling naturalist, like Sellow, who spent the late eighteenth and early nineteenth centuries criss-crossing the Atlantic. Born in Brazil in around 1760, he left home at the age of sixteen and travelled to Portugal to study mathematics at the famous medieval University of Coimbra. Though much younger than the other students, he caught the attention of his professors and the Portuguese authorities. In 1783, he was sent to the Cape Verde islands, a Portuguese colony off West Africa, as an official naturalist.[109]

He spent the following decade there, arguing with the bishop and local elites, witnessing a volcanic eruption on Fogo Island, and fighting off bouts of malaria, all while trying to breed flamingos in captivity, recording local customs, and collecting specimens of rocks, plants, insects and animals.

Disappointingly, he wasn't a very good husband or father: Feijó basically abandoned his wife and young son in Lisbon, leaving them destitute. Against his will, his Crown employers confiscated some of his salary to send to his wife as a form of child support.

In 1795, Feijó returned to Portugal, where he created a herbarium of his Cape Verde specimens, and in 1799 was sent home to Brazil to take up a job as sergeant-major and official naturalist of Ceará, a state in the northeast of the country. He began cataloguing the plants of the area in a document he envisioned would be his masterwork, the *Flora Cearense*. (He didn't become any more fatherly: when his son was expelled from school and sent to stay with him in Ceará, the pair clashed so much Feijó asked the military to dispatch his 'unruly and undignified' offspring to Angola or India 'for some time so that he would mend his ways'.)

Feijó died in 1824 and his work was largely forgotten. Even before his death, Napoleon Bonaparte had sent the French naturalist Étienne Geoffroy de Saint-Hilaire to pillage the Lisbon herbarium Feijó had founded, and the specimens were carried off to the Jardin des Plantes in Paris. Though Feijó and his Brazilian colleagues had carefully followed the Linnaean method and named all their new species, the French botanists erased their efforts and reclassified the plants themselves: perhaps it was this injustice Berg was trying to rectify when he gave the feijoa Feijó's name. Many of Feijó's extensive botanical writings soon fell into oblivion, too. The manuscripts of his precious *Flora Cearense* were rescued by a fellow naturalist from a bakery, where they were being used as wrapping paper.

———

Fortunately, the origins of the name feijoa don't quite stop at that sad ending.

Feijó was not the name the Brazilian naturalist was born with: his parents had actually called him João da Silva Barbosa. According to the most substantial biography I could find of him, when he was at university as a teenager in Portugal, the young Barbosa became 'so animated by Enlightenment science that he changed his name to Feijó, probably to signal his admiration for the famous Spanish naturalist and philosopher Benito Jerónimo Feijóo'.[110]

It's this Feijóo who we really have to thank for the strange word feijoa, then, and he turns out to be a pretty interesting person.[111] Feijóo – his full name was Benito Jerónimo Feijóo y Montenegro – was born in Galicia nearly a century before Feijó, in 1676. The oldest of ten children, he gave up his claim to the family wealth and entered a monastery at the age of fourteen, becoming a monk, scholar, essayist and myth-buster. Like other Enlightenment thinkers, he wanted to educate the masses about scientific discoveries and improve the human condition, but he was also a committed debunker of misinformation: he attacked such common superstitions as 'Jews have tails', 'goblins exist', 'bleeding and purging are good for every ailment' and 'menstrual blood is poisonous'.

What I like best about him is that he was also – incredibly, for an eighteenth-century man of the Spanish church – a feminist. Between 1726 and 1740, Feijóo published eight volumes of essays called *Teatro Crítico Universal*. In the first one, published in 1726, he wrote an essay defending women's intellect and promoting equal access to education: radical views at a time when even his French Enlightenment contemporaries Rousseau and Voltaire insisted on the natural inequality between the sexes.

The essay was later translated into English, with the catchy title 'An Essay on the Learning, Genius, and Abilities, of the

Fair-Sex: Proving them Not Inferior to Man, From a Variety of Examples, extracted from Ancient and Modern History'.[112] Over 227 pages, Feijóo set out to counter the 'common sayings' of the time, including that 'the most knowing woman knows as much as a raw school boy' and that women's skulls are 'as empty as a bladder full of soap-suds'. He also tried to convince the Spanish public that women could be trained in any field, from the military to medicine. 'It is time to strike out of the rugged paths of philosophy into the flowery walks of history, and prove by examples, that female intellects are equally capable of the most abstruse sciences, as those of men,' he wrote.

Feijóo gave examples of matriarchal societies in Borneo and Palestine, and highlighted the political nous of Queen Elizabeth I and Isabella of Castille. To witness women's bravery, he said, *'behold a maid of Orleans!'* (Joan of Arc). Then he provided a long list of learned women, where he gushed about their 'sublime and extensive genius' or their 'prodigy of erudition'. Anticipating a backlash – the view that his arguments might make women vain and presumptuous – he said:

> It is of use to display truth, and explode error. A true knowledge of things is valuable in itself, without regard to any other end ... If they really be our equals in mental faculties and in virtue, there is not the least harm in their knowing it and thinking so ... Let women therefore be intimately convinced, cherish a strong persuasion that they are not inferior in sagacity to men, then will they confidently encounter their sophisms, and confound their seducers.

It's no wonder that women are unfaithful to their husbands when they're treated so badly, he wrote, and he ended the essay by arguing that if men respected their wives' intelligence more, women would be less likely to commit adultery.

By Feijóo's death in 1764, half a million copies of his works had been sold. Sadly, it seems he didn't manage to change many minds. Women's rights didn't much improve during his lifetime, and women wouldn't get the vote in Spain for more than 200 years after Feijóo's essay was published.

Yet again, tugging on the loose threads of the feijoa's story – pulling them tight, right to the end – had revealed something completely unexpected. Names are just signs, sounds we use to call something or someone to mind. But with time, they accrete meanings of their own – the way barnacles and sponges encrust a wrecked ship. Hidden in the word 'feijoa' are stories, and lives – the life of Feijó, with his disappointments and his disappointing parenting, and the life, too, of Feijóo. He might have had nothing to do with the actual plant, but without 'feijoa', I would never have known of the existence of Feijóo – this enlightened and witty man who truly understood, before his time, what women were capable of.

RECIPE
Laura's Feijoa Mousse
Contributed by Laura Rosano, Uruguay

INGREDIENTS:
300 g feijoa pulp
1 tsp lemon juice
30 g of plain gelatine
1 egg white
50 g icing sugar
250 ml cream

INSTRUCTIONS:
In a bowl, beat the egg white together with the sugar and lemon juice until stiff peaks form.

In another bowl, whip the cream and set aside.

Dissolve the gelatine in ¼ cup of cold water. Heat ½ cup of the feijoa pulp in a saucepan to 80-90°C, then stir in the gelatine mixture. Add it to the rest of the feijoa pulp. Add the egg white mixture, then gently mix in the whipped cream.

Transfer to moulds or a baking dish and chill in the fridge for 6 hours. Serve with fresh feijoas, feijoa jam or Elizabete's feijoa compote.

COLLECTING
France & Italy

CHAPTER 10

A New Fruiting Tree

Friedrich Sellow sent his dead feijoa specimens across the Atlantic in the 1820s, but it would be another seven decades before the living plant would follow the same route. The feijoa was carried to Europe by the French landscape gardener Édouard André: the man who spurred its migration across the world and shaped its history more than any other person. Like Sellow, André was deeply influenced by Alexander von Humboldt and his tales of botany and adventure in South America, and like Humboldt, his life was shaped by a voyage to Colombia.[113]

Édouard André was born in the central French city of Bourges in 1840. He was the son of a horticulturalist, and followed in his father's green footsteps. By his mid-thirties, André was a successful landscape architect based in Paris. He was married, had two young sons – René and Paul – and his career was flourishing. He had served as the French capital's principal gardener for eight years, and had won a competition to design Liverpool's Sefton Park.

Then, in 1873, his wife Louise died, probably of appendicitis. She was just twenty-eight, and a few months earlier had given birth to their third child, Marie. André was devastated. Seeing his distress, Louise's older sister Cécile encouraged him to undertake the expedition he had long dreamed of: following in the footsteps of Humboldt and Bonpland in the tropical Andes of South

America. Cécile even offered to take care of the children while he was away, and the arrangement seemed to suit them both: four years later, he'd end up marrying her.

The aim of the expedition – as well as satisfying André's curiosity and distracting him from his grief – was to fill gaps in the scientific knowledge of the region, and collect specimens of plants, animals and minerals. But it was also commercial: on his return to Europe, André hoped to make a profit by selling seedlings of his botanical discoveries.

André left France in November 1875, aged thirty-five. After brief stops in Martinique and Caracas, he arrived in Baranquilla on Colombia's Caribbean coast, then travelled inland by boat on the Rio Magdalena as far as the Andes. He crossed forests, plateaus and plains to reach the volcano Chimborazo in Ecuador – the same mountain where, seventy years before, Humboldt had had his great epiphany about the interconnectedness of nature and the factors influencing the geographic distribution of plants.

Like Sellow, André collected thousands of specimens of plants, birds, butterflies, shells and animals, and recorded the customs and costumes of the peoples he encountered. But with his keen eye for landscape and design, he also took notes on the setting and layout of the city gardens of Bogotá, various Colombian towns and the promenade in Lima.

André's journey lasted around eight months. When he returned, his tales of adventure were serialised in the French newspaper *Le Tour du Monde* between 1878 and 1883.[114] Alongside André's travelogue, the newspaper included dramatised engravings made from his field sketches by other artists, including Édouard Riou, who had also illustrated the novels of Jules Verne.

The illustrations alone give a vivid picture of André's adventures, like a kind of graphic novel of plant hunting. They show canyons and waterfalls, distant volcanoes, forests of tree ferns and of towering palms, city gardens and streetscapes. There are sketches of children chasing butterflies, a tarantula capturing a hummingbird, and local men clad in wide-brimmed hats lighting each other's cigarettes while they cheer on a cock-fight.

We see André sleeping in a hammock in the jungle, surrounded by curious naked children as he peers into binoculars on the banks of the Rio Magdalena, and, disturbingly, being carried uphill on the back of a barefoot local porter in the rain, as though the man were a beast of burden: yet another reminder of the exploitation that often accompanied the naturalist project. (According to the text, André mostly walked himself or rode a horse, but this seems to have been a particularly difficult path, perhaps at high altitude. The image is titled 'La montée de l'agonie' – the climb of agony – but the agony pictured isn't André's.)

Wild weather was ever-present. The explorer leaned into a violent wind on a pass on Chimborazo, struggled up a mountain on horseback in a rainstorm as lightning sizzled above, and walked shin-deep through a swamp as torrential rain poured from his hat brim and the barrel of his gun. In other moments of drama, André is pictured abseiling down a cliff into a cave, unsuccessfully hunting a jaguar, and shooting a monkey from a tree, its frightened baby still clinging to its chest as it falls.

There are glimpses of his scientific work, too. One image shows André's field taxidermy workshop (what appears to be a small jaguar is tied to a table leg). Others show him collecting the giant, heart-shaped leaves of *Philodendron gloriosum* – now beloved by indoor-plant enthusiasts – and lying prostrate, high on a sloping cliff, reaching to collect a delicate *Schomburgkia* orchid for transplanting.

The most famous image shows André himself, bright-eyed and bearded, with a scientific instrument in one hand and a rifle in the other. He has a knife at his waist and a butterfly net at his feet. Over his shirt, pants and knee-high boots, he wears a woollen ruana – a traditional poncho-style garment with a vertical slit at the neck. Ruanas are worn to this day in the Colombian Andes, especially in the Boyacá region, where the locals celebrate the feijoa with an annual festival. (There, around 150 years later, also aged thirty-five, I would wear a ruana, too – though I'd skip the gun and knife.)

Colombia was paradise for a plant lover like André. The lush, undulating forests of the country's far southwest, between the Andes and the Pacific coast, were particularly exciting: 'the most fertile field of discoveries that the naturalist can dream of', as he described them in *L'Amérique equinoxiale*. 'Countless strange birds, new insects, and unknown plants will crowd around him. The vegetation, under the influence of the persistent humidity, equatorial heat and alluvial deposits torn from the summits, takes on an incredible luxuriance. The gigantic trees are covered with lianas from top to bottom.' Tree ferns 'gracefully tilt their arches of vegetal lace', he wrote, while filmy ferns 'line the steep walls with an adorable fringe of gauze in emerald and gold'.[115]

In one of these exuberant valleys, André first spied the plant that would help to make his name and his fortune. It was perched in the fork of a large fig tree, and it's easy to see why it would have caught his eye – the waxy, scarlet, heart-shaped flowers with their phallic golden spike would have contrasted perfectly with the plant's glossy dark leaves and the surrounding greenery. The species was later named after André by his Belgian business partner. *Anthurium andreanum* is now commonly called the flamingo flower, and is ubiquitous in garden centres and on windowsills worldwide. I have one in my bathroom – and recently spied a bouquet of them adorning the altar of a church in Tonga.

Of all the 4300 botanical specimens he collected on the voyage – 3600 of which were previously unknown to science – André considered the flamingo flower the most beautiful. 'Many samples found subsequently enabled me to send this bromeliad straightaway to Europe, where it became, and still is, a great success,' he wrote, glossing over some of the details – the first 40 plants sent to Europe died, and a second expedition had to be mounted to collect more. But the delay only added to its desirability: 'The whole horticultural press unanimously celebrates the beauty of this new species,' André wrote in 1877. 'Everywhere I am asked when it would be put up for sale.'[116]

Anthurium andreanum flowered in France for the first time in December 1880 and was finally available to buy in the spring of 1881. By autumn, André estimated the profit at between 60,000 and 80,000 francs (somewhere in the millions of $US today).[117] Colombia had made André's fortune, secured his reputation and fired up his imagination.

Over the next decade, he designed parks and gardens across Europe, including in Luxembourg, Lithuania, Rome, Monaco and Cannes. He wrote his magnum opus, *L'art des Jardins: Traité Général de la Composition des Parcs et Jardins*, a treatise on the art of landscape gardening. But he couldn't get South America out of his mind. In 1879, in the foreword to *L'art des Jardins*, he wrote: 'I can see in my mind images of these hot countries ... I was overwhelmed by these sites of wild nature a hundred times, and nothing could erase them from my memory.'[118] Sometime in the 1880s, André bought some land in Golfe-Juan, near Cannes on the French Riviera. (The city of Cannes later gifted him the adjacent ravine in recognition of the work he'd done to beautify the town.) There, André planted his own personal garden and built himself a house with a sweeping view of the Mediterranean, calling it 'Villa Colombia'.

A few years later – after André's second voyage to South America – Villa Colombia would become the feijoa's first home in Europe. And the descendants of the tree André planted in his garden in Golfe-Juan would spread around the world, its genes the basis for orchards from California to the Caucasus to New Zealand.

I wanted to find Villa Colombia. I had to know if the garden still existed, and if André's original mother feijoa tree was still there. Searching the web turned up no contemporary records of the place, but as I looked, I stumbled upon the blog of the Association Édouard André. I sent a message asking for more information about the man, the feijoa, and Villa Colombia. The secretary, Stéphanie de Courtois, a lecturer at the National School of Architecture of Versailles in Paris and an expert on André, replied in English. 'I am sorry to tell you that there is no more Villa Colombia,' she wrote. 'There has been a development on it. It's a pity!' But she put me in touch with someone else: her colleague Florence, who is André's great-granddaughter.

Florence André wasn't quite so categorical about the villa's fate. The family had sold the property in the 1920s, she said, but in the 1990s a friend of hers, Nadine, had walked the streets of Golfe-Juan looking for the spot and had found a house that looked intriguingly similar to the black-and-white photos of Villa Colombia in the old André family albums. For twenty years, Florence told me, she'd dreamed of going to investigate further, but she lived on the other side of France, and life had gotten in the way. Why don't we go together? I suggested.

So, we did. On a hot summer afternoon in 2019 – just after I'd visited Colombia, and before Berlin – I traipsed up a hill from the Cannes train station to meet Florence and her husband Paul Olivier at their hotel. We sat in the garden at a small table and shared a pot of coffee. Florence was in her sixties with black-rimmed glasses and her hair in a chestnut bob. She spoke excellent English – she had taught English and French in a former life – and her enthusiasm for gardens, history and the André story was infectious.

Florence was the baby of the family, the last of eleven children.

As a child, she wanted to become a florist and was fascinated by her famous great-grandfather. When she was in her early twenties, her father let her renovate a small billiard hall on the André family property in central France. (In later life, Édouard André split his time between Villa Colombia on the Riviera and the family home he had bought in La Croix-en-Touraine near Tours, in the Loire Valley.)

Florence noticed a little wooden door in the attic, and inside she found a big roll of brown craft paper. Nestled inside was one of André's original watercolour plans for a garden in the Netherlands. It had lain there undisturbed for a century. Her father told her, 'You found it, it's yours – but one day, you will have to do something for our ancestor.' Florence agreed, and in the 1990s she found a way to keep her promise. She founded the Association Édouard André, and began writing books and articles about his life and work. A friend once told her, 'Édouard André chose you', meaning he'd chosen her to preserve his legacy. She began to feel that perhaps he had.

Florence was now a landscape historian and lecturer at the National School of Architecture of Versailles – located in the former castle stables – and had recently written an academic paper with Stéphanie about André and the links he forged between Europe and South America. As we sipped our coffee, Florence told me more about his second trip to the continent, the time he brought the feijoa home.

———

In 1890, André and his eldest son René – Florence's grandfather – were invited to Uruguay to design a system of parks and promenades for the capital, Montevideo. They brought fashionable French landscape design to their plans for the transformation of the South American city, but André also stressed to local authorities the need to include indigenous plantings in the scheme.

'The taste for foreign plants will always prevail in private properties, but it is not the same in public areas, above all parks,' he later wrote. 'In order to achieve grand or picturesque effects that would be both satisfying to the eye and the mind, the main body of vegetation should be composed of indigenous species ... The landscape architect will come and discreetly add an exotic feature to an indigenous feature, detail to the mass, a contrasting touch to the general harmony. This is how I see the future of the rational approach to horticulture in these beautiful South American countries.'[119] With that in mind, he and René set off into the Uruguayan countryside in the southern spring to prospect for interesting native plants that would be suitable to plant in the public parks of Montevideo.

Surely, somewhere on that expedition André first laid eyes on the feijoa. At that time of year, it would have been in bloom, and just as the scarlet flamingo flower had drawn his attention in Colombia, the feijoa's unusual red-and-white blossoms would have been hard to miss. As a decorative native tree, it would have been just what he was looking for.

I feel certain that André wrote in his field journals about his first encounter with the feijoa. That moment, when the feijoa seduced him, was a turning point in the plant's history. The meeting between one man and one tree set in motion the feijoa's journey around the world, and its entry into an exclusive club: the small number of commercially cultivated food plants. I was dying to know what was going through André's mind at that moment, as well as where exactly he found the specimen that he brought back to Europe.

Sadly, André's diaries have never been located, Florence said. Could they be buried unlabelled in some archive or attic somewhere, like those plans you found? I asked. 'Unfortunately, what I suspect is worse,' she said. When Florence was a child, the La Croix house was under the tenure of her grandmother Claire, René's wife. Florence remembers the attic being stuffed full of plans and documents and books. But when Claire died in the late 1950s, Florence's mother took over, and wanted to put her own stamp on the house. Florence – still very young – remembers her elder brothers and sisters gleefully bringing the old things down the stairs, carrying them into the garden, and setting them on fire. 'We cannot imagine their mind, I think,' she said to me, seeing my horrified face. 'They had lived through the Second World War, and they wanted to go forward, not backward. They found all this old stuff very heavy. That's my feeling. So, unfortunately, I think Édouard André's little books disappeared in this great fire.'

Though the details of their collecting adventure have been forgotten, we know André and his son brought one layered feijoa plant home to France in 1890. (Layering is a method of propagating plants by causing their shoots to take root while still attached to the parent plant, producing a clone.) André planted his feijoa in the garden at Villa Colombia. In doing so, he was part of a cultural phenomenon – a craze for introducing exotic plants to the Côte d'Azur, the coastline also known as the French Riviera.

In the second half of the nineteenth century, the Côte d'Azur had become 'a sort of Garden of Eden for plant-lovers', according to the French garden historian Michel Racine.[120] Sandwiched between the Alps and the Mediterranean, the south-facing Provence coastline was bathed in a warm microclimate with mild winters that allowed gardeners to experiment with subtropical and tropical plants that wouldn't grow elsewhere in Europe.

As early as the 1840s and '50s, palms from North Africa were being planted on the French Riviera, helping to create the region's distinctive aesthetic. In an era when Instagram-happy tourists flock to places like New Zealand for selfies among mountains and lakes, it's hard to imagine a time before landscape tourism existed – but it was born here on the French Riviera in the nineteenth century, and the landscape that was its symbol was a globalised one.

Before 1850, according to Racine, 'pirates were legion' along the Côte d'Azur. The coastal road linking Nice and Genoa was so primitive carriages couldn't use it, and it was often cut off by flooding. But new road and rail links along the Provence coastline in the 1860s and '70s opened up the region from Cannes to the Italian border, attracting writers, musicians, journalists, painters, and 'the idle rich in search of perpetual springtime'.[121]

By 1887, a French writer travelled by boat between Antibes and Saint-Tropez and saw 'countless villas amid the shrubbery all along this endless shore, looking like white eggs laid during the night ... by monstrous birds from those snow-covered peaks visible beyond the coast'.[122] Many of the new arrivals were British, and the influx didn't always meet with local approval. In 1856, Prosper Mérimée, the inspector of historic monuments at Cannes, wrote that the English 'settled here as if in conquered territory ... They have built fifty villas or chateaux, each more extraordinary than the last, and deserve to be impaled upon the architecture which they have brought to the area.'[123]

The coast began to be seen as a kind of zone of transition between Europe and 'The Orient'.[124] British colonisers returning from the Empire's far-flung tropical outposts spent time on the Riviera reacclimatising to European soil, and invalids were sent there to recuperate from tuberculosis and other maladies. In testing whether the feijoa would grow on the French Riviera, André was part of a growing community experimenting with another form of acclimatisation: not of the human body, but of plants.

The expeditions of Humboldt to South America, Darwin's circumnavigation of the globe, and even earlier, the collections made by Joseph Banks and Daniel Solander on Captain Cook's voyages to the Pacific, had sparked a kind of 'botanical fever'. Many in the European aristocracy became fascinated with exotic plants. Rather than collecting, drawing and describing them, as the botanists did, a new generation of horticulturalists and landscape gardeners wanted to grow them instead.

Inspired by Humboldt's insight that the distribution of plant species is shaped by climate, elevation and latitude, they began the practical study of what could be grown where, filling their gardens with a riotous mélange of the world's subtropical species from Australia, South Africa, New Zealand, Asia, the near East and South America. All along the Riviera, they created a living display of the world's botanical treasures on the promenades and public squares and in the gardens of the wealthy.

———

André had to wait seven years, but in 1897 his feijoa tree finally fruited. When he broke one open and tasted it for the first time, he had only just found out what the fruit was actually called. A year earlier, in 1896, he had sent a flowering feijoa specimen to his friend Joseph Hooker, the former director of Kew Gardens in London. (As a young man in the 1830s and '40s, Hooker had collected plants all around New Zealand and the subantarctic islands and explored Antarctica, publishing a book on the region's plants, *Flora Novae-Zelandiae*, in 1853.)[125]

André asked the famous botanist to find out the Latin name of his Uruguayan fruit tree, saying he thought it must be a species of *Psidium*, a kind of guava. Figuring it out 'proved to be a very troublesome task' for Hooker: 'it was not until I undertook a systematic inspection of the whole vast tribe of Myrteae in the Kew

Herbarium that I was able to give M. André the name'.[126] Finally, André had all the information he needed to make a big splash in the *Revue Horticole*, the horticultural magazine of which he was the editor-in-chief.

In an article in its pages in 1898 he announced the feijoa to the world: 'A NEW FRUITING TREE: FEIJOA SELLOWIANA.'[127] Of all the woody plants that he brought back alive from Uruguay in 1890, André considered it 'one of the most important and useful for horticulture', he wrote. He provided a new scientific description of the plant, based on his own observations of the feijoa at Villa Colombia, which was now 3.5 metres high and equally wide. And he had clearly had an opportunity to try the fruit: 'Flesh thick, white, pulpy and watery, with a sweet and strongly perfumed flavour, reminiscent of Pineapple and Guava and exhaling an extremely sweet and penetrating smell, even before the fruit is ripe.' (Perhaps it's André we have to thank for the feijoa's common name in North America, 'pineapple guava'.)

The previous scientific descriptions and illustrations of the feijoa were not quite correct, André added. The black-and-white botanical drawing of the feijoa in *Flora Brasiliensis*, made nearly forty years earlier, showed the petals flat rather than hood-shaped, and Berg's description omits their contrasting colours – purplish-red inside, white outside. Those errors were rectified in the full-colour image accompanying the *Revue Horticole* article. With the luxury of having a living feijoa tree in his own garden, rather than having to refer to dried-up, decades-old herbaria, André was able to provide a much more vivid, accurate description of a plant that was of intense interest to botanists, horticulturists and home gardeners worldwide.

André summed up: 'So here we are in possession of a new fruit tree for the "Côte d'Azur" and the warm regions of the Mediterranean basin, and even for other regions of colonial

France.' Then he casually mentioned that young feijoa plants – propagated from his mother plant – would be available for sale in Lyon-Vaise from the following autumn.

Later in 1898, Joseph Hooker published another botanical drawing of the feijoa in *Curtis's Botanical Magazine*. (The image was drawn by Matilda Smith, a second cousin of Hooker's who was also the first botanical artist to illustrate the New Zealand flora. In the nineteenth century, botanical art was seen as one of the few scientific occupations suitably dainty enough for women.) André then wrote a follow-up piece in the *Revue Horticole*, describing the fruits in more detail: 'Their aroma was so intense that it filled the whole room in which they were placed, and the basket which held them is perfumed to this very hour.'[128]

André also sent a special package to *The Gardeners' Chronicle*, a British horticultural magazine, containing sprigs of leaves and a few ripe fruit from his feijoa tree 'on the sunny shores of Golfe Juan'. As he no doubt hoped, the *Chronicle* wrote a glowing, illustrated article: 'What the flowers and fruit are like may be judged from our illustrations; but to attempt to convey any description of the flavor of the fruit in words would be futile. Suffice it to say that it is – well, it is "fruity," acid, aromatic, spicy – we will add only one more adjective – delicious.'[129]

The story was then picked up by newspapers around the world, including the *Scientific American*, the *Geelong Advertiser*, the *Adelaide Chronicle*, the *Otago Witness* and the *New Zealand Herald*, where it featured in between an announcement for a sheep-dog trial and an advertorial for soap that supposedly cured 'scalp humours'. In March 1899, the *Australian Town and Country Journal* published a special follow-up note – no doubt quoting the *Chronicle*, rather than personal experience, as the feijoa had not yet arrived in Australia:

> A New Fruiting Tree.
> (FEIJOA SELLOWIANA)
> Since a figure and description of the above-named tree appeared in these columns many inquiries have been made about it, and not a few have asked what the flavor of the fruit is like. To the last query we may add that it is delicious – acid, aromatic, and spicy. We can only repeat our former suggestion that the tree is well worth introducing to cultivation in the warmer coastal districts of Australia.

By 1900, botanical gardens in Algeria and Russia had planted their own feijoas, and by 1903 they were being cultivated in Georgia, at Batumi on the eastern edge of the Black Sea.[130] In 1905, André received a letter from the head gardener of the Sultan in Constantinople, asking why his three-year-old feijoas were flowering abundantly but not fruiting. André responded in the *Revue Horticole* that Turkey was perhaps too dry during the spring flowering period, and asked whether the plants were seedlings or clones of his mother plant at Villa Colombia – seedlings were often slow to fruit, he explained.[131]

André's garden was ground zero for the feijoa as a cultivated plant, and the single tree he planted there was the direct ancestor of feijoa plantations in Europe, Asia, North America and New Zealand. But did it still exist in 2019? Had the land been bulldozed and developed into villas or hotels, as Stéphanie de Courtois from the Association Édouard André had suggested? Even if it had been razed, perhaps remnants of the old garden remained.

Florence André and I were determined to find out.

CHAPTER 11

The Hunt for Villa Colombia

Florence and Paul picked me up the next morning from the Cannes train station, and we began the search. First, we went to the Cannes municipal archives. They occupied a small room on the ground floor of a modern, peach-coloured building, hidden among fancy gated villas in the hills above the centre of town.

Florence had brought two clues with her. One was the André family photo album from the early 1900s, full of black-and-white images of Villa Colombia. The second was that someone – she couldn't remember who – had once told her that the property might have been renamed Villa Endymion. (I had already searched online for contemporary references to this name, and found none.) The archives held the complete records of the local Andrau real estate company, clearly the main game in town when it came to early twentieth-century property deals. As Florence suspected, there were no files under the name of Villa Colombia, but soon the archivist brought us the one for Villa Endymion. Around a centimetre thick, it contained correspondence between the property's various owners and the agency – photocopied photographs, typed letters, handwritten notes and folded site plans.

As Florence leafed through the documents, I looked at the André family album. Tiny photographs from February 1902 showed the approach to Villa Colombia, a large diagonal gate on the corner of two unsealed streets. The house itself was modest, a two-storey white rectangle with a tiled triangular roof and small balconies on the upper floor. By 1908, the André family had built a third storey with three shuttered windows looking out over a lush garden of palms, Australian wattles (also called mimosas or acacias) and eucalypts. On every page, I looked for plants that could be feijoas, but there wasn't enough detail in the images to be sure.

In one picture, dated April 1908, three women lounged on the terrace, a semicircular concrete platform on the hillside above the house. Beyond them, the coast curved away to the Antibes peninsula in the west. Another photo from around the same time was captioned 'Tout le monde aux fenétres', 'Everyone to the windows', and a family member stood framed in each one. Another Paul – André's second son – stood in the middle window on the first floor, surrounded by women in dresses with bishop sleeves that ballooned at the wrist, their dark hair piled in loose buns on their heads. In the doorway were a group collectively captioned as 'les Amalberti', the Italian family the Andrés hired as gardeners. The image was framed by a palm and what seemed to be a large eucalyptus tree. Many of the pictures showed Paul André's daughters and their friends in 'le ravin', the ravine, sketching or playing on a small bridge among dense vegetation. 'It must have been an amazing place for a child,' Florence said, looking over my shoulder.

The absence of Paul's elder brother René in the photos told another story, Florence said. René – Florence's grandfather – worked in his father's landscape design business and took it over after Édouard André died in 1911. He spent a lot of time travelling to work on gardens in Russia, Cuba and Egypt. Responsible for half the costs, but getting none of the enjoyment, he probably suggested selling the place.

There were photos in the Villa Endymion file, too, but the house labelled as such, with its circular features, didn't look anything like the rectangular Villa Colombia of the family album. Perhaps we hadn't found it after all. But as we worked our way through the documents, things started to fall into place. There were photographs of manicured gardens surrounded by mature palms, and of a bridge over a forested ravine. Another photo was even more promising. It seemed to be taken from the same vantage point as the picture of the André family at the windows: a palm and a eucalypt framing a house that *was* recognisable as Villa Colombia, with the addition of several balconies and some Grecian columns.

Next, Florence took out a map, showing plans to divide the property into five sections. It showed a 'Villa Endymion' near the bottom of the property, a watercourse marked 'ravin', and a curving half-moon structure near the top that looked just like the terrace where the André women had lounged. Further into the folder, we found a dog-eared, typewritten sales advertisement in English, describing 'a charming freehold residential property situate [sic] at Cannes-Eden on the slopes of a fine range of hills between Cannes and Golfe-Juan'. It detailed the 'pleasure grounds . . . of exceptional beauty', the 'beautiful terrace in a unique position for Villa site' and the mature acacia plantations, their fluffy sunshine-yellow pompoms sold for cut flowers. Then, the smoking gun:

> The lawns and gardens were laid out by Monsieur André, Horticultural gardener to the French Government, to whom the property originally belonged . . . The many walks on the property are bordered by a wonderful collection of exotic palms and rare shrubs collected from all parts of the world . . . The Washingtonia and other palms, and the giant Eucalyptus trees – named after Monsieur André – are a special feature of the property. Another exceptional feature is the ravine through which runs a mountain torrent bordered by sequestered walks.

Bingo. Rare shrubs, even! 'So, it's true,' Florence said. 'It really is this one.'

Gradually, the story emerged. In around 1923, the André brothers, René and Paul, sold the property to an English buyer, who – more interested in trendy Ancient Greece than in the obscure plants of Colombia – renamed it Villa Endymion after the handsome shepherd of Greek myth. (In one story, the goddess Diana fell in love with Endymion as he lay sleeping, and condemned him to eternal, immortal sleep so she could gaze on his youthful beauty forever.)

A second map of the property, on a large, creased sheet of builder's paper, showed what happened next. A larger villa was built on the site of that 'beautiful terrace', and this new house became known as Villa Endymion instead. André's Villa Colombia changed names for a second time, to Villa Diane. Those early plans to subdivide the property hadn't eventuated – but what had happened later in the twentieth century? The file showed the property had changed hands several times, but the records of the real estate company finished in 1979. Florence had heard rumours that a new villa development had been built on the site.

Well, now we would find out. The map showing the two villas had street names on it. The property seemed to be surrounded by Avenue Édith Joseph. I plugged it into Google Maps, and there it was: a curved road matching the contours on the plan. The satellite view even showed two houses in roughly the same positions, with plenty of vegetation around them. It was a fifteen-minute drive away. I was impatient to get there, to see what had become of André's paradise. Perhaps it hadn't been concreted over with apartments, after all – maybe his garden was still there, and the grandmother feijoa too.

Avenue Édith Joseph branched steeply off the main coast road, a jungly gully – the ravine! – falling away to the left towards the sea. Florence found a place to park near the crest of the hill, and she, Paul and I walked towards the house that had to be the heavily developed Villa Endymion. But the sign on the tall iron gate read 'Villa Eden Roc'. Next to it was a row of buzzers for half a dozen apartments. I pressed them, one by one. We waited. The early afternoon was hot and still, the cicadas whined, and the scent of pine and eucalyptus rose between the neatly clipped hedges. Eventually, a man with slicked-back silver hair emerged, wearing aviator sunglasses, a gold chain, an apricot-coloured collared shirt, and shorts so tiny that for a disturbing moment I thought he wasn't wearing any.

He seemed unimpressed with our quest. We had interrupted his siesta, after all. He had never heard of Édouard André, and besides, he said, he didn't care about the past. The neighbouring property – comprising the ravine and the house I thought must be Villa Diane, the original Villa Colombia – was abandoned, he said. 'Squatters are living there now.' We thanked him, apologised, and began walking back down the Avenue Édith Joseph towards the ravine. It was completely overgrown. Amongst the tangled vegetation I could make out figs, olives and bananas, and a row of tall palms. Webs of morning glory draped themselves over the trees.

At the bottom of the avenue was a white rectangular house with a tiled roof. As we rounded the corner onto the main coast road and arrived at the entrance, the gate opened to allow a woman through on a shiny black Vespa. She was wearing aviators, too – along with a leopard-print shirt, black miniskirt, high heels and heavy make-up. She was on her way to DJ at a local club, she said, when Florence stopped her to ask if we could have a look at the house. She agreed and zoomed off. Paul stood by the sensor to keep the gate open. But after a quick look around, it was clear it wasn't what we were looking for. It had to be the place next door.

A hundred metres further along the road we found the gate. Spray-painted graffiti was scrawled on the rusty metal. 'CHIEN MECHANT', it read, warning of a mean or vicious dog. Then, in English, 'NO ENTER'. I wasn't sure if I was brave enough to climb over this gate in search of feijoas. But I couldn't bear to turn back now. While we hesitated, the gate opened and a guy with missing teeth emerged, also on a scooter. (His accent was Algerian, Florence said afterwards.) We explained our story, and the squatter was friendly enough. He said we could look around, 'but don't go up the back, the dog's up there'.

Gingerly, we stepped inside. The light was dim under the canopy of vines, and fat mosquitoes swarmed about our legs. Abandoned among the bushes were the skeletal remains of old cars, bicycle parts and almost-fossilised washing-machine drums. The house loomed out of the trees on our left. The door was open, and the room inside was graffitied with Disney figures. Mickey, Goofy, Pinocchio and Donald Duck ran jauntily up the staircase in peeling pastel.

I climbed over some dead potted plants and nosed around the back to see the house from the other side, trying to mentally compare it to the image from the photo album. It didn't look quite right – there was a steep bank behind where there should have been a flat path. Had the original house been entirely destroyed? Returning to the front of the house, I climbed up the hillside into the blackberry-tangled undergrowth, anxiously listening for the 'mean dog', and looking everywhere for a big old feijoa tree. I found a decrepit house bus, more rubbish, and someone's washing hanging from a curious brick structure, but no feijoas.

Paul and Florence were sweaty and tired, and I felt bad for dragging them along on this mosquito-infested wild-goose chase in the heat of the afternoon. As we trudged back uphill to the car, I asked Florence how it made her feel: that André's beautiful vision had been reduced to this. 'I feel that my family would be very rich if they had kept it!' she said. She hadn't really answered my question, and I felt despondent. But then she said, 'I think it's not the right place. I don't know. I didn't feel anything about it – except for the little path up in the ravine.'

'But Avenue Édith Joseph was marked so clearly on the map,' I said. How could it not be here? I couldn't bear to give up, but there seemed to be nothing more we could do.

We were driving back to Cannes when all at once I saw a familiar house out of the window. It was the one Florence's friend Nadine had photographed twenty years earlier, thinking it could be Villa Colombia. Paul stopped the car and I hopped out, jumping up on a low wall to peek at the house. It had the same rectangular profile and rows of three shuttered windows, but no balconies, and the orientation to the road wasn't right. Then I noticed a slight woman around Florence's age sitting in the garden watching me as I balanced on her fence. She came to the gate, Florence explained our story, and the woman invited us in. Her name was Ghislaine, and this couldn't be Villa Colombia, she said – her own grandfather had built the place in 1912.

But when Florence mentioned Villa Endymion, she brightened. 'That's just up the road!' she said. 'Do you want me to take you?' Hardly daring to hope, we followed her back along the street the way we had come, past some bizarre mobile phone towers poorly disguised as metal conifers and Phoenix palms: 'The whole neighbourhood opposes them,' said Ghislaine. When she was a child, her father had worked as a gardener at villas all around Golfe-Juan, she said, and he used to bring home feijoas for her. 'It's like a little kiwi, you cut it open?' This suburb was called 'Little Africa' at the turn of the twentieth century, she said, because of its warm microclimate and exotic gardens.

Up ahead was a large black metal gate, decorated with gold curlicues and set diagonally across the corner of the avenue and a small street. Beside it was a little plaque reading 'Villa Endymion'. 'Et voilà,' said Ghislaine. Behind the gate towered (real) palms and cypresses, and nestled among them was a peach-coloured rectangular house with rows of three shuttered windows... I ran down the street towards it, and there, on the wall near another gate, a creeper climbed over a hand-painted tile: 'Villa Diane'.

Looking up, the house had the same scalloped balconies and Grecian columns as the photographs from the real estate file. Florence and I excitedly looked from the historic pictures to the house in front of us. It was clear this really was André's original Villa Colombia. While we were talking, the large gate up ahead began to open, revealing a mass of greenery beyond. A fit blond man in his fifties waved a visiting car out of the driveway. He had striking light blue eyes, and looked somehow familiar. (I realised later he reminded me of James Bond actor Daniel Craig.)

I ran over to him, and began a breathless and mangled French explanation of our mission. I called Florence over to help. The man's name was Brice, she translated, and he looked after the garden year-round for the wealthy, often-absent British owners. Yes, he said, there are still feijoas here. 'Come, I'll show you.' He set off briskly up the tidy stone path with his golden Labrador trotting behind. Ghislaine waved and walked home, but Florence, Paul and I followed Brice into André's garden.[132]

The original property had been divided in two, Brice said. Villa Diane, the original Villa Colombia, belonged to someone else, while his bosses owned the newer Villa Endymion and the majority of the garden. It wasn't always this neat. Brice started working here seventeen years ago – after serving in the French military in Africa, he had been searching for a more peaceful life. Back then, he said, the garden was a jungle, and it'd been his job to restore it. When the owners learned about André, they asked Brice to try to re-create the original garden. They even asked him to replace all the newer concrete paths with the original stone.

'Here's a eucalyptus your ancestor planted,' Brice said to Florence. 'It got hit by lightning five years ago, but it's growing again.' He pointed out three specimens of *Gunnera tinctoria*, the giant Chilean rhubarb, their massive upturned leaves a ridged topography of mountains and valleys. André planted them in the garden, too, he said, but they have become such an invasive pest that selling or propagating them in both New Zealand and the European Union is now illegal. There was a tiny *Araucaria angustifolia*, too – from the feijoa's native forest in Brazil – which Brice said he'd bought in England and brought back by car, part of an effort to collect every *Araucaria* species for the garden.

Then we crossed the ravine on a little wrought-iron bridge. 'There's the feijoa,' said Brice, waving. I turned back and squawked in excitement – I'd walked right past it. There it was indeed, blending into a wall of green on the uphill side of the bridge. I could see immediately, though, that this was no ancient grandmother feijoa. 'Is this the biggest one?' I asked. It was. There had been another one here, Brice said, but it had gotten sick, so they had cut it out in case it contaminated other trees.

'It has the most magnificent flower, so delicate!' he said. It only fruits every three years or so, and Brice hadn't tasted one, yet. But when it's windy, he said, the shaking branches reveal the undersides of the leaves, so they flash dark green and silver. 'That attracts the birds that pollinate it – isn't it genius?' I'd never heard that theory before, but it could be true. Birds are highly visual, after all.

I hadn't found André's original feijoa, but this was probably one of its children or grandchildren. Perhaps, on this very spot, André knelt in the soil and pressed his layered feijoa into the ground, or stood here to make the observations of the plant for his article in the *Revue Horticole*. I paused on the little bridge while the others went on ahead among beds of fragrant Provençal lavender. The mature trees, the feijoa, even the recurring weeds – they all bore André's imprint. On these few hectares of earth, he carried out his experiments and ate his first feijoa.

Eleanor Byrne, analysing what she calls the 'postcolonial gothic' in Jamaica Kincaid's work, writes that all gardens are haunted – that almost every garden must be made from the ruins of the one that preceded it. '[T]races of others' lives still remain deep in the soil, that may reveal themselves, uncannily, not uninvited guests to the property, not invaders, but ghosts ... introduced to the garden by other owners and gardeners, whose legacy must be reckoned with.'[133] I liked the idea of botanical ghosts, wriggling up through the earth after decades of dormancy, telling a subtle story of the people, like André, who had once gardened this same soil.

Brice led us around the corner towards the main house: the Villa Endymion, which had been built after the André brothers sold the property, on the site of the half-moon observation terrace where Florence's elegant aunts had strolled in 1908. It was still there, the semicircle deck just incorporated into the main house. Now, it overlooked a mature Chilean monkey puzzle tree (first cousin to Brazil's araucarias) and an inviting, crystal-clear infinity pool.

'Oh là là, all of this is very moving.' Florence was ebullient, her tiredness forgotten. 'I love seeing all this, it's incredible,' she said to Brice. 'How extraordinary that you opened the gate exactly at that moment. You can't imagine what it means for me to be here with you. When I think that my father played here as a child!' Until today, she had thought that Villa Colombia had been developed beyond all recognition, like so much of this glamorous coast. Then, for a brief moment, we had feared it had been mistreated and abandoned. But now, here was her patrimony, her ancestor's garden, still an oasis, uncovered by concrete, a living record of the exotic plants André had loved.

Looking back at the real estate map, it seemed clear that the roads had been mislabelled, or else the names had changed. Avenue Édith Joseph followed the same contours around the hillside and ravine, but was located a few hundred metres further down the slope than the actual street that curved around André's garden. Somehow, miraculously, we'd managed to find Villa Colombia anyway.

CHAPTER 12
Finding the Oldest Feijoa

The garden had survived the twentieth century, but André's mother feijoa had not: the sole disappointment of a serendipitous afternoon. It's possible feijoas don't even live as long as 130 years; no-one has ever studied their longevity. Still, perhaps somewhere I could find one of that original tree's earliest offspring, and get some idea of how old a feijoa can get. By now I was in the middle of my second 2019 feijoa trip, including visits to Colombia, France, a fragment of Italy and Berlin. Indigo was twenty months old, and I'd weaned her for good this time, breastfeeding for the last time in the check-in line at Auckland Airport. As I travelled around by train and on foot along the Côte d'Azur, I looked for ancient feijoas.

I had high hopes for Villa Thuret, a botanical garden on Cap d'Antibes. At the end of the nineteenth century, the director had been friends with André, and the garden's records showed a feijoa was planted there in 1903. But those I found at Villa Thuret were straggly and relatively young. In gritty Marseille, I unsuccessfully scoured the seaside gardens of Villa Valmer, trying to find the feijoa I'd seen pictured in a 1913 booklet; and in glitzy Monaco, I found young feijoas growing as trimmed box hedges bordering the steep street above the marina, their flowers fringing a view of the superyachts below. Around the corner, walking past shopfronts full of ugly Gucci bags, I entered the huge plaza in front of the famous Casino de Monte-Carlo. Valets collected wealthy gamblers in shiny convertibles, tourists posed for pouting selfies, and a couple climbed through a top-hinged door into a low-slung Lamborghini, the engine belching into life as they roared away. At the tables overlooking the square, an Aperol Spritz cost 18 euro.

In 1881, André designed both the park leading down the hillside towards the casino – called 'Le Boulingrin' after English bowling greens – and the next-door tropical gardens known as the Jardins de la Petite Afrique.[134] As I wandered the winding paths behind a gaggle of chatty Indian girls, among massive trees from all over the world, I felt I was beginning to understand something of the art form André helped to pioneer – landscape architecture. Stepping into his urban gardens from a city street can feel like an escape into nature. Yet they are completely manmade: a composition assembled from a global palette of fronds and foliage, twigs and trunks, flowers and fruit and form. There's something opulent and creative and over-the-top about the combination of plants from everywhere. Each tree invites you to look at it: to consider it as an individual species, rather than as an integrated part of a forest. It's the opposite of an ecosystem, in a way, but it's art.

A garden, writes Racine, 'is a space charged with meaning, a space that embodies an ideal or fuses ideas. It gives a faithful portrait of the gardener, revealing his intimacy with the site and surroundings and his ideas on the natural world. A garden is a system to be read, a living architectural composition representing the tastes and practices of a given society, full of allusions to the other arts: literature, painting, sculpture, and music.'[135] André's eclectic creation reveals the nineteenth-century European passion both for cataloguing and naming the world, and for thinking about plants and animals in isolation, rather than as part of an interconnected whole.

I walked beneath towering Moreton Bay figs, and massive New Zealand pōhutukawa with their familiar blood-red flowers and hairy armpits. There was also a rare, rather unhappy-looking Wollemi pine. A relative of both the kauri and the araucaria, Australia's Wollemi pine was thought to have gone extinct millions of years ago, until a singular grove was discovered in a canyon near Sydney in 1994. As a kind of insurance policy for the critically endangered species, clones were sent to botanical gardens around the world.

Near the bottom of the garden, past a group of ancient olives and a banana grove, I found another feijoa, mature and carefully topiaried, but quite young. It might have been planted in homage to André, but not a century ago.

―――

I kept looking. With Florence and Paul, I visited Square Mistral in downtown Cannes. Florence had discovered the square by chance a few years ago, and noticed green fruits covering the ground. She asked some local children what they were, and they told her: feijoas. Florence was thrilled; she had read André's articles about the plant in *Revue Horticole*, but had never tried one before. She gathered armfuls of fruit and took them back to Paris, where she was hosting a stand about André at a horticultural show. Florence filled a bowl with feijoas and gave them away to the surprised visitors, telling them of André's role in the plant's story. 'It was a great success,' she told me. 'Everyone said, "What's that?"'

As we walked past the ponds and fountains, dodging children playing on scooters and with water pistols, Paul told me the square was named after a contemporary of André's, the poet Frédéric Mistral. While André was busy creating gardens, the writer was rescuing a language. Mistral's epic poems were written in tribute to the landscape and language of Provence: Provençal, a dialect of Occitan.[136]

After the region was conquered by France in the fourteenth century, French rulers tried to repress the speaking of Occitan, just as successive New Zealand governments would later attempt with the Māori language. Through his poetry, the creation of a Provençal dictionary, a literary association and an ethnographic museum, Mistral took it upon himself to revive the language, and give the people of Provence a stronger connection to their heritage and stories. 'Lis aubre que van founs soun li que mounton aut,' he wrote: 'Trees with deep roots grow tall'. (The story also reminded me of Mónica Michelena's attempts to revive the Charrúa language in Uruguay.) In 1904, Mistral won a Nobel Prize for his efforts, and in 1963 the city of Cannes renamed this small square after him. Paul said his Marseille-born father knew many of Mistral's Provençal poems by heart: 'I used to listen to him recite them when I was young.'

'There it is!' interrupted Florence. On the far side, near a couple of park benches and a small playground, was one of the oldest feijoas I'd ever seen, its central trunk gnarled and twisted. Florence measured it with her hands. A metre around, she thought. 'I am very proud to have brought you here,' she said. 'I'm coming from a little far, and you from very far! C'est le jardin planétaire – the world is a garden.'[137] I climbed into the branches, wondering if this tree could have been planted by André, and thinking of Mistral. How deep did the roots of this tree go? But none of my subsequent investigations revealed any connection between André and Square Mistral, or any records of the park's design or plantings. The age of the Mistral feijoa remains a mystery.

Finally, past the eastern end of the French Riviera, just over the border in Italy, I found my ancient feijoa. It's probably not the truly oldest feijoa in the world: older trees almost certainly exist. But no-one has ever studied the dendrochronology of feijoas – whether their rings can be counted to determine their age – and few records survive from the early twentieth century about when and where particular feijoa trees were planted.

The sprawling Italian tree in the Hanbury Gardens in the tiny village of La Mortola is one of the only ones I found that can be persuasively dated back more than a century, to sometime before 1912. It's fitting, in a way – the place is replete with history, stuffed with stories, and the feijoa is just one of the celebrities to have made a cameo there.

After leaving Florence, I stayed the night in a palatial, turreted building that dominated the skyline of the town of Menton, on the French side of the border with Italy. First opened as a luxury hotel in 1903, the Winter Palace epitomised France's Belle Époque – the years of joie de vivre between the late 1800s and 1914, before the Great War reduced the continent to mud and trenches. In that optimistic era, English and Russian 'hivernants' – winterers – flocked here in the cooler months to enjoy the mild climate, the striking scenery and the luxurious tropical vegetation on their daily promenades.

The Winter Palace is now a private apartment building. My host, Jocelyne, was eighty years old, and seemed like she would have belonged among the Belle Époque plant-lovers. Her small apartment brimmed with houseplants and books. 'I've been reading about how trees talk to each other through the soil,' she said, spritzing a large drooping succulent with water. It was an orchid cactus from Mexico, she said, *Epiphyllum oxypetalum*, the Queen of the Night.

It only flowers one night a year, and when it does, Jocelyne throws a party for it, so her friends can watch the dazzling white blossoms turn towards the moon. 'It's pretty ugly, so I keep it growing here with its friends,' she told me, lifting an overlaying vine so I could see it better. 'No, you're not ugly!' she cooed, then whispered to me that it had sulked for a few years until she spoke nicely to it. The next morning, as I left via the Winter Garden's grand entrance hall, something caught my eye: a splash of red between the Grecian columns and the elegant marble staircase.

It was the flamingo plant, *Anthurium andreanum* – the bromeliad named after André, the one he had collected in Colombia. Florence believed André had chosen her to carry on his legacy. For a moment, it felt like maybe he had chosen me, too.

Later that morning, Carolyn Hanbury herself escorted me to Hanbury Gardens in La Mortola. Cicadas chainsawed from the pines, and beyond the arched gateway, palms and pathways tumbled down the arid hillside to the blue Mediterranean Sea beyond. 'I think it's one of the great entrances to a garden,' Carolyn said, as we set off down the steps between an avenue of cypresses. Blue jacaranda flowers offset the greenery and the peach-pink tones of the restored ancient palazzo. 'It's one hell of a vision for one man to have created,' she said.

That man was Thomas Hanbury, the great-grandfather of Carolyn's late husband, Simon. 'It's not my family, it's just that I obviously chose my husband quite well,' she joked, opening the wrought-iron gate to the small house within the garden where she now lives. 'We weren't meant to inherit it, but in a roundabout way we did.' When Simon died in 1997, Carolyn stayed on. She was now in her sixties, with short grey hair, a posh-sounding English accent and a funny, feisty sense of humour. We sat on the terrace overlooking the cypresses, the olives and the ocean, and sipped elderflower cordial while she told me the garden's story.

Thomas Hanbury was born in Clapham in southwest London in 1832, the fourth of seven children in a wealthy Quaker family.[138] When he left school, he worked in the tea trade in the city's docks, the comings and goings kindling his passion for adventure. In 1853, aged twenty-one, and with £6000 in his pocket, he left to make his fortune in Shanghai. He spent more than a decade in China, learning Mandarin and trading in tea, silk, cotton and property.

Hanbury first laid eyes on the promontory of La Mortola in the spring of 1867, while visiting Menton. The ruined Palazzo Orengo was surrounded by vineyards and olive terraces, and myrtles (the feijoa's only European relative) grew on the rocky point. It seems to have been love at first sight, Carolyn told me. 'They landed on this point by boat, and had a picnic. He was very Victorian, Thomas, he didn't do emotions. So, he just wrote in his diary, "my heart was lifted within me".' Hanbury bought the land that year, wound up his business interests in Shanghai, and came to live permanently at La Mortola with his new wife in 1871.

With the help of Thomas's brother, Daniel, a botanist and pharmacist, as well as a German landscape designer, they planted roses, citrus, palms, carob, aloes, yuccas and eucalypts. In 1885, a visitor spotted Australian banksias and grevilleas and New Zealand coprosmas and flax, 'all thriving well in the Antipodes of their native land'.[139] In 1893, the acclaimed British botanist Joseph Hooker described Hanbury's creation as 'a garden of Exotic plants . . . which in point of richness and interest has no rival among the principal collections of living plants in the world'.[140] As the garden's fame grew, it attracted the interest of European royalty: Queen Victoria herself visited and sketched the view.[141]

When Hanbury died in 1907, his ashes were buried beneath the cypresses, and 7000 people followed the funeral procession. According to Carolyn, locals still talk about him as though he left three months ago. Thomas's son Cecil then took over the garden;

but it was Cecil's wife, Dorothy Symons-Jeune, who preserved the garden's legacy. 'She was a difficult woman,' Carolyn said. 'She was my husband's grandmother, and she didn't like me – she'd be horrified I was here! She was obstinate, she was volatile, she was used to getting her own way. But she was a brilliant gardener.'

During World War I, the garden slept. It became overgrown and weedy but was undamaged. Between the wars, thanks to Dorothy, it flourished. 'She had a great philosophy – when in doubt, plant stout,' Carolyn said. 'In other words, don't just put one here and one there, plant a whole lot. She threw colour in – freesias, tulips, underplanting. She had 500 pots and vases and statues, masses of colour, masses of annuals.'

As World War II threatened, Dorothy was forced to retreat to England. When she returned to the garden after the war, she found it severely damaged. It had been taken over by the Fascists, mined, and bombed by the Americans from the sea. By 1947, she had it open to the public again – but to raise the money to restore it she had had to sell everything: most of the Hanbury property, houses, even some of her own jewellery. Eventually, in 1960, by then using a wheelchair, she was forced to sell it all. The Hanbury Gardens are now owned in perpetuity by the Italian state, and since 1983 have been run by the University of Genoa, which is slowly working to restore them. 'It is saved, and there are not many gardens that have lasted 150 years,' Carolyn said. 'Dorothy, I think, doesn't get enough credit for the fact she fought tooth and nail so it wasn't lost. It's had one or two teetering moments when it could have gone either way.'

———

The Hanburys kept three houses within the gardens, including the one where Carolyn now lives. On our way to see the feijoa, we passed through a small entrance hall. In the corner sat

Dorothy's wooden wheelchair, its seat no longer occupied by the formidable lady of the garden. A hefty torch and a pair of secateurs sat there instead. Nearby was an antique gong souvenired by Thomas Hanbury in China, and on the wall hung an 1828 drawing of the Mortola promontory, showing the property as it must have looked when Hanbury first set eyes on it.

In another corner, a dozen wide-brimmed garden hats sprouted on long dowels from a converted wine barrel, among butterfly nets and umbrellas. Forty-two gardeners worked in the gardens in La Mortola's heyday; these days, there are just ten.

I followed Carolyn down the garden's switchbacked paths, past cacti-covered hillsides and plants both familiar and foreign. I spied the glossy dark leaves of a New Zealand karaka, and spiky, black-trunked *Xanthorrhoea*, the Australian grass-trees I recognised from hikes around Canberra. Carolyn pointed out the oldest tree in the garden, a pomegranate that was already here in 1867 when Thomas Hanbury arrived. A small bridge led across a sunken Roman road: the Via Aurelia, built in 13 BC to link Nice to Genoa and Rome. A marble plaque lists some of the historic figures to have passed along it: Catherine of Siena in 1376, Niccolò Machiavelli in 1511, Napoleon Bonaparte in 1796. Just beyond it, and down another set of steps, we found the ancient feijoa.

It was an unwieldy, wayward thing, much bigger again than the one in Square Mistral, with four or five waist-thick trunks splaying from a central point. Ridged branches, thigh-wide, rambled outwards, unashamedly taking up space. Some doubled back, elbow-like, in their search for the sun. This was a tree that had not known much pruning. Every autumn, Carolyn comes down here to collect the fallen fruit. She became a feijoa convert when a fellow British gardener in Menton gave her some to try shortly after she moved in. 'A bit like Adam and Eve,' he said, "Try this." I loved it immediately.' I looked up through the tree's tangled branches, spying a few late flowers clinging on. The feijoa is recorded in the 1912 *Hortus Mortolensis*, a catalogue of the garden's plants, and is absent from the previous survey, made in 1897, so we can assume it was planted sometime in the intervening fifteen years.

As a small shrub, it had survived neglect during World War I. In the 1920s and '30s it had grown to maturity as the garden blossomed under Dorothy's surly stewardship. In 1941, two dictators strolled beneath its branches: Benito Mussolini and Francisco Franco met in the Hanbury Gardens on a February evening, the Italian trying to convince the Spaniard to enter the war. The growing feijoa tree continued flowering and fruiting through the conflict, and in the peaceful years that followed: when Prince Philip dropped in for a visit from his boat, and Winston Churchill was pushed up and down the steep paths in a wheelchair so he could paint the scenery. It stood steadfast during the years of decline, and it's still there today.

Feijoas have now been growing on the Côte d'Azur for at least 130 years. But while I found them in parks and gardens from La Mortola to Marseille, most of the locals I spoke with didn't know the plant. Even in the season, the fruit isn't widely sold or shared, and no French 'feijoa culture' seems to have developed. Instead, finding feijoas in the south of France felt like tracing a kind of secret history, known only to a few. Every time I laid eyes on those particular, well-loved leaves, I felt simultaneously the familiar and the strange. It gave me a jolt of New Zealand-ness in an exotic landscape. At the same time, each feijoa tree was like a message from Édouard André and the now-vanished world he inhabited: a living echo of a distant time.

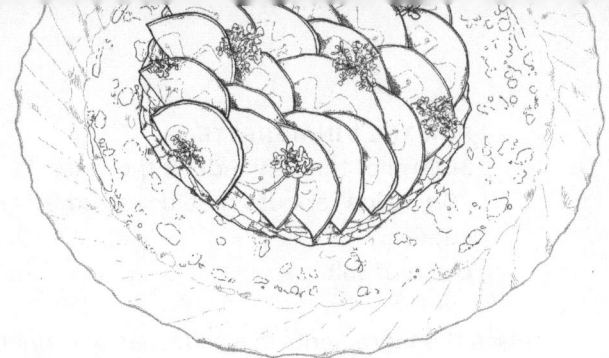

RECIPE
Mirazur's Fish and Feijoa Tartare in Feijoa Kefir Vinaigrette (serves 4)
Contributed by Laura Colagreco, Milton Fragozo and other Mirazur chefs

In 2019, the three-Michelin-starred restaurant Mirazur in Menton, France, was voted number one in the World's 50 Best Restaurants Awards. Mirazur's head chef, Mauro Colagreco, is an Argentinian with a love of feijoas. When I wrote to the restaurant team to share the feijoa's Riviera history, they were inspired to collaborate on this recipe.

In October 2023, Carolyn Hanbury delivered bags of fresh feijoas from the century-old Hanbury tree to nearby Mirazur. Mauro's sister Laura and a team of chefs used that same fruit to experiment and create this dish.

FOR THE KEFIR:
4–5 feijoas
1 litre water
90 g sugar
1 dried date
3 tablespoons of kefir grains

Begin the kefir several days in advance. Mix the sugar and water. Cut the feijoas into thin slices and pour the water over them, stirring well. Cover and leave to soak overnight.

The next day, strain and collect the liquid. Place in a bottle or jar and add the kefir grains and the date. Cover with a cloth and leave to ferment for 48–72 hours at 20–25°C in as much direct sunlight as possible.

Remove the date. Filter the liquid and collect the kefir grains for re-use (you'll normally get more grains than you put in, as they multiply with each fermentation). Keep the liquid in a bottle with a mechanical seal, in a cool place to stop fermentation.

Add a slice of feijoa to enhance the flavour, then keep in the fridge. For more fizz, leave the bottle on the bench for a day before refrigerating.

FOR THE VINAIGRETTE:
300 ml of the kefir – drink the rest!
70 g feijoa (about 1 medium-sized fruit) peeled and cut into cubes
pinch of salt

Place the ingredients in a saucepan and bring to a gentle boil for 5 minutes. Blend and strain until you obtain a fine coulis. Adjust the texture with more kefir if necessary.

FOR THE FISH TARTARE:
200 g fresh fish
1 finely chopped shallot
5 g chopped chives
Olive oil, salt and lime zest, to taste

Cut the fish into small tartare cubes. Mix with the shallot, chives, and lime zest. Season with olive oil and salt then set aside in the fridge to chill.

FOR THE FEIJOA CARPACCIO:
4-6 large ripe feijoas
1 g ascorbic acid (Vitamin C)
500 ml water

Cut the fruit into thin horizontal slices, then cut each into halves, making semicircles.
   Dissolve the ascorbic acid in the water and place the feijoa slices in the liquid.

FOR THE HERBAL OIL:
500 g leafy herbs – parsley, chives, coriander, tarragon
750 ml neutral oil

Heat oil in a pot to 85°C then add the finely chopped herbs, keeping the oil at temperature for 7 minutes. Transfer everything to a blender and mix at high speed, then filter through a fine strainer and decant, reserving only the green oil.

TO ASSEMBLE:
On a small plate, arrange ¼ of the fish tartare mixture in a flat circle 10 cm in diameter. Pour a little of the vinaigrette around the fish and add a sprinkle of herbal oil. Remove ¼ of the feijoa carpaccio from the water and arrange them on top of the tartare so that they overlap like fish scales. Decorate with coriander flowers. Repeat for the other 3 dishes and serve.

At home with Amalia and Indigo in Raglan, New Zealand (Lottie Hedley)

CLOCKWISE FROM TOP LEFT:

Feijoa scientist Rubens Nodari with chimarrão gourd in Santa Catarina, Brazil, 2019

Elizabete Aparecida de Lima at the Invernada dos Negros quilombo, Brazil, 2019

Feijoa scientist Juan Otálora Villamil in a forest of feijoas, Brazil, 2019

Friedrich Sellow's 200-year-old expedition diaries in Berlin's Natural History Museum, 2019

BELOW Chef Laura Rosano teaching children about feijoas, Uruguay, 2014

Museum curator Sabine Hackethal with one of Sellow's drawings from Brazil of *Araucaria angustifolia* trees, Berlin, 2019

Prince Maximilian of Wied-Neuwied's drawing of the 1815 expedition on the Rio Doce he and Sellow undertook together. The three Europeans pictured are Georg Freyreiss, Sellow and Wied himself, though he doesn't record which is which. (Biblioteca Brasiliana da Robert Bosch GmbH. Catálogo. Vol. 2. *O legado do Príncipe Maximiliano de Wied-Neuwied* / 1a. Parte: Ilustrações da viagem ao Brasil de 1815 a 1817. Petrópolis: Kapa Editorial, 2001.)

With Florence André (right) in Édouard André's former garden near Cannes, France, 2019

LEFT Édouard André, painted in 1902 by Édouard Debat-Ponsan. Behind him in a pot is a flowering *Anthurium andreanum*: the flamingo plant he collected in Colombia that bears his name and made his fortune.

ABOVE 'Everybody to the windows': Villa Colombia in the early 1900s, from the André family photograph album. (Édouard André Association)

BELOW Carolyn Hanbury with the century-old feijoa at the Hanbury Gardens, Italy, 2019

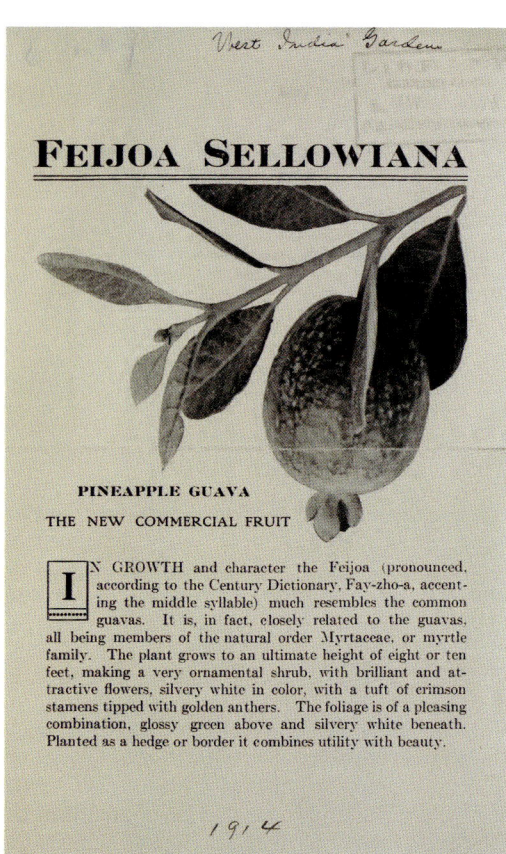

CLOCKWISE FROM TOP LEFT

'Dr Franceschi, wearing apron, shows original feijoa tree' in Santa Barbara, California, early 1900s. Photograph from the book *Southern California Gardens: An Illustrated History*, by Victoria Padilla. A limited edition reprint by Allen A. Knoll, Publishers, Santa Barbara, CA, 1994. Reprinted by arrangement with UC Press, Berkeley, CA, 1961

Feijoa advertisement from West India Gardens – Wilson Popenoe's father's nursery – in California, 1914

Ana Nelson and Phil Dynan with one of their feijoa bushes in Rancho Tehama, California, 2014

Mark Albert pruning his feijoas in Ukiah, California, 2014

Festival of the Feijoa, Tibasosa, Colombia, 2019

CLOCKWISE FROM TOP

Judging the feijoa desserts competition with Alberto Molano Zabala and Luz Marina; feijoa seller Cecilia Salamanca de Ramírez; and nurseryman Oscar Velandia

Joe MacLeod (Tūhoe) back home in Te Urewera, Aotearoa, 2022

BELOW Nigel Ritson's feijoa assessment system, Tākaka, Aotearoa, 2021

Omar Quintero's feijoa sorting centre in Bogotá, Colombia, 2019

Nigel Ritson with one of his improved feijoas, Tākaka, Aotearoa, 2021

BELOW All signs point to feijoas at Hinterland Feijoas, Queensland, Australia, 2015

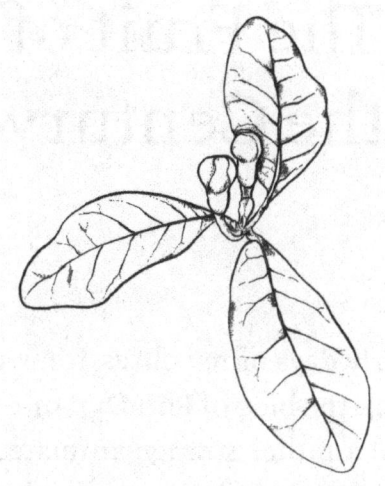

TAMING
California

CHAPTER 13

The Fruit of the Century

In 2014, in the early days of my obsession with the feijoa's history, I stumbled on the blog of Phil Dynan, a Californian artist. He had just posted a rather strange animated video, aiming to entice people to come to a feijoa festival at his place: or, according to the video, to a 'Feijoa Festival on the Island of Guayabo on the Planet of Kakariki'. Colourful, hand-painted creatures cavorted in a psychedelic landscape against a backdrop of feijoa fruit and flowers. 'Welcome to the enchanted island of Guayabo' appeared in rainbow-coloured text; '842 days of feasting on an eternal paradise island . . . Live music, free snacks, feijoa wine, pleasure-bots . . . Taste the magical feijoa flower and breathe in the intoxicating aroma.'

Naturally, I got in touch.

Phil wrote back straight away. He seemed surprisingly normal, albeit with a healthy feijoa fixation. In one email, he told me he spends part of the year working in an art studio in London, where he has to buy feijoas from the greengrocer. 'They go for about five quid each and I have to buy the whole crate,' he wrote. 'I CANNOT LIVE WITHOUT THEM!!!!!!' Six feijoa-related exclamation points! Surely, this was one of my tribe.

That year, I had also connected online with Mark Albert, a part-time feijoa breeder at Ukiah, on the Pacific Coast just over the Mendocino Range from Phil's place. If Phil approached the feijoa as a whimsical artist, Mark was a scientist and a poet, and seemed as interested in the feijoa's history, biology and cultural meaning as I was. 'Yeah, if you want to learn about the feijoa in the US, Kate, you probably should come to my house,' he wrote. 'I seem to be the holder of the feijoa knowledge here.'

I'd missed Phil's feijoa festival, but decided to go and visit him and Mark anyway. TVNZ had axed one of the shows I was working on, and I no longer had a full-time job. But the research centre I'd worked for in Indonesia had offered to send me to report on a deforestation conference in New York. I decided to commit to this wild feijoa book idea, and stop off for a few days in California on the way.

The US state, I knew, was an important staging post in the feijoa's story. Just as aspiring actors and musicians move to Los Angeles to make it big, the Golden State is where fruits go to get famous. The avocado and the kiwifruit arguably both became international household names after ad campaigns launched in California.[142] In the early twentieth century, the feijoa seemed poised to do the same.

———

Red Bluff, CA, was flat, suburban and bone dry: California was in the grip of its worst drought since records began. Phil had asked me to meet him at the small art gallery he owns with his wife, Ana Nelson. When I pulled up at the address he'd given me in the rented red Volkswagen Beetle I had already managed to dent, it was obvious I was in the right place – if not yet reliably driving on the right side of the road. The side wall of the gallery was covered in a huge mural that featured a bug-eyed goat, a horse, a donkey and a dog, all painted in the same bright style as the feijoa video's mythical animals.

Inside, I met Ana, an artist's apron tied around her colourful print dress. She reminded me of my aunty Beth, and I immediately felt comfortable. She was around forty, I guessed, and had light brown hair with a fringe. Then Phil arrived to show me the way to their place while Ana closed up the gallery. He was in his sixties, tall and rangy, wearing a Hawaiian shirt and sporting a small, neat moustache. 'Come on,' he said. 'I want to show you something.' On the edge of town, we stopped at a nondescript car park outside a small shopping centre. Phil loped over to a patch of bushes growing in between the rows of cars: they were feijoas, roughly pruned, but with a few unripe fruits dangling from the internal branches. 'I'm keeping an eye on them,' he said.

He and Ana are feijoa scavengers. Years ago, when they were living in Sacramento, the place they rented had a feijoa hedge. Phil still remembers the first one he bit into. 'It just exploded with flavour. I'd never had a fruit like that before. It was intensely good.' Ana loved them, too, and they were immediately hooked. Phil is a marathon runner – he's done more than fifty – and when he ran, his body seemed to crave feijoas. 'There's something in my chemistry that really wants that fruit.' So, they started cruising the neighbourhood streets, making offers to the owners of feijoa trees to 'clean up the mess'.

They still scavenge, but now it's to supplement their own supply. At the time of my visit, they had about fifty feijoa trees – as well as around twenty cats, eight dogs, a donkey, a goat and a horse – at their home in Rancho Tehama, a remote, private reserve in the foothills to the west of Red Bluff. That's where we headed next, driving on straight roads through walnut plantations to the edge of the hills. Scrawled in shouty capitals, an array of notices on the fence near the entrance advised: 'WE NEED VOLUNTEERS FOR THE TEHAMA COUNTY FIRE DEPT' and 'REPORT ALL ILLEGAL MARIJUANA GROWS'.

Phil said there were hundreds of cannabis farmers, both

legal and illegal, living in what he nicknamed 'Rancho Marijuana'. In the fall, apparently, the scent of the buds hangs thick in the air, and you can smell the community before you reach it. It's the kind of place that attracts outsiders, a bit of a world apart.

———

By the time we arrived at Phil and Ana's home it was late afternoon. First, they showed me their art studio, on a ridge looking out across a dried-up stream to the angled planes of the Mendocino Range. Coyotes roam up there, Phil said. Mountain lions, too, and racoons and rattlesnakes. The evening sun lit up the strawberries in a patch Ana was using to shade the roots of some feijoa seedlings. A tiny jewelled hummingbird hovered over a sprinkler. And there, between the climbing morning glory and pumpkin vines, was the pride of the garden: two very healthy feijoa bushes and a flourishing cannabis plant.

This was no illegal grow. Ana is licensed to breed low-THC medical marijuana, and uses it to treat her own chronic headaches. 'Smell it,' she urged. I sniffed the spiky, tightly packed head of buds. The scent was pungent, powerful, but also remarkably fruity. 'What does it remind you of?' Ana asked. Well, it was probably the power of suggestion, but it did have a hint of feijoa. 'Exactly! They're sharing the best soil in the garden, so maybe they've shared some chemicals as well,' she said.

We headed home to eat Ana's (unlaced) feijoa muffins. The cats lounged on the couches, and the freezer was stuffed with whole feijoas, labelled by month: a rationing system to ensure they never have to go too long without tasting one. 'We're not taking any chances with a bad season or a short season. We can't afford to run out!' said Phil.

As we ate, Phil told stories. He's had as many lives as one of his cats. Ana is his third wife, though they've been married since

1998. He's worked as a journalist and an IT guy; owned a greeting card company; run for the California State Assembly; and self-published a novel about the Iraq War. As a nineteen-year-old in the mid-1960s, he joined the US Army Security Agency, and was posted to Asmara, Ethiopia – now Eritrea – where he taught tennis at the summer palace of Haile Selassie and reported back on any interesting conversations he overheard. (He couldn't tell me what they were about, though: 'I'm still under oath.') He even met the emperor himself. Phil towered over him, but Selassie, he said, radiated a frightening sense of power.

These days, Phil and Ana just wanted to make art, grow enough feijoas that they would never be caught short, and if there were enough to spare, share the joy with others. But feijoas in California are a niche interest. The fruit on those Sacramento street trees rotted into the grass, and the Rancho Tehama Feijoa Festival was a bit of a flop. 'We had two people come from Santa Cruz...' Phil trailed off.

'But it did bring *you* here,' added Ana. 'So, there's person three.'

Feijoas weren't always treated with such indifference in California. At the start of the twentieth century, their future seemed bright.

It was fall 1908, and sixteen-year-old Frederick Wilson Popenoe was about to come face to face with his idol: 'with nothing to recommend me save an enthusiastic interest in rare plants, I ascended the slopes of Mission Ridge, feeling considerably in awe of the man I was about to meet, for we of California looked to Doctor Franceschi ... as our foremost authority on rare plants', he later wrote.[143]

The nurseryman Douglas William Coolidge had secured Popenoe an introduction to Dr Francesco Franceschi, an Italian horticulturist in Santa Barbara – then considered 'the Mecca of California plantsmen'.[144] Franceschi's home, Montarioso, was perched above the city, and his orchard of more than 150 exotic fruit trees provided a rare splash of brighter green among the native sage scrub.[145]

Franceschi made Coolidge and Popenoe welcome, and together they rambled over the dry hills[146] behind the Italian-style house, admiring his tropical and subtropical plants. In the study, Popenoe marvelled at the piles of European horticultural and botanical journals, jostling for space with books in French and Italian. The Doctor's 'inexhaustible enthusiasm' and 'strikingly foreign' costume made an impression on the young Popenoe, too – Franceschi wore a 'small tam-o'-shanter tilted on one side of his head, a peculiar European jacket', and light, baggy trousers.[147] Over the delicious Italian dinner, the three men almost certainly discussed feijoas. Each, in his own way, played a critical role in the fruit's arrival and establishment in the United States – and all three were genuine feijoa fans.

Franceschi was born Emanuele Orazio Fenzi in 1843, the scion of a wealthy Florentine family. He obtained a doctorate of laws at the University of Pisa, then took over the family bank – but when the Fenzi fortune was lost in an economic crisis, he sailed for California with his wife and some of his children. In 1893, aged fifty, he settled in Santa Barbara, set up a nursery business, and began experimenting with new and exotic plant species. He invented a new name for his new life: Dr Francesco Franceschi.[148]

The week I visited Phil, I spent a day in the Bancroft Library at the University of California at Berkeley, where Franceschi's extensive correspondence is kept. His California letters and documents – written between 1904 and 1913 – are held in twenty brown cardboard boxes in the library's archives, and can only be viewed in person. Inside these boxes is the story of how the feijoa came to the United States.

In 1901, Franceschi received a package of feijoa seedlings from the south of France. They were reportedly descendants of André's mother tree at Villa Colombia,[149] and he planted them in a few locations in Central and Southern California. It was just one of the hundreds of new species of plant that Franceschi introduced into the United States at the start of the 1900s. He corresponded in English, Italian, Spanish, German and French with nurseries and botanical gardens all over the world: Java, Guam, Cartagena and Quito. He wrote to northern India for figs, and to the director of the Auckland Museum to procure New Zealand tree ferns and a flowering Rarotongan shrub.

Reading the letters, his passion for the endeavour is obvious. 'If only a few of them will prove on experience to be suitable for California, one ought to feel proud to have made them known,' he wrote to a correspondent in 1904.[150] In this he was part of a long tradition dating back to before US independence: the art of introducing and acclimating foreign plants that could make some contribution to the economy. 'The greatest service which can be rendered any country is to add a useful plant to its culture', wrote the Union's third president, Thomas Jefferson, in 1800.[151] Discovering and promoting exotic 'useful plants' was Franceschi's mission in North America – and the feijoa was one of his favourites.

'FEIJOA SELLOWIANA, the coming fruit of the century,' Franceschi wrote in a letter in 1906.[152] Admittedly, he was trying to induce a prospective buyer to buy plants for $5 each, ten or twenty times the price of the other Uruguayan Myrtaceae he recommended, the pitanga and arazá. Franceschi was intensely curious about the plant, and sent feijoa questionnaires to plantsmen in Uruguay, Argentina and France, trying to find out more about the species. The Uruguayan contact returned the completed questionnaire (along with some feijoa seeds), informing Franceschi that the fruit was 'not kept in high esteem there'. Franceschi replied: 'Perhaps for that old reason, *Nemo propheta in patria*' – a Latin saying meaning 'No man is a prophet in his own country'. Then he added: 'Let's see what future it could have in California!'[153]

In 1913, Franceschi printed a special pamphlet listing feijoa plants for sale. He included a photograph of the flowers and fruit, and sung the feijoa's praises: 'The pulp is white and juicy, sweet, with a little acidity, in flavor and perfume an indescribable blend of pineapple, raspberry and banana; and not more than twenty tiny seeds are found in each fruit. All persons who have had the chance of tasting the fruit of FEIJOA are unanimous in stating that is the best introduction in its line during the last ten years.'[154]

He may have been exaggerating a little. In the letters I found addressed to Franceschi, the reports about feijoas were mixed. One early Californian adopter was Scott Way, who planted one of Franceschi's first imported André feijoas at his home in Altadena in 1902. Three years later, it produced seventy-five fruits, and he wrote to Franceschi pronouncing the feijoa a splendid commercial proposition, 'by far the most valuable new fruit that has been introduced into California in years'. The fruit was delicious, the seeds unobtrusive, the skin 'as thin as ordinary writing paper', he wrote. 'I should say that the fruit is all that is claimed for it, and more ... There would be no trouble to find a ready market at high prices if the fruit could be furnished in quantities.'[155] But another correspondent, Thomas Morris Carnegie – the nephew of steel magnate and philanthropist Andrew Carnegie, one of the richest Americans in history – was less impressed with the taste. 'The fruit trees "Feijoa sellowiana" have grown strongly and well at my place in south-east Georgia,' he wrote to Franceschi in 1908. 'The fruit is about the size of an egg and entirely unfit to eat.'[156] Hmph!

If Franceschi was the feijoa's prophet in North America, Frederick Wilson Popenoe was his greatest disciple. Born in Kansas, Popenoe came from a family of fruit lovers. His grandfather Willis grew apples, his brother Paul wrote a book about dates, and his father Frederick became a pioneer of the fledgling Californian avocado industry. Popenoe would go on to be a renowned botanist and fruit explorer in his own right. In 1901, when Popenoe was nine years old, his father moved the family to Costa Rica, where he had opened a gold mine. The venture was an abysmal failure, but that year in the tropics had a profound impact on the young Popenoe; it was where he first encountered avocados, learned Spanish, and developed a passion for plants and Latin America.

In 1904, the Popenoe family moved to Los Angeles, and then in 1906 to nearby Altadena, where Frederick senior set up a nursery business he called West India Gardens, selling tropical and subtropical plants. His son went to Pasadena High School, but according to his biographer, 'he spent more time propagating plants than burning the midnight oil studying'. The schoolbooks might not have interested him, but accounts of what he called 'the great plant hunters' did. Popenoe read about Lieutenant William Bligh and his voyage on the *Bounty*, and how the expedition's aim of bringing breadfruit from Tahiti to the West Indies was frustrated by mutiny. He followed the exploits of explorers who combed the Andes for quinine-yielding *Cinchona* trees, and admired Frank N. Meyer, who had just returned from China with what became known as the Meyer lemon.

'All this inspired me, and I began to feel that plant hunting was just about the most romantic occupation imaginable,' Popenoe wrote, looking back on this time later in life. 'Not only did a chap get to travel in out-of-the-way corners of the world, but he stood a good chance of bringing home some new fruit, or food plant, which would add materially to his country's wealth and happiness.'[157]

And so teenage Popenoe set about, as he called it, 'making friends with plants'. He took over a patch of soil in the garden, grew rose bushes from cuttings and sold them to rich neighbours for 'a dollar and a half in hard cash ... just about the easiest money, it seemed to me, that anyone could hope to earn'.[158] He also made friends with a human – a fellow plant-nerd called Knowles Ryerson who had become an orphan at the age of eleven and was living with one of his teachers.[159] Popenoe's father sent the boys out around Southern California on bicycles looking for promising avocado seedlings worth propagating. It was the start of what Ryerson later called 'a most intimate friendship'.[160]

Ryerson got a job working for Douglas Coolidge at his Pasadena Rare Plant Gardens in 1908, while still in high school. Coolidge introduced Ryerson to his first feijoa,[161] and must have befriended Popenoe, too, since he took him to meet Franceschi that fateful day on Mission Ridge. After that meeting, the 'mere lad' and the Italian nurseryman became frequent correspondents: there are eighty-five letters from Popenoe in the Franceschi boxes. In what seems to be the first one, in 1909, Popenoe asked advice about budding the feijoa. 'You will probably recall a young man visited your place last fall with Mr Coolidge. I am that young man, and look back with much pleasure to my visit at your place. I am just starting to grow the avocado, the Feijoa, and a few other specialties on a commercial scale, and am much interested in them.'[162]

Other conversations concerned the avocado, which they agreed should be renamed ahuacate, as it was called in Mexico, and definitely not alligator pear, as it was called in the Los Angeles markets.[163] Many of Popenoe's letters are actually addressed to Franceschi's son Cammillo, who was of a similar age. On picking up one of Popenoe's letters - usually written on his father's nursery letterhead - I could immediately tell if he was writing to Franceschi the elder or the younger. In the letters to Cam, there are glimpses of teenage life amongst all the botanical talk, and I can hear the way he must have spoken, with that old Hollywood American slang: 'That sure was too bad about Stanford losing the game,' he said in one. 'I want to thank you again for the plants, old kid, they sure do look good to me.'[164] Cam, Popenoe and Ryerson seem to have knocked around together. The three adolescent boys would send each other feijoas they found in the market,[165] jump on the 'electric car' - the LA streetcar or tram - to go to plant shows, and enjoy 'many a subtropical fruit jaunt together'.[166]

From the letters, it's also obvious that Popenoe shared Franceschi's passion for the feijoa. He got very worked up that 'some dope at the Scientific American' had credited the famous botanist Luther Burbank (rather than Franceschi) with the feijoa's introduction into the US, and decided to write a lengthy paper on the plant to set the record straight. 'Say, I wish when you get a little time you would make up some pretty complete notes about the most important of your father's introductions,' he wrote to Cam, 'so that I can get up an article covering them in a satisfactory way.'[167]

That year, 1911, Popenoe's older brother Paul had been sent to Europe and North Africa by their father to collect date specimens for the family nursery. He also spent a month in Europe investigating the feijoa. Paul's interest in feijoas would soon be superseded by his passion for eugenics and marriage counselling, but in 1911, aged twenty-three, Paul visited the French Riviera in search of feijoas, just as I did a century later. A black-and-white image shows the young Paul – dressed in suit, hat and bright white collar – gazing at the original feijoa tree Édouard André planted at Villa Colombia. As Florence André and I discovered, that tree no longer stands, but back then it was bushy, healthy and twice Paul's height, and fruits carpeted the ground beneath it. André's hired gardeners showed Paul around the property, but it seems they couldn't satisfactorily answer all his feijoa questions. André himself was unable to be consulted. He had been ill for some time, and that very day, while Paul was visiting, the postman arrived at Villa Colombia with the news of André's death.

In February 1912, nineteen-year-old Frederick Wilson Popenoe's 'Feijoa Sellowiana; Its History, Culture and Varieties' was published in the *Pomona College Journal of Economic Botany*.[168] It remains the major historical source for the feijoa's early days in France and the United States. It is also a heartfelt advertisement for what Popenoe sincerely believed was 'a fruit of rare merit ... a magnificent fruit'. He began: 'Among the fruits which have been offered as commercial possibilities in California there are few which possess such intrinsic merit as the one here considered ... Certainly few plants can offer such an appeal to public favor ... It is a fruiting shrub of sterling excellence.'

In the paper, Popenoe described what was known about the feijoa's botany and history, and made sure Franceschi got the credit for bringing it to the US. He gave growing tips: '[a] liberal supply of water during the first few years results in much greater growth and more fruit' and advice on both propagation and pronunciation: 'according to the very best authorities', it should be pronounced *Fay-zho-a*, as the name derives from Portuguese, not Spanish (the point is arguable).[169] Mystifyingly, he vastly overstated the feijoa's keeping and shipping qualities, claiming fruit can be kept in the house for three to four weeks, or shipped from France to California and still remain in perfect condition for eating. Growers today dream of such longevity!

Popenoe was also very enthusiastic about the crop's 'first class' commercial prospects in California, declaring the state 'better adapted' to the feijoa than Southern France.[170] Partly, it was marketing. Both Franceschi and the Popenoe family stood to make a bit of money from a rush on feijoa plants. But from their letters and writings, it's also clear they believed their own hype.

CHAPTER 14

It's All About the Cultivar

At this point in its history, the feijoa was essentially wild. The early American nurserymen knew that for the feijoa to achieve celebrity status, or at least to make money on commercial plantations, it needed to be tamed. And it was Mark Albert – a modern-day Franceschi or Coolidge living in Ukiah, Northern California – who first taught me what it means to domesticate a plant.[171]

I visited Mark right after leaving Phil's place. Fingers of cloud reached into the dry valleys from the Pacific Ocean, and the air on this side of the Mendocino Range was oppressive, humid and hot. Mark's gravel driveway was lined with feijoas on one side and pomegranates on the other. As I drove along it, looking for the house, a family of turkey vultures circled overhead, and a woodpecker quarrelled with another bird atop a pole. After five months with no rain, the drought was about to break.

Mark answered the door, and offered me a deep-purple glass of his homemade grape juice. He was in his late sixties, thin and self-possessed, and, possibly because he had just injured himself falling off his roof, a little quieter than he'd seemed over email. 'I am very verbose and will rant at the drop of a hat, so I hoot about my feijoa cultivars,' he'd written in an early one, and signed off every time 'in abundance'.

In defiance of the approaching storm, we went to the garden: Mark's 'Heaven on Earth'. Despite the long dry summer and my host's profuse apologies, it was green and bountiful: lavender, olives, grapes, plum trees, pears, neat rows of vegetables. The feijoas made a long border, and Mark had meticulously labelled and mapped each one.

Mark spent his youth living in a commune in the Haight-Ashbury district, San Francisco's hippy heart. He was a conscientious objector to the war in Vietnam, and then with his wife Judy he travelled through Iran, Afghanistan and India, where he became 'a complete mango freak'. Back home in California, he trained as a nurseryman and worked in the avocado business. It was the late 1970s, and avocados were booming: 'All these wealthy doctors and real estate people were buying vast tracts of land and paying for it with avocados,' he said.

Mark's job was to trawl the existing avocado orchards in the hills around Santa Barbara, collecting scions – young fruit-bearing shoots – for the nursery to graft. One day, on a very large estate in Montecito, Mark came across an old, landscaped row of a dozen unfamiliar bushes: feijoas. He tasted a fruit, and it was immediately appealing, like nothing he'd ever eaten before. So, he pocketed some, and grew the seeds at his nursery. 'They came up like hair on a dog's back, and very soon I had 200 to 300 seedlings growing.' Mark liked to think that row of trees was planted by Franceschi himself, or at least by people he'd sold the plants to.

When Mark and Judy moved to Ukiah, the feijoas came, too. By then, Mark had retrained as a nurse, but he couldn't get rid of the nursery habit. Via the California Rare Fruit Growers organisation, he met other feijoa growers from around the state and acquired some older cultivars, planning to graft them onto his scrumped seedlings. But as they grew, he realised some of those chance seedlings produced delicious, sweet feijoas. He planted some of those seeds, and when they were grown, again selected the ones with the best-tasting fruit.

This is how plants get tamed. It is a process as old as farming itself. As humans settled in one place and starting growing crops, they picked the plants they liked best – the fastest-growing, the ones producing the biggest or the tastiest fruit – and grew more of those. They chose the offspring they liked even more, and repeated the process. Through selective breeding, people have been able to completely transform the agricultural plants we now rely on. It first happened around 11,500 years ago, in Southwest Asia's Fertile Crescent (today's Middle East), possibly because many easily domesticated species were naturally found in that landscape: wild wheat, barley, peas, sheep, goats, cows and pigs. But agriculture also began independently in a handful of other homelands, including China, the African Sahel, and the island of New Guinea in the western Pacific.[172] In the Andes, people domesticated potatoes, beans, coca, llamas, alpacas, guinea pigs, peanuts, tomatoes, tobacco and pineapples. In the Amazon, it was sweet potatoes and squash. Mesoamericans, meanwhile, transformed the meagre seedheads of a spiky grass called teosinte into the fat, nutritious corncobs of maize. Breeding and cultivar selection is one of the most enduring and important plant relationships we have.

Over generations, humans have taken tiny wild apples and turned them into sugary orbs, made peaches sixty-four times larger, turned skinny white roots into fat orange carrots, and shrunk the banana's seeds until they are practically microscopic. In selecting for different characteristics of the wild cabbage – by favouring leaves, stems, flowers or buds – breeders turned that one species into kale, collard greens, kohlrabi, broccoli, cauliflower and brussels sprouts. And in the 1700s they crossed two species of wild strawberry – one from Chile, the other from the eastern US – to produce the large garden strawberry we know today.

The feijoa, in contrast, remains relatively unchanged by human hands. A domesticated plant is considered to be one that has been so genetically altered through artificial selection that it looks recognisably different from its wild ancestors. We have no way of knowing what the feijoa was like before the Southern Proto-Jê started eating it, but while I noticed more diversity among the feijoa trees that I saw growing wild in Brazil, much of the fruit I collected looked indistinguishable from the ones that fall in my New Zealand garden, though many were smaller, and some certainly tasted more bitter. Rubens Nodari's team of geneticists in Brazil believe a small amount of domestication has taken place there, through selection by the feijoa's first Indigenous eaters, and more recently by rural and quilombola communities.

The first step in the more formal process of domestication is the selection of one or more cultivars. The word is short for 'cultivated variety', Mark told me. While the words are often used interchangeably, a variety is a naturally occurring type within a species, whereas a cultivar is one maintained by human intervention. That can require more or less work: some plants produce offspring that turn out just like their parents, and varieties of those species can be kept by simply collecting seeds and growing them. Other plants, including the feijoa, are much more variable when grown from seed. Seedlings from the same parent may produce at different times of the season, have fruits of different sizes and shapes, and vary in flavour and yield. As an evolutionary strategy, this diversity makes sense, and is part of the reason the feijoa is able to thrive in so many environments: the variability helps the species make the best of whatever conditions it finds itself facing. To succeed commercially, though, more uniformity is needed, and so the feijoa must be cloned – by grafting, making cuttings, or layering – in order to produce genetically identical trees that will produce the kind of fruit the grower wants. That clone is a cultivar.

―――

Outside of Brazil, Édouard André's mother feijoa in Golfe-Juan was probably the first feijoa cultivar. By now, it seems unlikely that any clones of that plant still exist, nor any of the other French introduction from Uruguay, 'Besson'. Historical research carried out by Mark and another Californian collaborator, Glen Woodmansee, indicates that the feijoas grown in California in the early twentieth century were likely a genetic mix of Andre and Besson ancestry, as well as a third importation of seed from Argentina made by H. Hehre of Los Angeles, and perhaps a couple of other introductions as well.[173]

Out of that cross-pollination emerged the first North American cultivars. The most significant was selected by Douglas Coolidge. Now better remembered as 'an ardent advocate of the avocado',[174] Coolidge was also obsessed with feijoas. He first encountered them in 1905 – thanks to Franceschi – and from then on, Coolidge said, his enthusiasm grew every year. In 1909, wanting to 'thoroughly test its hold on the public', he handed them out to forty people to try. 'Man, woman, and child, American, Mongolian, Latin and Ethiopian, and with but one exception, everyone pronouncing it the most delicious fruit they had ever tasted.'[175] (The exception was an American who thought it was okay, but no better than other fruits – which in retrospect seems significant!)

In a 1914 catalogue, Coolidge declared the feijoa 'charming' and 'the most desirable fruit introduction in many years ... We really feel that too much cannot be said of the Feijoa, and we confidently predict that it will be planted on thousands of acres for commercial purposes, and surely no home collection of plants is complete without one to a dozen of them.'[176] And though his collection of rare plants numbered in the thousands, he chose an image of a feijoa to adorn the letterhead on his nursery stationery.[177]

But Coolidge wasn't just a feijoa booster. He also planted out and observed thousands of seedlings, looking for the best individual plant he could find, a cultivar good enough to name after himself. By 1917, he had found it: self-fertile, fast-growing, with 'uniformly large fruits of the finest flavor'. Feijoa seedlings normally sold for just 25 cents, but he offered grafted 'Coolidge' specimens for $10 – the equivalent of more than US$200 today. Grafting feijoas and growing them from cuttings isn't easy, but after four or five years, the nursery managed to produce enough potted cultivars to meet demand and sell to other nurseries.

'Coolidge' was eventually introduced into Australia and New Zealand, along with two other Californian varieties, 'Choiceana' and 'Superba' (Mark Albert tried growing both, and found them neither choice nor superb: 'Wow, was that a good feijoa in 1920? Seems like a joke by today's standard!') Together they became the grandparents of the feijoa cultivars subsequently developed in New Zealand.

But in the US, as the century progressed, the pioneers' grand hopes for the feijoa were never realised. A few commercial plantations were attempted, but most failed. Reports became more cautious. In 1919, one California plantsman wrote that the feijoa was 'Another of our semi-tropical fruits ... which was boomed to the limit by over-zealous nurserymen without testing out its value fully. This fruit is simply another example of having its value extolled before determining some of the salient facts concerning it. It was widely distributed, and although it bloomed profusely the bushes failed in most instances to set fruit, and in consequence of this it lost its popularity.'[178]

The reason for these fruiting failures was discovered by Popenoe's bestie Knowles Ryerson. He went to the University of California to study horticulture, and in 1914 made a study of a mysterious feijoa tree in Pasadena – apparently a layer, or clone, of André's original at Villa Colombia. Each spring, the Pasadena tree would shimmer with thousands of blossoms; by the fall, there would be no fruit at all. Ryerson carefully gathered pollen from another feijoa, and used it to hand-pollinate the blooms. The tree produced fruit for the first time in eight years, and they were 'of large size and of very fine quality'.[179] Ryerson had discovered something that is still true of feijoas today: most trees – though not all – require cross-pollination from another genetically distinct individual.

But, shortly afterwards, Ryerson swapped the university nursery for the battlefields of Europe – he served two years in France during World War I. And as the century progressed, the feijoa's other great advocates were no longer around to defend it. Franceschi returned to Italy in 1913 and two years later, aged seventy-two, moved to Libya to set up a new nursery and herbarium. Popenoe spent many years exploring South and Central America as an official fruit explorer, eventually settling in Honduras, where his wife Dorothy – the mother of his five children – would die tragically at just thirty-three.

Bizarrely in keeping with the theme of Popenoe's life, Dorothy was killed by a fruit: she's believed to have been poisoned by eating an unripe or improperly prepared ackee.[180] This plant, *Blighia sapida*, was brought to the Americas from West Africa in the eighteenth century, most likely on a slave ship. It is now the official national fruit of Jamaica, where – just like the feijoa in New Zealand – it is associated with wellbeing, pleasure and national identity. But, unlike the feijoa, the plant has a poisonous dark side. Ackee fruits are reportedly delicious when ripe and cooked properly, but can be fatally toxic when underripe.

The consequences of eating a too-young feijoa are a lot less dire. However, Popenoe did fear that a lack of public knowledge about when to eat the fruit might be hampering the feijoa's chance at world domination. In his 1920 *Manual of Tropical and Subtropical Fruits* – his last publication concerning the feijoa – he defended feijoas against detractors who, he believed, simply hadn't tasted them at their best: 'Everyone knows that the finest pears are only turnips if eaten a trifle too soon or a trifle too late. The observation is applicable also to the feijoa.'[181]

Four years later, Ryerson wrote a long article in the *Los Angeles Times* on 'That Popular Fruiting Ornamental, the Feijoa.' Ryerson was now a horticulturist at the Agricultural Extension Service, and he quashed his old friends' hopes for any great commercial success for the 'fruit of the century'. The feijoa was still unknown, he wrote, had to compete with many other fruits, and wasn't much to look at. 'The buying public is not too prone to try new things which are not particularly attractive, especially when the price is rather high.' Ryerson still clearly had a soft spot for the fruit, but he thought it was best suited for the home garden. 'The feijoa will doubtless continue to find its greatest usefulness as an attractive and showy ornamental in small plantings rather than as a commercial plant put out in extensive acreage.'[182]

———

That was exactly what happened. The feijoa – now more commonly called the pineapple guava – did not became a commercial success in the United States, and the vast majority of Americans have never heard of it. As the esteemed botanist Julia Morton wrote (crushingly) in 1987: 'Few fruit bearers have received as much initial high-level attention and yet have amounted to so little as this member of the Myrtaceae, *Feijoa sellowiana* Berg.'[183] Ouch! Writing in 1993, a group of horticulturists in Florida cited pollination issues, failure to fruit in warm areas, the difficulty of propagation and the problem of judging fruit maturity to explain the feijoa's lack of success there: 'it is little wonder the plant has not lived up to its potential or expectations'.[184]

Perhaps Franceschi and Popenoe *were* over-zealous: maybe their early hype backfired and set North Americans against the feijoa before it was really ready to be released. I asked amateur feijoa historian Glen Woodmansee what he thought. Glen drove around New Zealand in a campervan for three years in succession, visiting feijoa growers, and he's thought about this question a lot. He reckons the boosters hadn't yet learned the feijoa's limitations: the fact that 'seedling plants produce unreliable crops, cloned plants are hard to reproduce without a lot of skill, shelf life is very short for a big country or even a big state like California to transport fresh fruit to market, and learning to avoid bruising when the fruit falls, or to carefully touch pick, is an expensive art'.

In the century since Coolidge, there have been no US scientific or government efforts to breed feijoas. On the rare occasions Glen has seen the fruit in a California grocery bin, 'they're expensive and already overripe, guaranteeing that anyone who tries one will never repeat the mistake', he said. Attempts in the 1980s to import New Zealand cultivars ended badly, too - probably, I was told, because of a cock-up by the exporters, who mislabelled random seedlings as cultivars. Or perhaps it was just that individual feijoa trees selected for how well they performed in the particular soil and climate of a South Pacific archipelago did not thrive as expected in continental California.

Ultimately, despite the best efforts of the early nurserymen, the feijoa failed to make its fortune in California, and never became a cultural phenomenon anywhere in the United States. Somehow along the way, the original cultivars were lost - a mystery that fascinated Mark Albert. 'Where did they go: Andre, Besson, Hehre? Were they even worth keeping?'

And in 2003, the feijoa reached a new low. That year, New Zealand entrepreneur Geoff Ross applied to the US Food and Drug Administration for permission to import new flavours of 42 Below vodka, which was already a hit in American bars. The passionfruit, mānuka honey, and kiwifruit vodkas were quickly approved, but the feijoa one stalled. Eventually, Geoff received a fax from the FDA: 'We can't approve this product,' it said.

The reason? 'Feijoas don't exist.'[185]

I was interested in the places where the feijoa had succeeded, of course, but also where it did not. What does it say about the dance between people and plants that the feijoa *didn't* become a household name in the very place where the first cultivar was selected, and where there were such high hopes for it?

Many factors have to come together for a new fruit to make it big, and only a few have managed it in the past century: blueberries, kiwifruit, macadamias and avocados - Coolidge's other great passion. There are now 3000 commercial avocado growers in California, while just a handful grow feijoas. The reasons for the fruit's obscurity could be as simple as its biological limitations combined with bad press and a lack of investment: the North American stars simply not quite aligning for the feijoa.

But I also wonder whether the pioneers' focus on the plant being 'useful' - by which they meant lucrative - wasn't enough on its own. Californians needed to fall in love with the feijoa, not just make money from it, and that's not something that can be measured in acreage or annual return. Perhaps we can't force a connection with a plant or a fruit simply through growing it commercially, and we can't always bend it to our will. Another kind of alchemy needs to take place for a plant to become part of our identity.

Anyway, perhaps it was for the best. If the feijoa had achieved North American glory and become an economically 'useful plant', it would certainly stand proud in thousands of rows of uniform plantations. But something else might have been lost. The fruits might be too valuable to give away – and global ubiquity would surely have changed the special meaning the tree has for New Zealanders (and others).

Mark Albert had a different dream for the feijoa in California. 'My big thrust is getting people to grow their own fruit in their own backyard,' he told me, as the storm gathered over his garden. After two decades of selecting his favourites, he had identified some of his own cultivars, naming them 'Albert's Supreme' and 'Albert's Pride' – believing them much tastier than the older cultivars. 'The plant is easy to improve flavour-wise, but not very changeable in its other qualities,' he said.

In Brazil, Rubens Nodari is trying to encourage farmers to select their own local varieties, in order to safeguard the feijoa's genetic diversity. Likewise, Mark thought the feijoa's future in North America was in hyper-local cultivars that are perfectly adapted to certain climatic and soil conditions. His feijoas love Ukiah's mist-and-mushroom season, he reckoned. 'If you've never tasted a feijoa ripened in the cool misty season, you may not have tasted true feijoa heaven. They sweeten under low light and cool conditions.' His guiding philosophy? There has to be a match between cultivar and climate. Individuals can't do much about the climate, 'so it's all about the cultivar'.

Before he died in 2023, Mark gave away hundreds of free feijoa seedlings every year at the Bay Area scion exchange, and gave talks and workshops where he extolled the virtues of the fruit. When he got caught crawling under people's feijoa trees at the edge of their gardens, he got the tree-owner to taste one. Some have had a feijoa in their garden for thirty years and never known the fruit was edible.[186]

'The feijoa is remarkable, and no-one should be without one. It comes at a really nice time of year, after every other fruit. It's just stunning it's not in every yard,' he said now, warming to a favourite theme. Best of all: 'They pick themselves! You don't even have to figure out when the fruit is ripe!' In doing so, Mark believed, the tree forces humans into humility. Every day, we must go down on our hands and knees and, in gathering up the abundance, worship at its feet. 'That is man's proper place in the garden. One comes to love such a tree.'

RECIPE
Phil's Great-grandmother's American-style Feijoa Pancakes
contributed by Phil Dynan, California

INGREDIENTS:
1 cup flour
2 tsp baking powder
1 tbsp sugar
½ tsp salt
⅔ cup milk
1 egg
1 large feijoa
optional: dash of cinnamon to taste
optional: ⅓ cup of cornmeal for grainy texture

INSTRUCTIONS:
Dice the feijoa into small pieces. (Phil leaves the skin on, but you can peel if you prefer.)

Mix all the ingredients together and test on a hot griddle at a medium heat. If too thick, add a small amount of water to the mix.

Pour out 10-cm-round pancakes into the pan and flip once bubbles appear. Once golden brown on both sides, enjoy with the toppings of your choice.

Phil says: 'There is nothing particularly mysterious about the ingredients – this recipe is the same one my great-grandmother Rose used, except for the feijoas.'

CELEBRATING
Colombia

CHAPTER 15

The Tropical Feijoa

On my first afternoon in Bogotá, the chilly, cloud-shrouded capital of Colombia, I went to the market at Paloquemao to look for feijoas. I had been planning to walk from my hostel in the city's historic tourist precinct, La Candelaria, but I felt tired after the long series of flights from Auckland, and from the altitude - Bogotá is 2640 metres above sea level - so, instead, I took an Uber. I sat in the front so as to look less suspicious, as the service is technically illegal in Colombia, though considered safer than taking a taxi. The driver was horrified I'd thought of walking, saying I would have passed through a 'tolerance zone', where the police apparently turn a blind eye to sex work, drugs and homelessness.

'No des papaya,' he insisted. Don't give them a papaya? Was he warning against handing out fruit to homeless people on my way home? But no; it turned out that in Colombia, fruits are so important they've become part of the language. 'Dar papaya' is local slang for making yourself an easy target, for giving an opportunity to thieves. (Colombians also use the word guayabo - meaning guava, not feijoa - for a hangover, either because guavas often look fine on the outside when inside they are swarming with tiny caterpillars,[187] or referring to a person so incapacitated that all they can do is sit under a guava tree and wait for the fruit to fall. Sounds kind of like a feijoa tree to me!)

I promised to give no-one any papaya, and the driver let me out right in front of Paloquemao. I was soon swallowed up by one of Bogotá's largest fruit and vegetable markets, a huge, labyrinthine building filled to the brim with sound, colour and commerce. There was a stall selling a dozen different kinds of medicinal bark, and one featuring a bucket of fluorescent fuchsia-pink ullucos, a native root vegetable. Another sold only chillies: fat red ones, round orange ones, shiny bottle-green ones and tiny unassuming pale yellow ones that, according to the señora selling them, were the spiciest of them all.

Two old men with very few teeth sat chatting and shelling beans in one of the narrow alleyways that led between the shops. Cuban rap blared from one stall, while another showed a Copa América football game on a large TV screen. Deeper inside, I found the fruit stalls. Each was a rainbow feast of colour, the produce stacked in neat, glistening pyramids: a tower of oranges next to magenta plums, yellow dragonfruits piled up by deep-purple mangosteens, and yes – fat familiar feijoas. But they were just one attraction among the overwhelming cornucopia.

There were apples, peaches, pears, tamarillos, cherimoyas, prickly pears, cape gooseberries (called uchuva, there), limes, kiwifruits, watermelons, rock melons, mandarins, avocados, strawberries, passionfruit, guavas, real-life papayas, giant guanábanas and four kinds of mango. Above, the pyramids were crowned with rows of ripening bananas and spiky pineapples. A boy of about eight or nine worked at his parents' stall, reaching on tiptoes to grab a plastic bag from a huge roll then rapidly filling it with mangosteens.

One especially well-presented shop was just begging to be photographed, but a 'no cameras' sign hung above. 'The owner doesn't like foreigners,' said one of the young uniformed attendants. But other shopkeepers were willing to indulge a gringa, and introduced me to other fruits I'd never seen before. There was the tiny, blueberry-like agraz, a Colombian native. I popped one in my mouth straight away, and it was sour but juicy. I also tried a kind of banana passionfruit with bright orange pulp called a curuba, and bought a shiny, round, orange lulo, a member of the nightshade family, like eggplants and tomatoes. Later, I cut it into quarters to suck out the insides, which looked like those of an unripe tomato but tasted like sour rhubarb and citrus.

The reason for all this abundance is Colombia's unique geography. Located on the equator, at the boundary between South and Central America, the country's coasts are washed by both the Pacific Ocean and the Caribbean Sea. Its lowlands are carpeted in tropical forests and swamped in wetlands, and its mountains reach to more than 5000 metres above sea level. That collision of ecosystems has made Colombia the second-most biodiverse country in the world – after Brazil, which is eight times the size. The place is home to nearly 2000 species of birds, more than any other nation on Earth, and twice the number found in the entirety of North America. There are 26,000 native species of flowering plants, including more endemics than in any other country. The intricate variation in climates also makes it possible to grow a wide variety of native and exotic fruits, from temperate peaches and wine grapes to tropical coffee and cacao. You just have to pick the right place.

In Bogotá, the equatorial climate means it remains much the same temperature all year round. But unlike the sweltering cities of the Caribbean coast, the capital's high altitude makes it cool and overcast, stuck in a kind of perennial early spring. Bogotanos I spoke with explained that when they tire of the city's monotonous weather and grey skies, they can 'go to summer' by driving to lower altitudes for the weekend, or heading higher up into the Andes for a dose of winter. It's as though seasons there are less a temporal phenomenon than a spatial one.

All this means that different crops thrive at different altitudes – and there is a 'goldilocks zone' in Colombia for feijoas, too. It turns out that growing them on the equator does some strange and wonderful things to the plant's behaviour that I had never seen before. This, along with the world's longest-running feijoa festival in a town calling itself 'El Pueblo de la Feijoa' is what had brought me to Colombia.

———

By visiting Bogotá – in June 2019, a few months after my Brazil trip – I was following in the footsteps of several other feijoa people in this book. It is the hometown of Juan Manuel Otálora Villamil, the Colombian feijoa geneticist living in Florianópolis, who insisted I try the city's famous dish, ajiaco. (It turned out to be an extremely filling and delicious soup made of chicken, corn, capers, a dainty local herb called guasca, and three kinds of potatoes.) Landscape gardener Édouard André was there in 1876, and later named his Riviera home 'Villa Colombia' in memory of his travels in the country. And in 1920, a century before I arrived in the city, Californian feijoa disciple Frederick Wilson Popenoe went there too.

Like me, he marvelled at the city's market, which he considered 'one of the most complete in tropical America', and took up the local method of enjoying hot chocolate: 'the Colombians accustom their chocolate (as you would put it in Spanish) with broken bits of cheese in it. Try it,' he wrote to his patron, the agricultural explorer David Fairchild.[188] At a café on a cobbled street in La Candelaria, I took Popenoe's advice, and can confirm that customising one's chocolate in this way is both tasty and entertaining – the triangles of white cheese get all stringy and stretchy as they melt.

Colombia has endured much in the 100 years between

Popenoe's visit and mine. In the 1940s and '50s, there was 'La Violencia', a ten-year civil war between Liberal and Conservative factions that killed an estimated 300,000 people and displaced more than a million. Later, violence between leftist guerrillas, conservative paramilitaries, drug cartels and the army trapped civilians in a deadly web of uncertainty and terror, and resulted, by the end of the 1980s, in a homicide rate that was the highest in the world. Children were recruited as fighters, and there were massacres, assassinations, torture, kidnappings and sexual violence on all sides. Finally, after a drawn-out peace process lasting decades, in 2016 the government signed a ceasefire deal with the last remaining guerrilla group, the Fuerzas Armadas Revolucionarias de Colombia (FARC), formally ending fifty-two years of civil war. The half-century of violence had left 260,000 people dead and sent seven million fleeing from their homes.[189]

The peace remains fragile. According to Human Rights Watch, since 2016, more than 1000 human rights defenders and social leaders have been killed in the country. Still, Colombia has begun to grapple with its past, and in 2021 embarked on a truth commission to face up to the war's atrocities. Tourists have returned, and many natural wonders that were out of bounds for decades can now be visited once again. In the places I went to, I felt completely safe.

Feijoas must have arrived in Colombia sometime in the 1930s or earlier, as their presence is mentioned in a book published in 1937 by the local botanist, physician and politician Emilio Robledo Correa.[190] They could not have been widespread in 1920, or the feijoa-mad Popenoe would have mentioned them in his detailed letters. In any case, it wasn't until around the 1980s – as war flared in the countryside and Pablo Escobar built his multi-billion-dollar narco-empire – that feijoas became a part of Colombian commerce, culture and identity.

Many people had told me that if I wanted to know about feijoas in Colombia, I needed to meet grower and enthusiast Omar Camilo Quintero. So, while I waited for the feijoa festival to begin, I spent a few days with him, touring his plantations and learning how the plant had adapted to the tropics. Omar picked me up early in the morning outside my Bogotá hostel. He was short-haired and clean-shaven, wearing black-rimmed glasses and sensible jeans, and the first thing he did was hand me a bag of feijoas to keep me going on the journey. Then, as we drove north and west across the Sabana de Bogotá, the wide altiplano or 'savanna' that surrounds the city, he told me stories in rapid, clear Spanish.

He explained why many of my Uber drivers had pronounced feijoa 'frey-hoa', inserting an *r* that wasn't there. 'Feijoa sounds weird in Spanish,' he said. Adding the *r* makes the word feel more natural. (So it turns out that 'feijoa' sounds strange and foreign in every language – and to me, it implies that there is no 'correct' pronunciation of the name.)

Omar also filled me in on local idiosyncrasies (Colombians measure fuel consumption in 'gallons per kilometre', a mash-up of metric and imperial systems), gestures (it's common to point to things with your mouth, by stretching your pursed lips in different directions) and his family history – a personal story deeply entwined with a certain fruit.

'I was born surrounded by feijoas, I grew up eating feijoas, and now I make my living from feijoas – they have been present at all the stages of my life,' he said. 'I have the greatest affection for feijoas, and everything about them awakens my interest, my curiosity, and my desire to continue learning about the species.' When he went with his wife and kids to Disneyland in California, and Disney World in Florida, Omar was more excited about discovering feijoa plants growing in both places than he was about any of the cartoon attractions. It's possible he is even more of a feijoa obsessive than I am.

Omar's father, Over Quintero Castillo, was the original feijoa pioneer. The sixth of sixteen children, he was the first in his working-class rural family to go to university. Over's parents were among the many displaced from their homes during the civil war in the 1950s, and money was tight. Over worked as a teacher to support his studies, completed a biology degree, and eventually became a researcher specialising in biotechnology at the Universidad INCCA de Colombia. At around the same time, Over's half-brother, Fabio Barrero Castillo, was working in the Federación Nacional de Cafeteros, the agricultural organisation that had helped to make Colombia synonymous with coffee.

By the 1980s, it was becoming clear that being so reliant on one (legal) crop was making Colombia's fortunes too dependent on the international coffee price. Over and Fabio set about identifying and developing other potential crops that could help the country to diversify, Omar explained, 'and the one my father was most interested in was the feijoa'. Partly, that was because few people had worked on it before. But he also just liked the taste.

In 1987, the half-brothers purchased a piece of steep, stony land overlooked by cloud-shrouded mountains in La Vega, about 35 kilometres from Bogotá, and began work on a germplasm bank: a kind of living museum collection of genetically distinct feijoas. They called it the Centro Nacional de la Feijoa - the national feijoa centre, or CENAF. Over and Fabio imported and planted New Zealand cultivars - Mammoth, Apollo, Gemini, Unique, Triumph - alongside plants collected in Colombia. They observed them closely, and selected fifteen individuals that in the first three years gave an average harvest of at least 20 kilograms per tree, with an average fruit size of at least 60 grams. (None of the New Zealand varieties distinguished themselves.) Because Colombians like to eat them skin-and-all, Over's team also prioritised those that had thinner, sweeter skins. Today, there are more than 1500 genetically distinct feijoa plants growing at CENAF, and four main cultivars discovered there that are now in widespread commercial use.[191]

Alongside the breeding and research, Over started making deals with interested landowners, encouraging them to grow the best varieties and sell the fruit. As a young child, Omar played among the feijoa plants, and helped fill bags with soil for the seedlings. His mother made feijoa smoothies from the fruit and milk, and decorated them with feijoa petals. Where other children would bring an apple to school as a present for the teacher, Omar and his brother would bring bags of feijoas to share. Over taught his children to love feijoas, hoping the fruit would also bring them more opportunities than he had had in his own childhood.

But in 2003, Over died of cancer, aged just fifty-two. Omar was twenty-three, a recently graduated biologist himself. He abandoned his plans to study overseas, and stayed in Colombia so he could take over the family business and continue his father's feijoa legacy. Now, he oversees eight different commercial feijoa orchards, including CENAF, and a Bogotá factory where the fruit is brought and sorted into juicing, local and export grades.

Around mid-morning, the car crested a range of hills, the suburbs gave way to dairy farms and haciendas, and, near the town of Tenjo, we arrived at the first of Omar's orchards.

He pulled up outside some colourful wood-and-adobe

houses and introduced me to the friendly landowners, Carlos Mario Castro and Janet Ricaurte, just as a heavy rain started to fall. Sheltering in the packing shed, we met Manuel Vanegas – a small, older man with sun-browned skin, bright eyes and a shy, beaming smile. He had worked for Omar's family for a decade, and also tended the feijoas at CENAF alongside his wife and daughters. While we waited for the rain to stop, Omar explained to Manuel that I came from an exotic country with defined seasons. Here in Andean Colombia, in contrast, people call it 'winter' when it rains a lot, and 'summer' during periods of drought, he said.

So, what happens to the feijoa when there is no spring warming to trigger flowering? As the rain eased and we walked out into the orchard, I found out. Though the trees were covered in ripe fruit, they were also glistening with bright flowers. On the same branch, I saw buds, flowers, tiny fruits and fully ripe ones. In New Zealand and other temperate countries, the winter chill inhibits blossoms from forming, and spring's rising temperatures and lengthening days spur all the plants to flower more or less at once. But in Colombia, they can bloom all year round – which is how Omar's mother could garnish her fresh smoothies with feijoa flower petals. Here, you can eat a ripe feijoa straight from the tree at practically any time of year, something that seems almost miraculous to a feijoa-loving New Zealander who is starved of them from June to February!

There aren't always large quantities of fruit, though. Typically, there are two drier periods each year – both called 'summer' – which stimulate more flowers to grow at once. Following each drought, the rains return, and help to swell the developing fruit. But many Colombian growers are convinced they are already experiencing the effects of climate change. For the past few years, the dry and wet periods have become less marked, and more unpredictable.[192]

Still, Omar and Manuel have a secret weapon that allows

them to more or less control fruiting despite the climate, and to coordinate peaks of production for the most useful times of year: pruning. 'We can make the trees flower whenever we want,' Omar said. Manuel – who is, according to Omar, 'a genius at pruning' – took up his secateurs to demonstrate the technique.

Manuel prunes boldly, leaving a central leader and several tiers of four or five horizontal branches. Twenty to thirty days after pruning, new buds will grow, and if the plants are well fertilised, a profusion of flowers will burst forth. Six months after pruning, fruit production will peak. That control is a significant competitive advantage. Colombia has continuity of supply, leading to more stable prices, and can export feijoas to Europe during the times of year when neither the northern nor southern hemisphere orchards are producing. (The downside is that the trees must be tended all year round, meaning more labour is required.) In the first six months of 2019, feijoa production in Colombia reached more than 9000 tonnes – compared with an estimated 1200 tonnes in New Zealand the same year.[193]

Pruning has other benefits, too. Opening up the tree's canopy also increases air flow, inhibiting the growth of fungal pathogens, and allows easy access for the blooms' avian pollinators. Omar advises landowners to keep plenty of forest cover around their plantations to encourage the presence of birds. Although there are a number of species that visit the flowers, he said, the most important is called the mirla, a cousin of the blackbird also called *Turdus fuscater* or the great thrush. Right on cue, a large brown bird with bright orange legs flew across the orchard. 'That's a mirla,' our hostess said – off to snack on the feijoa's tasty petals and transport its pollen at the same time, setting in motion the next crop of fruit.

In the afternoon, we headed further west. The Tenjo farm we'd visited was at 2600 metres above sea level, Omar said, near the upper limit for decent feijoa production in Colombia. Above 3000 metres, the páramos begin – the spongy, rain-drenched mountaintops where the majority of the country's water supply and rivers originate. Below 1800 metres, introduced Mediterranean fruit flies thrive and cause severe damage to the fruit. In between is the 'goldilocks zone' that is perfect for the feijoa: not too hot, not too cold. The place we were to spend the night was a few hundred metres down the mountain. 'Finca El Cortijo', Omar said, at 2300 metres above sea level, was a place of happy childhood memories for him – but it was also touched by Colombia's violent recent past.

Grey wisps of waterlogged cloud hung about the mountains, and 10,000 feijoa trees fell away across twenty-five sloping hectares between the highway and a small stream. The farm is so steep tractors are impractical; I watched one of Omar's employees transport the harvest with a horse and cart instead. Before it was a feijoa farm, it was a cattle ranch belonging to Donald Lee Cary, a Texan who spent much of his life in Colombia as an executive for ExxonMobil.

When Cary retired to La Vega, he met Omar's father Over, who convinced him to turn the pasture into a feijoa orchard. The pair formed a partnership where Cary provided the land and Over took charge of the cultivation. But at sunset one Saturday in March 1998, Cary was snatched by three gunmen as he left the farm. The kidnappers drove him through Bogotá in his own car, revealing as they left the city that they were members of the FARC. Ransoms were one of the guerillas' main sources of revenue at the time, and they are estimated to have kidnapped or taken hostage more than 20,000 people between 1990 and 2015.[194]

For the next five months, Cary was their captive, made to march for hours through jungle and mountains as government mortars exploded nearby.[195] The constant walking and the diet of 'guerrilla soup' – pasta and rice in broth – trimmed his waistline by two inches, and he grew a grey beard. Eventually, after 170 days on the march, his family paid the ransom, and Cary was released to the Red Cross. Soon afterwards, he decided he no longer wanted to stay in Colombia and left the country. He died in 2017.

Omar remains in business with Cary's descendants and was reluctant to talk much about these events. 'The history of Colombia is very complicated,' he kept saying, and quickly moved the conversation back to feijoas: they could potentially contribute to Colombia's rehabilitation, Omar believes. The worst effects of the war and the illicit drug trade happened in rural areas, where people had few economic opportunities and were frequently displaced by the violence or the cartels. Omar would like to see the coca fields replaced by feijoa orchards. 'Part of the solution to the conflict is to provide opportunities for rural people to do other kinds of things, to give them alternatives to the things we wish did not exist in Colombia.'

There are some challenges to overcome, he concedes: coca thrives at slightly lower elevations, and the fact that feijoa trees take three to five years to start producing commercial quantities of fruit will prevent many small farmers from investing. For now, Omar is focused on showing by example that feijoas can be a viable business. In 2019, he sold 320 tonnes of fruit – a quarter of New Zealand's entire commercial feijoa production that year – to buyers in Colombia, the Netherlands, Germany and Russia. But it's not just business. For Omar, feijoas are an inheritance; his passion for the plant is a way of honouring and remembering his father.

As dusk fell, Omar led the way to a low, whitewashed house with a fading russet roof and red-painted wooden verandahs hung with geraniums in pots. He stayed here a lot as a child, he said, and used to play in the river while his father checked on the crop. That night, I went to sleep in a single bed in a room at the end of the corridor. All around was cold and quiet, and a photograph of Over – a small, gentle-looking man with kind eyes – watched over me in a frame on the bedside table.

Finally, I'd found somewhere where feijoas were as widely known and warmly appreciated as they were in New Zealand. And yet this was a different feijoa again – different from the New Zealand one I knew, from the Brazilian one under the araucarias, the cryptic French feijoa, or the invisible Californian one. This was a tropical feijoa, with a strange biology of its own. Until I'd seen it with my own eyes, I'd never have imagined a feijoa tree could simultaneously be covered in fruit and flowers.

While the biological and commercial novelties were fascinating, I was also deeply curious about the cultural significance of the fruit here. What do feijoas mean to Colombians? Why and how have they become a part of people's identity?

The following day, Omar dropped me at the bus station in the north of Bogotá, and I jumped on the afternoon coach to Tibasosa, the small Andean village in the department of Boyacá, which has adopted the feijoa as its symbol and holds a festival every year in its honour.

CHAPTER 16

The Festival of the Feijoa

Three and a half hours later, the bus shuddered to a stop on the side of the highway. 'Tibasosa!' called the driver. The girl sitting next to me pointed out a well-dressed sixty-something woman standing by the bus stop: 'que tiene cara de esperar alguién', one of those lovely expressions that should exist in English, but does not. It was true: the woman did have a 'waiting-for-someone face', and she was waiting for me. It was María Fernanda Olano, this year's president of the Corporación Festival de la Feijoa, who had agreed to host me in her home and act as my guide to Tibasosa.

Though she grew up in Bogotá and spent nearly two decades living in Arizona, San Diego and London, María Fernanda has a family connection to Tibasosa that dates back at least two centuries. The house she now lived in – where she took care of her ageing mother – was built by an ancestor on her father's side around 200 years ago. (It was abandoned for several decades while the family lived south of Bogotá, until María's father, Noel Olano, returned in 1989 to do it up.)

We went there first to drop off my bags. The dark, old-fashioned rooms overlooked a beautiful patio with a lichen-draped lemon tree and a stone fountain embedded with coiled ammonite fossils. In my upstairs room, the window opened onto a view of red-tiled roofs, lush bougainvilleas, distant hills and feijoa trees in the neighbours' walled gardens.

Before it got dark, María Fernanda wanted to show me around, so we walked the few cobblestoned blocks to Tibasosa's plaza, or main square. Like many small Andean villages, the plaza was gigantic compared with the size of the town: a great expanse of public space, hundreds of metres from one end to the other. The twin stone belltowers of Our Lady of the Rosary, the eighteenth-century church, dominated the eastern end, the hands of its clock face stuck at twenty-five minutes past seven. Elderly couples in ruanas walked arm in arm, teenagers took selfies, and kids raced each other to the three flagpoles at the western end, the bright banners signifying nation (Colombia), department (Boyacá) and municipality (Tibasosa). A horseshoe of hills encircled the town on three sides, and the setting sun lit up the storm clouds swirling around the high, flat-topped páramo in the distance.

As we walked past the church, René Vargas Cuellar rushed out of a doorway. He and I had been corresponding for years, ever since I stumbled on the festival's existence online and knew that, one day, I just had to go. María Fernanda called out to him, and René gave me a huge bear hug of welcome. But he couldn't stay and chat; he was part of the organising team for the Festival of the Feijoa. It was just four days away, and there was a lot to do.

―――

Dusk was falling, and on the far corner of the plaza a brightly lit sign beckoned: *Tierra de Feijoa* – Land of the Feijoa – a restaurant housed in a colonial building with whitewashed walls and dark timber lintels. Inside, a hand-painted frieze of feijoa fruit, leaves and flowers led the way into a small courtyard, where María Fernanda and I sat down at a table. The leather-bound menus, embossed with feijoas in green thread, contained a variety of dishes featuring the hero ingredient – trout a là feijoa, pork with feijoa salsa – but neither of us were very hungry, so we ordered tomato soup instead. There would be plenty of feijoa action in the coming days, and I didn't want to peak too soon.

Before long, the ruler of the restaurant – this tiny feijoa kingdom – came bustling out of the kitchen in his chef's uniform and stripy bandanna: Jaiver Leandro Pérez Alfonso, thirty years old, all smiles and charisma and boundless energy. Tonight, a Tuesday, the restaurant was relatively quiet, so he sat down with us for a while, talking rapidly of his plans for the festival. 'You can be a celebrity judge of the feijoa dessert competition,' he said to me. 'And I want you to do a live cooking demonstration. Can you make a traditional New Zealand feijoa dish?' The idea of such on-the-spot multitasking terrified me. The only thing I could think of to make was feijoa and apple crumble. But how could I say no in the face of such friendly enthusiasm?

The conversation ranged widely, and Jaiver and María Fernanda seemed to enjoy each other's company. When she went home, I stayed at the table, and Jaiver told me how he'd ended up in the land of the feijoa.

He was born 200 kilometres away in a different world, down on the Llanos: the vast tropical grasslands that stretch from the eastern foothills of the Andes across the Orinoco River into Venezuela. Jaiver's father left school aged seven to work in the fields and on construction sites, while his mother waited in restaurants, taught Jaiver to cook, and instilled in her son a strong work ethic. His entrepreneurial soul was revealed young. By his early teens, he was making arepas, popcorn and rosquitas de arroz – ring-shaped crackers made of rice flour and cheese – and selling them at school.

But growing up on the Llanos in the 1990s and 2000s meant that Colombia's civil conflict was an unavoidable part of life.

Jaiver remembers hiding under the bed and praying while the army and the guerrillas shot at each other outside. Armed groups – both guerillas and paramilitaries – would show up and demand shopkeepers give them money, food, perhaps a pair of boots. If the people didn't comply, they risked death. If they did, the rival group could accuse them of collaborating with the enemy. There was no way to win. In Jaiver's small community, people he knew were murdered in broad daylight in the butcher's shop or the supermarket. 'We knew that it could happen to anyone,' he said.

When Jaiver was twelve, he was taken hostage by the FARC one day as he arrived at school. The guerillas forced the entire town into the plaza at gunpoint. They were looking for some people, and took them away. That night, he hid in his teacher's house, with no way to tell his parents where he was, as the guerillas had cut the phone lines and disabled the mobile phone signal. But when the students and teachers cautiously emerged in the morning, the FARC had gone.

───

By seventeen, Jaiver wanted something different for his life. In primary school, he had gone on a school trip to the Tibasosa area – the first time he'd felt cold weather. But the town had seemed peaceful, a place of opportunity, so he farewelled his parents and moved to the mountains. He stayed with an aunt in Tibasosa, invented an elaborate work-experience history, and landed a job as a shoe salesman in nearby Duitama, where he worked from 8 am until 8 pm every single day, with only two days off a month. After a year and a half, he had saved enough money to buy a couple of computers and open his own internet café. Not that he knew anything about computers – at his high school the guerillas had blown up the electricity supply so often they mostly didn't work – but he set about teaching himself how to take them apart and put them back together, and how to install software, and before long, three computers had become twelve.

After that, he started a low-cost travel agency, aimed at showing locals the sights of their own backyard. The tours would often finish in Tibasosa, sampling feijoa sabajón – a kind of creamy fruit liqueur made in the town. Next, he got a job in Tibasosa's city hall, working as a private assistant to the mayor. He fixed her computers, and travelled with her to meetings in the department capital Tunja and in Bogotá. Then he worked in a sabajón factory, selling sabajón and feijoa champagne, and then he worked in a bank for a while . . . By now, I was practically open-mouthed at this string of achievements, the constant reinvention, the fake-it-till-you-make-it, self-made audacity – but Jaiver told his story straightforwardly, as though anyone would have done the same.

Finally, realising tourists were always looking for 'algo típico' – something typical or particular from a certain place – he came up with the idea of Tierra de Feijoa: a place where visitors to Tibasosa could go to eat dishes featuring the feijoa. With a business partner, he started the restaurant. In the evenings, Jaiver ran the show on his own, working simultaneously as waiter and chef: taking orders, then running back to the kitchen to make the food. He started inventing feijoa desserts – sponges, mousse, cakes – and salsas for meat dishes. He figured out how to preserve feijoas in syrup, how to use lemon juice to stop the fruit from oxidising, and how to make an alcoholic feijoa chicha (the signature fermented drink of the Andes, usually made from maize). Introducing people to a new flavour was a source of deep satisfaction for him.

Now, six years on, he employed five people during the week and eleven on the weekends. 'Tibasosa opened a lot of doors for me,' he said. 'I was a very rural and humble person, I didn't have any resources. I imagined many things for myself, but I never thought I could have a restaurant.' The feijoa itself is a symbol of his transformation, of the new existence he has forged for himself. 'The feijoa changed my life. At this moment it represents everything to me – it gives me food, it gives me economic stability, it means I can offer employment to others. I never thought that the feijoa could give me so much.'

Jaiver had to get back to the kitchen. He made me promise to come back the next day and help him to make his latest invention, envueltos de feijoa. I said goodnight and walked home to María Fernanda's. Crossing the plaza, I hugged myself against the cold night air, and felt a wild surge of excitement. High in the tropical Andes, so far from home, I'd found an entire town of people just as obsessed as me.

―――

Idiosyncratic small towns play an outsize role in Colombian storytelling – from Macondo in Gabriel García Márquez's novel *One Hundred Years of Solitude* to the *Encanto* town in 2021's Disney movie. Tibasosa, too, oozed with a personality of its own. It wore its history on its whitewashed walls: murals recalled the supposed visit of Colombian independence hero Simón Bolívar, lionised the town's 'matriarchal' succession of six female mayors[196] and paid homage to the feijoa in all its forms.

As the week progressed, I watched a muralist complete a new work just in time for the festival. Between the shuttered wooden windows and lintel-topped doors on the two-storey government building that lines the southern side of the square, he was painting delicate, full-length portraits of Tibasosa's mayors: ten women and two men, all smiling in smart suits. Several of the women held books, another had the green, red and white municipal flag draped over her arm – and one lifted aloft a laden plate of feijoas.

To learn about the plant's history in the town, María Fernanda took me to meet local nurseryman and feijoa grower Oscar

Velandia. As he showed me around his huge nursery, where he and his daughters tend no fewer than 20,000 feijoa seedlings, he told me the story. In 1935, a señor called Antonio Maria Tamayo Palacios brought three plants from the Bogotá area and planted them in the gardens of various wealthy Tibasosa families. They grew so well in the town's climate that they soon caught on, and by the 1980s most well-to-do Tibasosa houses had a feijoa tree or two in the garden.

Oscar himself arrived in Tibasosa in 1962, from another small Boyacá town called Tinjacá. Alexander von Humboldt apparently visited Tinjacá in the early 1800s and declared it 'the best climate in the world'. Still, once Oscar found Tibasosa, nothing could persuade him to leave. 'This village is a paradise. It's very healthy, very quiet, you can live here without complications.' When he tasted his first feijoa, he was hooked. He began growing his own, about forty plants to start with, and discovered for himself how variable the plant is from seed. Only a few of the seedlings produced decent fruit. In the 1990s, Over Quintero brought him some cultivars from New Zealand – Triumph, Mammoth, and one he just called Nueva Zelanda. He selected another cultivar called Tibasosa, and those are the four varieties he sells today.

Oscar had a small grey moustache, a straw hat and a neat checked shirt tucked into belted jeans. He was eighty-three years old, but seemed much younger. 'That's because I eat feijoas every day,' he said. 'It's the fruit of eternal youth!' This was something I heard quite often in Colombia – including from Oscar's daughter Pilar, a food engineer, who told me that the feijoa is 'the second or third fruit in the universe' that helps the body restore cells and slow down ageing – a claim I couldn't quite back up in the scientific literature. Certainly, Oscar considered it his job to promote the feijoa to others. 'As a service to humanity,' he said, 'the feijoa is a great thing.'

In the 1980s, other Tibasoseños began to experiment with the feijoas that were abundantly growing in the town's gardens.

Back then, Margarita Rojas López was a newlywed. Her husband, courting her, used to bring her little presents of feijoas, which his father sold in his Tibasosa store. Once they married, and Margarita moved to the town, she started making feijoa cakes and sweets. This was during the period of the 'matriarchy', and Margarita said she was inspired by the fact that women were in charge. 'I came from a home where the father was the authority. But when I arrived in Tibasosa, the work of women was very much emphasised, and it gave me more confidence. It made me think, what can I do? What can I contribute?' The small business she started then has grown into Agroindustrias las Margaritas, a tiny, modern, hygiene-conscious processing factory hidden inside a colonial building on the corner of the square. There, her staff distil feijoa essence from the raw fruits and make a wide range of feijoa products including sabajón: the Baileys-like liqueur made from milk, egg, fruit extract, aguardiente (Colombia's national anise-flavoured firewater)... and a few secret ingredients.

In the steaming kitchen at Tierra de Feijoa, a huge steel pan was heating on the gas stovetop, half-full of feijoas cut into quarters with the skin still on. Jaiver poured two kilos of sugar over the fruit, then stirred the mound of white crystals in with a wooden spoon. Music blasted on the stereo, a mix of international and Colombian pop and hip-hop. Jaiver sang along to ChocQuib-Town, Andrés Cepeda and Juanes as he added a squeeze of lemon juice to the mixture to stop the fruit oxidising and turning brown. This is how you make feijoas in almíbar, he said, a kind of viscous sugar syrup that forms the basis of many other dishes.

First on the list was envueltos de feijoa. Sold as street food around Colombia, envueltos are similar to Mexican tamales: little steamed packets of maize and cheese, wrapped – or enveloped, the word's origin – in corn husks. Out the back, several of Jaiver's kitchenhands and their young children were peeling the husks from the corncobs and grinding the kernels into a fine paste. Jaiver crumbled a mozzarella-like white cheese into the maize mix, and added melted butter, salt, baking powder and more sugar. He whizzed some of the feijoas in syrup in the blender, then poured the resulting green smoothie into the maize mix as well. Then we started making the envueltos: taking a pale green corn husk, spooning the maize mix into it, adding a little piece of cheese and a caramelised quarter-feijoa from the almíbar, then wrapping it up tight and placing it in another large pot. Jaiver had lined the bottom with water and the empty corncobs to add flavour and prevent burning. When it was full of envueltos, he covered the top with leftover corn husks to help trap the steam.

We still had some maize-and-feijoa mix left. 'I know! We can make arepas!' Jaiver announced, pouring little circles of the batter onto a hot frying pan. When they were brown, we tasted them. Not bad. 'Tell the customers we have a special,' Jaiver said to the head waitress. 'Arepas de feijoa!' She raised a sceptical eyebrow – an expression I read as 'here-he-goes-again-with-his-last-minute-inventions'.

But Jaiver's enthusiasm was irresistible, and the customers were convinced. The orders came in, and soon we were helping to crack eggs into the mixture. 'Arepas need eggs,' the waitress said to Jaiver. 'And how much sugar did you put in?'

'A kilo and a half? Too sweet?'

'Very sweet,' she said. Jaiver wasn't in the habit of measuring anything. He just chucked ingredients in by eye, tasting the mixture, adding more of something else. Then he had another idea. 'Ooh, we could make ice cream! Mix the almíbar with milk or cream and freeze it!' The waitress rolled her eyes, but Jaiver was unperturbed. 'That's what I like about the feijoa,' he said. 'The possibilities are wide open. There is room for experimentation and innovation. It's all new.'

———

Finally, Saturday morning arrived. The thirty-second annual Festival of the Feijoa was under way at last. A huge stage stood in the plaza, and people were putting out long rows of white plastic chairs in front of it. Stalls sold local feijoa products and clothes made in China, and a cheesy festival jingle played repeatedly on the loudspeaker.

Margarita's company store had a prominent location on the corner of the square, selling fresh feijoa smoothies and sweets and bottles of pale green feijoa sabajón, each one 'dressed' in a tiny woollen ruana and a little knitted hat. Other shops, including one called Feijolandia, also advertised their feijoa wares. I tried several different kinds of feijoa ice cream. On the pavement outside were feijoa seedlings in pots, probably grown in Oscar's nursery.

Presiding over one of the fresh-fruit stalls was eighty-seven-year-old Cecilia Salamanca de Ramírez. She had a lined and beautiful face and a naughty gleam in her eye, and was delighted to pose for photographs. Cecilia had been selling feijoas at the festival every single year since it started thirty-two years ago, she told me. 'I give thanks to my God for inventing the feijoa,' she said. 'It's what's given me my bread every day. I like to eat it, and I like to see others enjoy it.'

That first Festival of the Feijoa was held in Tibasosa in 1987. Like other aspects of the town's history, the origins are a little contested – but suffice to say it was started by a group of Tibasoseños who wanted to attract tourist dollars to their town and give locals a sense of municipal pride. The strategy had worked for other Colombian towns before. Every year, in some corner of the country or other, you can attend the Festival of the Mango, the Festival of Honey, the Festival of the Egg Arepa and the Pineapple Fair. There are towns that hold festivals for donkeys, for crabs, for sugarcane and for the cebú cattle that form the backbone of Colombia's rural economy.

Barrancabermeja, an oil-rich city on the Magdalena River, holds an annual Festival of Petroleum, while in Bucaramanga in Santander they celebrate the Festival of the Golden Ant. I was sorry to miss that one – a homage to a peculiar local delicacy called hormigas culonas, or big-assed ants. For a few weeks in April and May, the queens of this leafcutter ant species (*Atta laevigata*) emerge from the ground in flying hordes, their round abdomens swollen with eggs. Locals risk being bitten as they harvest them, then fry their crunchy bodies with salt: a protein-packed aphrodisiac snack.

So, there was a precedent for the Festival of the Feijoa. The first one in 1987 was small, Margarita said, just a few stalls with feijoa cakes, snacks and fresh fruit. But after three hours they had sold everything. 'People loved it, because it was something new.' Margarita served as the festival's president for several of the early ones, as did María Fernanda's mother. They began to include a musical programme, featuring folkloric musicians from around the Andean region, an annual folk music and dance competition for children and teenagers, and a luthiers' exhibition of handmade musical instruments. But every year, it's a challenge to find the money needed to put it on. 'It's very hard to raise money for cultural events in a country where many people don't have enough to eat,' María Fernanda explained.

On the festival's first morning, the organisers were busy problem-solving. The power went out for at least an hour, leaving the stage quiet. An unanticipated cycling event closed the road between Duitama and Tibasosa for most of the morning, preventing visitors from arriving, jamming traffic and stranding Jaiver, who had gone to Duitama to pick up supplies. A child performer dropped and broke a microphone and the rental company wanted the festival to pay a million Colombian pesos for it – the equivalent of US$250.

But by the evening, the troubles were forgotten as the music soared above the square. The festival always features traditional Andean Colombian folk music – the humorous, storytelling carranga; the syncopated, polyrhythmic bambuco; the pasillo, a kind of sped-up version of the European waltz; and the torbellino, meaning 'whirlwind', describing the light, rapid steps of the accompanying dance.

On the stage sat half a dozen ruana-wearing musical maestros, all men, who took turns to sing love ballads, solo or in duets, accompanying themselves on guitar and a number of other stringed instruments I didn't recognise. Some were new originals, while others seemed to be traditional favourites, with audience members singing along. There were songs about destiny, unrequited desire, infidelity and passion – even one about falling for a woman on Bogotá's public bus system, the TransMilenio.

One of the maestros, Javier Peña, was staying at María Fernanda's as well, with his wife and seven-year-old daughter. After the performance, he invited me to come to a tertullio, a kind of late-night musical after-party (or folk session) in someone's nearby house. The intimate tertullio, he assured me, was just as much a part of the festival as the public performances in the plaza – I couldn't miss it.

Javier was in his fifties, charming and lively in person, and assured and passionate on stage (one song he'd played was called 'Beautiful Obsession', and though it seemed to be about his wife, made me think of the feijoa). As we walked to the venue, Javier took great delight in educating me about Colombian Andean music, which originated in the mixture of Indigenous Muisca, Spanish and (to a lesser extent) African culture that took place in these parts in the centuries after colonisation. The gaita is a long flute of Indigenous origin, made of cane and feathers, and the stringed instruments the Spanish brought from Europe evolved over the years to become something typically Colombian: there is the tiple, guitar-shaped but slightly smaller, with twelve metal strings and a harpsichord-like sound. Then there's the 'tiple's little brother', the requinto, which is ten-stringed, smaller again, bright and melodic. The pear-shaped bandola andina is related to the mandolin.[197]

When we arrived at the tertullio, we sat in a large circle in the lounge with dozens of other guests, while the hosts served pizza and hot aguapanela, a sweet drink made from sugarcane, and someone passed around a bottle of whisky. Accompanied by a young woman on guitar, the eldest maestro – a man in his late seventies or eighties in a grey ruana – began to sing emotive, narrative songs in a still-powerful voice, each of which he introduced with a story about how he came to write it. It was clear he was a well-known and much-loved artist: some people sang along, while others asked respectful questions. Javier nodded along, smiling, with his arms folded over his requinto.

The songs were rural and nostalgic, parochial and gently nationalistic. They often ended with a punchline that everyone laughed at, and I invariably didn't quite catch. The maestro kept his hands hidden beneath his ruana most of the time, and later I noticed he was missing two or three fingers. Soon other maestros took their turn. A requinto was passed around the room. Other musicians joined in on guitar, tiple and the spoons. By 1 am I was fading, and Javier walked me back to María Fernanda's – but he told me the next day that the music went on until dawn.

'The other two judges have fallen through,' chef Jaiver said on Sunday morning – 'so you'll need to find two more people to help judge the feijoa desserts competition.' I recruited Alberto Molano Zabala, a psychologist friend of María Fernanda's who I'd met the day before, and Luz Marina, the wife of one of the luthiers, who claimed to have 'experience in desserts'. I had plenty of experience in, well . . . eating desserts, and I supposed by now I was a feijoa expert, so I guessed I was vaguely qualified? Jaiver sat us down at a table under a marquee on the edge of the plaza, gave us a briefing, and made us sign a pile of paperwork. Clearly, we were to take this very seriously.

Two nervous women carried their desserts up to the table. The dishes were exquisite, the most beautiful things I'd ever seen made with feijoas. One was an ice-cream cake: a pale green frozen hemisphere decorated with a feijoa flower and four feijoa slices arranged in a cross, surrounded by squirts of Chantilly cream and spherical globes of frozen feijoa. Inside, on a biscuit base, were two different kinds of homemade feijoa ice cream (one involving the skins, the other without) separated with a layer of sweet arequipe (caramel).

The other dessert consisted of three individual portions of feijoa marshmallow, heart-shaped and drizzled with white and milk chocolate. I thought they were all gorgeous and delicious, but Luz Marina had lots of opinions and advice about the proper consistency of the marshmallow, and the texture of the cake base.

We waited two hours for the next contestant to appear. He was a young Bogotá chef with a name-badged uniform, earring and tattooed forearms, and had made an elaborate construction he called 'Tierra de Feijoa'. It featured a drizzled chocolate tree decorated with crystallised feijoa flowers, and two white-chocolate 'feijoas' painted green and filled with feijoa-flavoured cream, surrounded by dollops of feijoa jam and custard. A quinoa-and-chia-seed crumble represented the 'soil of Tibasosa', he said.

It was very impressive, but we found ourselves resistant to picking the city wunderkind who had arrived late over the women from the local microenterprise. Besides, despite the elaborate presentation, the dessert itself didn't taste much like feijoa. 'And it's not really the right shade of green,' added Alberto. We chose the feijoa ice-cream cake, presented by the shy, smiling Lina.

I had never seen such feijoa-related culinary creativity. In New Zealand, you can buy feijoa beer, feijoa wine, feijoa yoghurts and drinks and chocolates and breakfast cereals. At home, we make feijoa muffins and feijoa cakes. But that's about it. The sheer variety and constant innovation in Tibasosa was something else – savoury dishes, alcoholic drinks, desserts and salsas and sweets. 'Colombians in general are very creative people, we are skilful and enterprising,' Jaiver said. 'If Tibasosa is the land of the feijoa, then many things have to be made of feijoa.' It seemed obvious when he put it like that.

On Sunday afternoon, the clouds rolled in from the páramo. For an hour, heavy rain pooled in the cobblestones. The downpour drove many of the visitors away, and postponed the festival closing ceremony until late into the evening. Eventually, though, I found myself standing at the end of the sodden 'green carpet' with Javier and the other musical maestros, wearing my new, handwoven sheep's-wool ruana in an attempt to fit in. Above me, the stage was already crowded with bright-costumed performers and familiar faces.

When the man on the microphone called our names from the stage, Javier took my arm and paraded me jubilantly down the green carpet as though we were a celebrity couple. 'In recognition of the writer and journalist Kate Evans, from New Zealand, for her connection with the festival,' purred the MC in melodramatic radio-announcer tones. María Fernanda hugged me as I climbed onstage, and René presented me with a hand-carved trophy, topped with a green-painted, larger-than-life wooden feijoa. On the base was a small metal plaque, inscribed with my name and Escritora – writer. I was touched and embarrassed all at once. All I'd done was show up! It was a prize just for being here: gracias por existir, as I'd heard Colombians frequently say: thank you for existing.

This was the climax of the Festival of the Feijoa – a celebration of the mere existence of this small green fruit. But it was more than that. Everyone I'd met here had a kidnapping story, or had been touched by the civil war in some way – Jaiver hijacked as a child, Omar's American business partner snatched by the FARC, and in 1980 María Fernanda's mother and sister spent three days as hostages of the M-19 guerrillas in the siege of the Dominican Republic Embassy in Bogotá. In a country that had been so riven by conflict, this determination to create a wholesome local identity felt like such a hopeful, optimistic thing. The effort was quite explicit: the festival's programme proudly celebrated '32 years creating identity and history and tasting the fruits the land gives us, to the sound of Bambucos, Pasillos and Torbellinos'.

In adopting the feijoa as their symbol, I wondered if the people of Tibasosa were reaching for something inoffensive and neutral, something that everyone, regardless of their politics, could get behind. The architects of the festival had braided together food, music, movement and a sense of place, and started a new tradition their community had embraced – and it didn't seem to matter that the feijoa wasn't originally Colombian.

Back when I first began this project, one of the reasons this particular plant had captured my curiosity was that I perceived its story as surprising, even ironic: here was this deeply exotic fruit from a far-off continent that my country had somehow adopted as its own. And yet, in following the feijoa around the world, I was starting to see that this kind of thing happens all the time. Culture is created, in part, from these chance collisions and borrowings: a fragment of music from here, a plant adopted from there. Some aspects of culture can remain unchanged for millennia; but our local, regional and national identities are also continually being forged from a mix of what we carry with us and what we find when we get there.

Having such heterogeneous origins doesn't mean that these symbols of culture are inauthentic, or don't hold real significance: if they didn't, feijoas wouldn't be able to make people cry. It's just that their meanings are not singular, and they are not static, either. The ways we weave music, plants and food into our lives are constantly evolving.

———

The bright stage lights reflected off the wet cobblestones, and everything felt overexposed and surreal. A musician standing behind me tapped me on the shoulder. His guitar was slung around his neck, and his ankle-length black cape was lined with red silk and decorated with colourful badges and rosettes. 'Eres de Nueva Zelandia?' he asked – are you from New Zealand? I nodded. He swept his black bowler hat off his head and pointed inside at the label. There was a picture of a kiwi, and a 'Made in NZ' logo. He'd bought it on a trip to Christchurch, he said, when his son was studying there.

It was a common enough little coincidence. But in that moment, as I stood among the earnest local dignitaries, the musicians in their ruanas, and the kind people who had taken me into their homes and lives for a week, it felt symbolic. The story of the feijoa was ripe with these kinds of convergences: invisible threads connecting people across time and space, a kaleidoscopic array of stories and connections that already stretched far beyond my expectations. Made in New Zealand: perhaps it was a sign. It was time to follow the feijoa home.

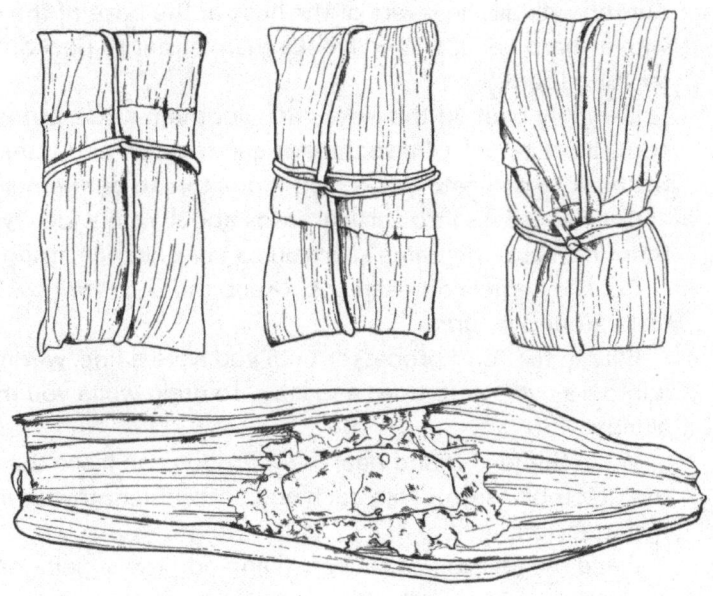

RECIPE
Jaiver's Feijoa Envueltos
Contributed by Jaiver Leandro Pérez Alfonso

Savoury-sweet envueltos, also called bollos, are a popular street snack in Colombia.

INGREDIENTS:
For the dough:
6 large sweetcorn cobs in the husk
200 g/2 cups grated mozzarella
3 tbsp softened butter
½ tsp salt
1 ½ tsp sugar
1 tsp baking powder

For the almíbar:
500 g feijoas (about 6 to 10 depending on size)
⅓ cup sugar

INSTRUCTIONS:

Cut through all the layers of the husk at the base of the corncobs with a sharp knife. This will make them easier to peel off without splitting them.

Carefully peel off the leaves and set them aside, but discard the corn silk or tassel. (These threads catch pollen and transfer it inside the husk to pollinate the kernels – one thread per kernel!)

Cut two leaves into vertical strips about 1 cm wide – you'll use these to tie up the parcels, or you can use kitchen string instead.

Cut the kernels off each cob. (Keep the cobs for now.) This should yield around 4 cups.

Blitz in the food processor until you have a fine, wet meal. Tip it into a sieve over a bowl and leave to drain while you make the almíbar.

Wash the feijoas and peel them (or you can leave the skins on, like the Colombians do). Trim each end and cut lengthwise into halves, then quarters.

Place the feijoas in a saucepan and add the sugar. Heat over a low heat, stirring. They will release some water.

Cook gently for around 10 minutes until they are soft but still retain their shape, and the sauce has reduced by about half.

Squeeze a bit more water out of the corn meal, then transfer it to a bowl. Stir in the cheese, butter, salt and sugar, and taste to test. (Jaiver says: 'It should be a little more sweet than salty.') Add more salt or sugar to your taste. If it's too dry, add a little of the corn-water.

Take one good-sized husk leaf and place a couple of spoonfuls of corn mixture in the middle. Add one feijoa quarter and an extra pinch or cube of mozzarella, and spoon a little more corn mixture on top.

Cover with another leaf and wrap it around so that the filling is completely enclosed. Fold down the top third of the parcel into the middle. Fold up the bottom third so that it overlaps. Then use the strip of husk or string to tie it in place.

Steam the envueltos for an hour. Jaiver lines a large pot with the corncobs, covers them with a layer of leftover husks, pours boiling water on top to just below the level of the cobs, then arranges the envueltos on top and cover with a tight-fitting lid. Continually add more water as they cook. The husks prevent burning and keep the envueltos from soaking in the water. You could also use a large steamer pot.

Open one of the packets to check whether it's cooked through and the cheese is melted.

Serve the envueltos warm, still in their packets, and eat with a spoon.

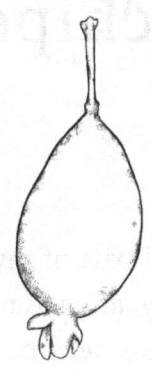

CLAIMING
New Zealand

CHAPTER 17

This Remote Archipelago

I'd left the New Zealand part of my story for last, but I was soon grateful I had. Shortly after I returned from Colombia and Europe, travelling overseas became impossible. In the autumn of 2020, Covid-19 arrived in New Zealand as the feijoas were swelling. As the fruit began to drop, so did the government announcements, until, by the end of March, the country was in lockdown, one of the world's most restrictive. For a full month, we were ensconced in our homes, and the usual networks of feijoa exchange were stymied. Instead, people occupied their time by preserving feijoas, or making them into muffins, cakes, pancakes and chutneys.

One of the foreigners caught in New Zealand, unable to return home, was the British writer Neil Gaiman. After panic-buying some chickens, he spent the lockdown holed up with his wife and four-year-old son in a series of Airbnbs in the Hawke's Bay, where, without fail, there was always a feijoa tree in the garden. Feijoas were something of a revelation, Neil told me later: 'It was amazing for me that I had lived to be almost sixty on this planet, travelling around and eating things, and had just never encountered them before.' Over seven or eight weeks, Neil got to experience the full feijoa-season cycle New Zealanders go through each year: from excitement, to abundance, to addiction, to overwhelm.

On Twitter, he begged the nation for advice about what to do with the mounting buckets of fruit: 'The sheer quantity of feijoa here is defeating us.' New Zealanders rushed to enlighten him, and the hundreds of responses illustrated some of the passion the fruit inspires here, and the special place it holds in our culture. 'When you have eaten as many as you can safely hold, they also make excellent ammunition for backyard warfare,' advised Professor Richard Easther, an eminent theoretical cosmologist at the University of Auckland. 'Might be harder during a lockdown, but they are nature's own organic Nerf guns.'

Software developer and musician Nat Torkington advocated giving 'the people's fruit' to neighbours without trees, as a form of socialist redistribution. Another person replied that the new no-contact rules were a godsend for unsolicited feijoa gifting: 'We fill shopping bags with them and leave them on the doorsteps of friends and family when they are out as "a gift".' Someone else admitted: 'I may be the only person I know who doesn't like feijoas.' New Zealanders overseas chastised everyone else for making them homesick. But most people responded with something along these lines: 'You eat ALL of it. Or you drop it off on my doorstep.'

In Raglan, our commune really came into its own. When the lockdown started, Amalia was four, Indigo was two, and so was Monica's and Manu's daughter Skye, who had been born just thirty-six hours before Indi. Our lives were already so entwined – we cooked for each other four nights a week – that it made sense for us to be one large 'bubble'. We isolated from the world together, and took turns looking after all the kids, which meant we could keep working online (most of us were contractors, working remotely). We were privileged in other ways, too. We all stayed healthy, and the Whāingaroa harbour was a short walk away, so we could spend time in nature. And it was feijoa season. Our trees were still relatively small and not producing much fruit, so every few days I'd take the girls on a treasure hunt.

I knew of an enormous feijoa tree in the centre of Raglan, hidden away behind the now-empty offices of our co-working space. A bounty of ripe fruit carpeted the ground beneath. Amalia would climb high into the branches and send more raining down, while the little ones proudly threw them into the shopping bag and the double pram. These free green gifts, the abundance, the breath of autumn in the air – in these unsettling times, here at least were things that hadn't changed since my childhood. We'd walk home through the eerily silent streets and eat feijoas by the dozen. At night, when I cuddled Indi to sleep, I could still smell the sticky-sweet scent on her skin.

I returned to my research on how the feijoa had got to this remote archipelago in the first place. Its arrival here was part of a wholesale transformation of these islands' vegetation that took less than 200 years. Apart from the Arctic and Antarctica, New Zealand was the last major landmass to be discovered and settled by humans. At least 80 per cent of its plants were found nowhere else, and it was largely covered with forest. Around 700 years ago, when Māori arrived from the Pacific islands, they brought a handful of new plants stashed in their voyaging canoes – taro, yams, paper mulberry and kūmara. But with European colonisation, the trickle of exotics became a flood.

The settlers brought fruit and vegetables, pasture and timber crops – apples, potatoes, pines and clover – and began remaking the landscape to remind themselves of their far-off homelands. Like the colonists in southern Brazil, they cut down most of the forests, and between 1840 and 2000, 8 million hectares of native forest were toppled for timber and to make way for farms and settlements.[198]

By the early twentieth century, some enterprising nurserymen had begun to import and experiment with plants that were completely new to everyone – plants like the feijoa. So, when exactly did it get here, and who was responsible for beginning the nation's feijoa obsession? It had seemed a simple question, but it was one without an easy answer – the early nurserymen and breeders didn't leave much of a paper trail. Ross Ferguson, a scientist and kiwifruit expert at Plant & Food Research, had followed their faint tracks in a 1983 journal article, and so I chased down all his references, trying to find more details.[199] But though I combed through dozens of gardening and horticulture journals from the first half of the twentieth century, the accounts were frustratingly short on detail, and often contradictory.

An article in the *Manawatu Standard*, written in 1932, gave credit for importing the 'rare Brazilian plant Feijoa Sellowiana' to Whanganui nurseryman Alexander Allison. 'Quite recently he told [this] writer that some hybrids he had got from California would popularise this fruit and that in a few years it would be universally grown in New Zealand.'[200] It also said Allison was the first person in New Zealand to grow the kiwifruit. Much more is known of that story: the principal of Wanganui Girls' College, Mary Isabel Fraser, had collected the seeds while visiting her sister on a mission trip to China in 1903, and given them to Allison to grow.

I could find no date for Allison's supposed feijoa introduction, but by 1934 another source says there were four feijoas growing in the neighbouring garden of Allison's brother James, and that they were already 10 to 12 feet high, 'with a spread equal to the height'.[201] Today, on Allison's old property – now a thoroughbred horse stud – an enormous feijoa tree still grows.

I went there in spring 2019, and it was at least ten metres high and almost as wide, adorned in a thousand flowers, with a thick, knobbled trunk that I could barely get my arms around. It was easily the biggest feijoa I'd seen on all my travels, adding more weight to the theory that Allison was among the earliest New Zealanders to grow one.

However, another account claimed that an unnamed Auckland nurseryman imported the first plants from Australia in 1908.[202] A third correspondent, writing in 1946, said 'there is one planting that was made in the Bay of Plenty about 40 years ago . . . yet these old trees continue to bear regular and heavy crops of a good type of fruit'.[203] Whoever introduced them first, it wasn't until the 1920s and '30s that feijoas became more widely known. The man responsible for that was Hayward Wright – once described as 'New Zealand's greatest plantsman',[204] and best known for developing the 'Hayward' kiwifruit cultivar that kick-started the modern global kiwifruit industry.

Wright was an austere, forbidding man, cantankerous and intolerant with a legendary temper – but given his family life, perhaps that's not surprising.[205] He was born in 1873 in the Far North of New Zealand, and moved to the island of Munia in Fiji as a young teenager, where his parents Ernest and Sarah were running a plantation.

His father Ernest was apparently 'the black sheep of a good family' and an alcoholic, who would lounge about reading the Greek classics, while Hayward, aged thirteen, had to supervise the Fijian workers on the plantation. Ernest was known as a cruel man, and later, while working as a trader in the Solomon Islands, so mistreated some of the islanders he hired that they eventually turned on him with their 'tomahawks' and killed him.[206]

His father's death wasn't the end of Wright's troubles. Back in New Zealand, he apprenticed to a well-known nurseryman and eventually bought land of his own in the Auckland suburb of Avondale. He set up a nursery and 25-acre orchard, married, and had three children. But in 1921, his two sons died less than a month apart. Wright never recovered from the loss, became intensely religious and buried himself in his plants.

In his orchard, according to one contemporary correspondent, 'Portuguese, Japanese, and Algerian lemons, Bengal citrons, Californian mandarins, Chinese and German cherries, Spanish and Fiji oranges, South American guavas and the Maltese blood orange flourished in rich profusion'.[207] The house was always overflowing with seedlings and cuttings, and he could 'talk of nothing but plants'. He spent excessive amounts of money buying new cultivars and species, and though he was generally difficult and stern, his daughter remembered him as 'like a kid with a new toy' whenever a novel plant arrived from overseas. Wright crossed limes with kumquats to make a limequat, and grew bunches of 'pineapple oranges' on long stems.

In around 1920, he imported his first feijoa seeds. They came from the El Saff Botanic Garden in Egypt, of all places, and in 1925 Wright advertised 'Feijoa sellowiana' in his nursery catalogue – although at first he wasn't especially complimentary, describing the fruit as resembling 'a half-withered green passionfruit'.

By 1930, he had managed to import the Californian cultivars 'Superba' and 'Coolidge' from Adelaide in South Australia.[208] Wright also acquired 'Choiceana' from California. When it fruited, he planted out the seeds and selected a few of the most promising. Two of those cultivars – 'Mammoth' and 'Triumph' – became the ancestors of most subsequent New Zealand cultivars, and are still extensively planted in the commercial feijoa industry in New Zealand. They can now also be found growing in Colombia, California, Brazil, Argentina, Italy, France and my own garden.

By 1932, Wright was convinced of the feijoa's potential, and wrote a glowing article entitled 'Valuable Fruit' for the *New Zealand Herald*: 'This is truly a dual purpose shrub. It is bushy and symmetrical in shape, and in the spring is a mass of blossom, a fact which should win a place for it in every garden as a shrub, to say nothing of its fruit, which is destined to become one of the very best for jams or jellies. It has a flavour quite its own, which can only be described as delicious.'[209]

I quite agree.

On his own property, Wright planted a long feijoa hedge, which survived for nearly eighty years. By the time I found out about them, I was two years too late to see the trees for myself; they had all been cut down to make way for high-density housing. A new government policy that came into force in 2015 removed any protections for urban trees, and by 2021 more than 250,000 trees across Auckland city had been lost: 1000 trees a week.[210] When the property was sold to developers, Wright's historic feijoas were among the casualties.[211]

Still, it was Wright's advocacy – and his superior cultivars – that helped feijoas to quietly win over New Zealand. By 1937, they adorned a number of private gardens around Auckland, one grower was selling feijoas to fruit shops in the inner-city suburb of Newmarket,[212] and the *New Zealand Herald* published recipes for feijoa jam, jelly, and something called 'feijoa fool': a mixture of the raw pulp with ground walnuts, honey and crisped wheat flakes.[213]

That same year, Wright made a present of 200 feijoa trees to the city council, which planted them all along Alberton Avenue in Mount Albert, just a block away from my father's childhood home on Summit Drive.[214] Dad remembers hooning past them on his half-size bike on his way to high school in the 1950s – he was always late, so there was no time to scrump any feijoas for his lunchbox. I went back to check, and was relieved to discover that some of those trees, at least, are still there.

In 1939, a department store in Palmerston North offered customers the choice of a 'DAPHNE or FEIJOA, FREE with cash purchases 10/- or over from the MANCHESTER and FURNISHING sections'.[215] In 1941, under the headline 'Fruit Hedges, Lovely and Useful, Women Should Insist', the *Auckland Star* advised the government to plant feijoa hedges around state houses, as it 'is an abundant bearer of delicious fruit which is good for both jelly and salads ... In the planting of the garden the woman can have an enormous influence, and any woman knows the advantage of having fruit right on the spot for her table and preserves.'[216]

Over the following decades, feijoas became a part of New Zealand life. Low-maintenance and easy to grow, feijoa trees often occupied a corner of the typical suburban 'quarter-acre block', where they fringed the lawn and the Hills Hoist rotary washing line. But since they were mostly eaten fresh under the tree or served in fruit salads, they took a little while to show up in formal recipe books.

Culinary anthropologist Helen Leach, an emeritus professor at the University of Otago, looked through her database of historic cookbooks for me. A 1947 recipe for feijoa jam is the first one she found, in the Auckland Diocesan High School Old Girls' League recipe book. Another cookbook, prepared by the Otago University Association of Home Science Alumnae in 1960, has a recipe for scrumptious-sounding feijoa dumplings – laden with sugar and lard like all good mid-century British desserts.[217] These days, New Zealand newspapers and magazines frequently feature articles with titles like 'Ten Great Ways to Use up a Feijoa Glut', providing more inventive recipes like feijoa salsa, feijoa muffins, feijoa pickle, feijoa massaman curry and feijoa 'fizz': a fermented, kombucha-like drink made from the skins.

In the late 1990s, commercial feijoa products began appearing in supermarkets, too: breakfast cereals, sweets, yoghurts, chocolates, ice creams and ice blocks, bottled smoothies and juices. As a teenager in the early 2000s, I drank sweet Lothlorien sparkling feijoa wine in the sand dunes and at parties with my friends. The same company now sells a feijoa and mānuka honey liqueur, which I took to Brazil and Colombia to share with the feijoa scientists and festival organisers. The 8 Wired brewery in Matakana, near my parents' home, makes a delicious feijoa sour ale. And 42 Below's feijoa vodka – though it faced such existential hurdles in the US – quickly became a bestseller in New Zealand, selling three times as many bottles as the company's plain vodka.

As I neared the end of my investigations, I thought I knew, more or less, the long journey that feijoas had taken to arrive in New Zealand, and how they had taken hold here. By this time, I'd become 'the mad feijoa lady of Raglan', as my publisher at *New Zealand Geographic* had predicted. People from Argentina and China asked my advice about sourcing New Zealand cultivars, while feijoa lovers I had never met began sending me things – a beautiful set of feijoa watercolours from Oregon, a pair of resin paperweights with feijoa flowers caught inside.

But I felt there was something missing. I still didn't have a sense of what it meant that an exotic plant had been adopted as a Kiwi symbol. It also troubled me that the history I had found in the recipe books and newspaper archives seemed overwhelmingly white. I knew that feijoas gave a feeling of 'home', and formed part of my connection to place, landscape and nation. But as a descendant of Pākehā settlers, living on land that was probably dubiously acquired (if not outright stolen) by people who looked like me, I also had some awkward feelings I was struggling to name.

Overseas, I'd sought out the feijoa stories of Indigenous peoples, and of Brazil's quilombolas, and had loved learning about what the feijoa meant to Elizabete, Laura and Mónica. I knew that feijoas were meaningful to many Māori New Zealanders, too, and were often included in dishes served at restaurants like Monique Fiso's Hiakai in Wellington – the leading edge of the new high-end, modern Māori cuisine. It felt incomplete to write a story about plants and New Zealand and belonging without including any Māori perspectives. Still, feijoas are not native, and they haven't been here for all that long. Could they have any connection with our nation's history, or teach me anything about how to belong in Aotearoa?

During lockdown, I'd connected with the chef Peter Gordon, a feijoa lover who has both Māori and Scottish ancestry, and had just returned to New Zealand after three decades running successful restaurants in London. When I asked for advice, he suggested I call Hamuera Orupe McLeod. Commonly known as Joe, he has worked as a chef all over the world, and is also a television presenter, a rescuer of traditional Māori cuisine and plant knowledge, and a direct descendant of the famed Ngāi Tūhoe prophet Rua Kēnana.

In our very first conversation, Joe dropped a bombshell. 'My ancestors spoke about feijoas,' he said over the phone. 'They talked about bottling them, up in the failed commune of Rua Kēnana at Maungapōhatu. By 1908 they had these things growing.'

I was gobsmacked. Could it be that feijoas had arrived in New Zealand sometime in the first decade of the twentieth century, immediately proved themselves in the Bay of Plenty (as one of my journal sources suggested) and then very quickly made it to

Rua Kēnana's Maungapōhatu, in the heart of Te Urewera – a place that had no road access until the 1960s,[218] and is still one of the most remote settlements in the North Island? I had my doubts, but it wasn't impossible.

I asked Joe if he'd take me with him to Te Urewera so I could learn more – about the possible feijoa connection, but also about the importance of plants and place to him and other Tūhoe. He said yes, but the second Covid-19 lockdown and subsequent community outbreaks delayed our meeting for another year.

CHAPTER 18

The People's Fruit

By the time I called Joe again in the spring of 2022, the feijoas at our Raglan home were head-high. The Kakapo had turned up its toes – the spot I'd planted it turned out to be mainly gravel – and the Mammoth was suffering, bent at a permanent angle after a cyclone knocked it over the previous summer. The Kaiteri was enormous, though the fruit tended to be bitter. But the Unique was laden with flowers, and in the autumn, I expected it would drop its small tasty fruit all season long.

Joe told me he was travelling the following week from his house in Wellington to the ancestral home of his Tamakaimoana hapū, Maungapōhatu. There was to be a ceremony to rededicate the refurbished Tānenuiarangi meeting house at Te Māpou Marae, and he invited me to come with him. 'That way you can talk to the old people,' he said. We arranged to meet near Waimangu, at the intersection of State Highways 5 and 38, right on the border of the Waikato and Bay of Plenty districts. Though I was driving from Raglan, and Joe from Wellington, we arrived within five minutes of each other.

He climbed out of his black hatchback wearing his trademark black beret and the all-black Māori warden uniform he wears everywhere in public.[219] Now sixty-four, Joe is accustomed to moving between worlds – as comfortable hobnobbing with presidents and diplomats as he is with gang members. With me, he was friendly, and we hugged in greeting. Still, I could tell he was sussing me out. In conversation, he jumped rapidly from one topic to another as easily as he switched between Māori and English – at times mid-sentence – but over our two days together, he told me some of his life story.

He was born in Murupara, but grew up on the Bay of Plenty side of Te Urewera, at Matahī in the Waimana Valley. In the 1950s and '60s, every marae had an orchard. His grandparents taught him te reo Māori, and his mother showed him how to harvest and bottle the abundant fruit: apples, cherries, plums, peaches – and feijoas.

Within Tūhoe, Joe's Tamakaimoana hapū were known as food providers. 'Our role was to feed our tribe . . . The scholars and practitioners of the craft were all alive, were all around us. But I think I was the only one who broke away to become a fully trained professional chef.' He got his first job as a luggage boy in a hotel during the school holidays, then worked his way up from pot washer to silver polisher to vegetable peeler to chef. Then he travelled the world, working in Papua New Guinea, Singapore and Japan, before landing a job at The Ritz in London under chef Michael Quinn. By the mid-1980s, he was back in New Zealand as the executive chef at the Beehive's clutch of restaurants and cafés, where he served feijoa ice cream to Wellington politicians.

Following his diplomat wife overseas again in the 1990s, Joe worked for New Zealand ambassadors in Germany, Japan and the UK. When he could get hold of them, he served feijoas to the ambassador's guests, too. 'When I saw them, I bought what I could carry. Bloody things weigh a tonne when you load your bag up!' The possibilities were endless: 'feijoa tart, feijoa pie, feijoa flummery . . . trifles, crumble, tartelettes, creams, jellies, cheese cakes . . . It's a people's fruit. I'd class it as one of our favourites.'

In 2004, Joe and his family came home for good. 'I came back to my people, because I needed to reconnect. I knew a lot of them weren't going to be with us that much longer, and I was right.' He wanted to recover and preserve traditional knowledge about native foods, plants and cuisine – bottle it up for the future like a juicy feijoa – but he needed to get permission from his uncles to share that information more widely. At first, they were reluctant, but Joe eventually convinced the elders that the best way to keep knowledge alive is to share it. Now, he spends much of his time travelling from marae to marae, teaching Māori the old ways to forage, identify plants, combine flavours and prepare food.

I couldn't have found a better guide to the feijoas of Tūhoe country.

———

We got back into our cars and I followed Joe to his auntie's place in nearby Kāingaroa, a flat and faded forestry village enclosed in a vast radiata pine forest. Carpeting 2900 square kilometres of the central North Island, the exotic Kāingaroa Forest is the second-largest plantation in the southern hemisphere. In 2008, the government returned a large portion of the forestlands to seven iwi, including Tūhoe, in a Treaty of Waitangi settlement nicknamed the 'Treelords deal'.[220] (Until their leases run out, the forestry companies still own the trees.)

Joe's auntie, Pamela Hitaua, welcomed us and gave me a bed for the night, but said she didn't know anything about feijoas. Joe, undeterred, made a phone call in Māori. He hung up, excited. 'We'll go and see Uncle Tahae, he knows about some old feijoas in Ruatāhuna,' he said. By now, it was late afternoon, and we drove a few blocks down the road to visit James Doherty, known as Tahae – the name means 'mover', Joe said, 'because he got things done'. The house was surrounded by a picket fence and a neat garden. A kindly, lucid man in his eighties with white hair answered the door, alongside a beautiful elderly Māori woman wearing a straw hat decorated with flowers: Tahae and his wife, Myra Heurea.

Joe is related to Tahae on his father's side and Myra through his mother's, he explained. They both seemed happy to see him, and invited us in. We sat down in the living room by a wall of embossed encyclopedias (one was headed 'Sylt to Uruguay', which I took as a good omen). Joe struck up a conversation in Māori with Myra while I talked to Tahae.

He told me many stories in his old-fashioned accent, almost all of them involving trees – a green thread running through his life like sap. Tahae was born in 1937 and raised in Ngaputahi, a loose hamlet of homesteads on the Ruatāhuna road. His father had given him a Pākehā name, hoping it would bring him advantages, but in his early years he spoke only Māori at home. The closest primary school was 7 miles (11 kilometres) away over the hill, so Tahae didn't start until he was ten – old enough to walk there and back each day.

The family lived off the land and the bush, only buying sugar, flour and butter. When someone was injured, Tahae's grandmother would send him out to gather native medicinal plants – wharangi and hangehange, tutu and karamū (coprosma). He kept an eye on the flocks of kererū, the fat native wood pigeons, to see which trees they were visiting, so he could help to shoot, trap and preserve them for ceremonial purposes on the marae.

When Tahae was thirteen, his father sent him into the bush to fell giant rimu trees, with nothing but a splitting gun, wedges, a crosscut saw and his little brother – whose job it was to hang on to the other end of the saw until the blade had bit into the massive trunks.

Once the groove was deep enough, Tahae could cut through them alone. He split the logs into battens and sold them to farmers for fence posts. The proceeds funded his boarding school fees at

St Peter's Māori College for boys in Auckland, and his siblings' education, too. He got a job in management with the Forest Service in Kāingaroa – the Pākehā name helped – and spent most of his career moving around the country, far from the lands and people of Tūhoe.

When the Forest Service was disbanded in the 1980s, he happened to be posted back in Kāingaroa, so he and Myra stayed. Now, he tends his garden – kale, a winding grapevine, lots of flowers and a solitary feijoa tree. 'I'd be one of the first to admit that it is a really special fruit,' he said, showing me how he hand-pollinates the flowers to ensure a maximum haul. 'I look forward to them. I can eat and eat and eat! Can't beat the old feijoa!'

And yet, though he and his siblings spent their childhoods roaming Te Urewera's abandoned homesteads, standing on horseback to fill sugar bags with raided fruit – apples, pears, cherries, Golden Queen peaches, Black Boy peaches, Black Doris plums, greengage plums, even kiwifruit – back then there were never any feijoas, he said.

Tahae only encountered them later in life: perhaps in the 1980s, he reckons, when he returned to live in Kāingaroa. There were some old trees in Ruatāhuna, he said, and told us where to look. But they weren't there when he was a schoolboy – when his teachers punished him for speaking Māori, but the skies were still alive with kererū, and the rivers full of fish.

The next morning, I followed Joe into Te Urewera. Leaving Kāingaroa, we drove east on straight forestry roads through conifer tunnels, the waysides lined with yellow-flowering broom and gorse, splashes of weedy colour in the green and grey. When the rows of pines receded, in the distance I could see a cloud-capped wall, forbidding and aloof: the bush-clad ranges of Te

Urewera – Te Manawa o te Ika a Māui, the heart of the great fish of Māui, the 'encircled lands' of Tūhoe.[221]

In 2014, as part of the Tūhoe Treaty settlement, Te Urewera ceased to be a National Park, as it had been for sixty years. It no longer belongs to the state. An Act of Parliament designated the 2127-square-kilometre landscape a 'legal person' instead. Now, it owns itself, and is represented by a board made up of Tūhoe and government officials. The precedent was the inspiration for New Zealand's Whanganui River also gaining legal rights, and subsequently rivers in India, Bangladesh, Colombia, Australia and Canada.

When I looked up the Te Urewera Act 2014 I was moved to discover that it begins not with legalistic jargon, but with poetry:

> Te Urewera is ancient and enduring, a fortress of nature, alive with history; its scenery is abundant with mystery, adventure, and remote beauty.
>
> Te Urewera is a place of spiritual value, with its own mana and mauri.
>
> Te Urewera has an identity in and of itself, inspiring people to commit to its care.[222]

It also explicitly lays out that the new law is intended to 'contribute to resolving the grief of Tūhoe'.[223] There are many sources of that grief.

In the 1860s, the colonial government confiscated the tribe's productive Bay of Plenty lowlands, then invaded its heartlands. In historian Judith Binney's words: 'This was to be a war to destroy a homeland.'[224] Tūhoe resisted, and the conflict took 'a huge toll on the lives of the Urewera people. It is impossible to assess the deaths from the military campaigns, as starvation and disease found their own victims.'[225] As the century turned, more Pākehā land-grabbing, famines, epidemics and conflict ensued – including, in 1916, a deadly and illegal armed attack by police on Maungapōhatu itself. Throughout, and to this day, the people of Te Urewera clung tightly to their culture and language and continued to assert their autonomy and their sovereignty over their sacred lands.

The sense of entering another country was palpable as I followed Joe's car into the mountains. Road signs warned of wandering stock, of the 72 kilometres of winding unsealed road ahead – and, as we got closer to the culturally and historically significant community of Ruatāhuna, they were written in Māori. In most parts of New Zealand, Pākehā like me are used to feeling at home, like the country is ours to roam over as we wish. Te Urewera is different: an important, if uncomfortable, reminder that this entire archipelago was Māori first. In the past, driving the Ruatāhuna road to tramp around Lake Waikaremoana, I'd felt like an interloper – a foreigner, even. I still felt like one now, but travelling with Joe changed everything.

Over our two days together, I would come to feel like one of his students or apprentices. He would give me orders – chop the onions, set the table, open the gate, wash the dishes – and I found myself jumping to obey. At the same time, a few words from him transformed the expression of anyone we met from suspicious to welcoming, as he explained my odd mission with a touch of wry amusement.

It started to spit as we drove into the Ruatāhuna valley. The bush loomed on either side of the road. Some giant rimu remained – the long-lived podocarps so sought after by loggers – but the lower reaches were dominated by tawa. Many of their long leaves appeared burned, a legacy of the previous hot, dry summer, Joe said. But today, a cool mist settled on the hilltops, rendering them invisible. Our first stop was at the headquarters of Manawa Honey, an award-winning Tūhoe social enterprise that aims to address endemic social and environmental problems by nourishing the local economy, culture and ecosystem at once.

Manawa's bees feast on the Urewera forest's flowers – mānuka on the flats, rewarewa on the ridges, māhoe in the gullies, and tāwari deep in the mountains – and its people learn beekeeping, business support and marketing. In 2021, Manawa's rewarewa honey was named the 'Best Tasting Honey in the World' by blindfolded judges in a prestigious international contest.[226]

I followed Joe across the grass to the back entrance of the unassuming building, its long deck affording a view across the foggy hills. The founder and CEO, Brenda Tahi (Ngāti Porou), offered us a hot honey-and-lime drink. Brenda, a small and authoritative great-grandmother in her sixties, had a neat braid holding her long grey-and-auburn hair off her face. While she and Joe discussed their respective projects – they're both using food to bolster their people's connection to nature and culture – I savoured the steaming cup of honey-lime: a welcome, warming sugar rush after the wet and winding drive. ('You should do feijoa-and-honey next,' I suggested.) When the drizzle stopped, Brenda slipped into her Crocs and took us outside to show us her feijoas.

Brenda is from Gisborne, but she's lived in Ruatāhuna for the best part of forty years with her Tūhoe tāne (husband) and raised her family in the valley. In the early 1980s, they lived here, in the house that's now the Manawa office, and Brenda planted a row of feijoas along the fenceline. 'Nobody else had feijoas,' she said. 'I pretty much knew there were no feijoas in Ruatāhuna.' They now form a tall, bushy hedge, visible from the main road – these were the old trees that Tahae had told us to look for. Why did she plant them? I asked. Was it part of asserting a sense of independence up here? 'Yeah, that's the kaupapa' – the idea, the way of doing things – 'who wants to buy feijoas in town? It's really cool to grow your own kai.' She chuckled. 'I'm actually proud of them now. You make me proud of them!'

As happened so often on my travels, feijoas had forged a friendly connection between us, and Brenda was looking at her everyday trees with new appreciation. But so far, nothing I was learning supported Joe's theory of the feijoa's early arrival in Te Urewera. If they had arrived in 1908, I thought, surely they would be more widespread around here, and Tahae and his friends would have seen them in some of the old gardens. Would this mission to Maungapōhatu turn out to be a fruitless quest?

The rain was still falling. Ghostly wisps of mist slipped between the ridges, even between individual trees, occasionally outlining a single dark rimu against the pale breath of the mountain. Up ahead, Joe's car kept disappearing into clouds. The narrow gravel road was dotted with puddles and potholes and occasional steaming piles of horse poo, and as it climbed, it seemed to cling to the side of the mountain. A metre beyond my driver's-side window, a precipitous cliff fell away into the fog.

We turned onto a private road, marked by a hand-carved wooden sign: 'Private property. Entry by permission only. No shooting.' To me, it felt like we were heading into the middle of nowhere – but for Joe, it was the centre of the world. He pulled over, got out, and beckoned me over. I followed him across a clearing to the edge of the bush. The rain had stopped, but it was freezing. 'This is where we bring everyone to say hi to the mountain,' Joe said. Maungapōhatu (1366 metres) is the sacred mountain of Tūhoe; a mist-maiden, Hine-pūkohu-rangi, is said to have enticed him to earth. Tūhoe descend from their union – an ancestry deriving from the land itself and its ubiquitous mists.

'And there it is!' Joe said, grinning and gesturing.

Maungapōhatu doesn't often reveal himself. We could see nothing but thick white cloud. 'When that happens, we say the mountain's wearing his hat,' Joe said. Pōhatu means stone, and Joe has had a piece of its unique white rock shaped into a medallion he can pin to his own hat - he had it set in silver while travelling in Indonesia. It's a way of carrying the mountain with him, he said.

I looked out into the ether, shivering, trying to imagine its sacred bulk. Mountain cabbage trees, with thick glossy leaves and hairy tummies, leaned out from the cliffside. They are called tōī in Māori, Joe explained, and the heart of each spiky pompom is edible - 'one big potato'. Up here, beech trees have replaced the tawa. 'You'll notice the change in foliage and tree growth because we're climbing up into the snowline,' Joe said. In winter, the drifts are so deep they block the road.

'So, this is my home,' he said. 'This is the heart of Te Urewera. You'll see the isolation, and why we treasure it.' We walked back to the cars. 'Nearly there, kiddo!'

The road got even narrower and more rugged. The trees now were plush and monstery - their trunks covered entirely in moss, topped off with a layer of lichen. Everything was completely saturated. Starlike clematis flowers glowed white in the midday gloom, and the roadsides were lined with crown ferns and tutu. For once, there was not a weed in sight.

An hour and a half after we'd left Ruatāhuna, we emerged into a kind of perched valley, with a few cleared fields, a small pine plantation and a cluster of buildings. It was beginning to rain again, and all around the clouds were closing in. Joe pulled up next to the renovated meeting house - Tānenuiarangi, first built in 1914. The wooden carvings framing the rain-spattered door had been freshly repainted in red-brown, orange, white and green, and featured a tiny image of Rua Kēnana's face among the koru patterns. We peered through the window, but couldn't go inside, Joe said, until it had been blessed the day after tomorrow – by which time I needed to be back home.

I followed Joe next door to a wood-lined building with an industrial kitchen. He'd expected that we would help with the preparations for the weekend's feast, then stay the night, but the place was deserted. One of the uncles had made the three-hour trip to Rotorua to buy supplies, and hadn't yet returned. Instead, Joe boiled a worn cast-iron kettle on the huge gas stove, made tea, and as the rain sheeted down outside, told me about Maungapōhatu. 'This is the stronghold of Rua Kēnana,' he said.

Rua Kēnana Hepetipa was born in 1869, probably here in Maungapōhatu, and rose to national prominence in his thirties after a series of visions foretelling the peaceful end of Pākehā rule confirmed him as a prophet. By 1906, he had amassed a group of Tūhoe followers who grew their hair long and called themselves the Iharaira, or Israelites. The biblical story of a people exiled and oppressed in their own land resonated with Māori,[227] just as it had for enslaved African Americans a century earlier. Rua encouraged his followers to sell their stock, possessions and land, and migrate from the coastal valleys and the interior to Maungapōhatu. In the middle of 1907, at least 500 people lived there full time.

'They built a marae from scratch in seven days,' Joe said. Rua ran a tight ship, in the early years banning both alcohol and tobacco. Leaders gave children scripture verses to learn, and inspected each family's home twice a week; a dusty fireplace, poorly stacked woodpile, loose dog or chicken could incur a threepence fine.

The community endured for the better part of a decade. But in 1916, as war raged in Europe, the New Zealand government began recruiting Tūhoe for a Māori contingent. Rua opposed participation in the war, Joe said. 'He said, it's not our fight.' Though his teachings were pacifist, rumours spread that Rua was arming his followers and had prophesied a German victory.

In January 1916, the Minister for Native Affairs revived Rua's years-old 'sly-grog' charges, and on 2 April 1916 an armed force of sixty-seven policemen marched into Maungapōhatu to arrest him. In the confusion that followed, police shot dead Rua's son Toko and another man, and Rua was hauled off to Mount Eden Prison in Auckland.

After one of the longest trials in New Zealand history, the jury cleared him of sedition, but found him 'morally guilty' of one fairly dubious charge of resisting arrest. For this, he was sentenced to a year's hard labour and eighteen months in prison, and the community was forced to sell livestock and land to pay the legal fees. Even after Rua returned, Maungapōhatu never regained the vitality and population of the early years, and the police attack left a lasting legacy of mistrust.

But the place remains spiritually, culturally and historically significant for Tūhoe. As a child in the 1960s, Joe helped bring in supplies from Waimana by horseback to the few people living there. His great-grandmother on his mother's side was the eldest child of Rua and his first wife Pinepine (Rua had twelve wives in all) – a direct ancestral line to the prophet. 'Do you wish you'd met him?' I asked. 'Well, we live with him, spiritually. His body's, like, over there,' Joe said, pointing. 'And we are the succession plan to his dream.'

———

The wind howled outside, the afternoon was edging into evening, and no-one else had arrived. Joe asked if I still had his phone in my pocket, and I groaned. I knew exactly where it was: on top of a fence post outside Manawa Honey, where I'd left it after taking a photo of him and Brenda. When I confessed, Joe seemed pretty relaxed, but my stomach clenched. What a way to repay his generosity!

We'd planned to stay the night in Maungapōhatu, sleeping marae-style on mattresses in the hall and helping out. But, as no-one had shown up, Joe thought it made more sense to head back to Ruatāhuna, to look for his phone and meet up with the event organisers. I was disappointed. There was nobody around to even ask about feijoas. Though I knew hundreds were due to gather for the celebrations on the weekend, for now, the place felt lonely, lost in the past and the clouds.

We drove out on the gravel road, passing the one remaining ancient thatched whare. Joe noticed a car parked outside a little house further up the hill, and pulled over to check if anyone was home. He knocked on the door. After a minute, it opened to reveal a tiny old woman in polar fleece, slippers and a knitted bottle-green headband. On the duck-egg-blue walls of the kitchen behind her was a framed panorama of the sacred mountain.

Joe introduced me to Erana Manihera, a retired Presbyterian minister he called Nana. They were talking in Māori, and when she switched to English, she spoke slowly, and with a strong accent. She lives in Ruatāhuna now, she said, and had arrived that afternoon to tidy up for the ceremony, but she was born in Maungapōhatu in 1938. 'In that little house,' she said, pointing down the slope to the old whare. 'Three of us were born in that little house.'

As children, she and her siblings loved climbing the fruit trees, seeing who could get the highest. 'There's pear, all the shapes of pear. And grapes, the purple and green. And walnut, chestnut. Cherries. Christmas plums, the little one, the yellow one, and the big red one.' 'Did you bottle the fruits, too?' I asked.

'Yes, with our mummy. Mummy keeps the boys in house to learn all about the woman work. And Daddy take us girls out in the paddock to do gardening and woodcutting. Our daddy make a garden for everybody right through the year. Pūhā grow anywhere, watercress anywhere.' It was only in the 1950s, when the little community school closed down, that Erana left Maungapōhatu for the first time, to finish her education among strangers who teased her for her mountain origins. 'To us growing up, this was the only world.'

Were there feijoas in that world? 'I never saw feijoas,' she said. 'But now my brother has planted some, over there.' She pointed to the road. Right next to my car were two scruffy little feijoa trees I had completely overlooked. I ran down to them, and Joe and Erana followed. The bushes were a couple of years old, just the height of a person, growing among raspberry canes and comfrey. Though my feijoas at home were already flowering, these didn't yet have any blooms. 'It doesn't grow so well here,' said Erana. 'That's how our dad was, too. Experiment with what grows here and what doesn't.' Her brother has planted olives and figs as well, she said. 'Last year the fig tree, it had fruit. I said, "One for you, God – and the rest for me."'

There were feijoas in Maungapōhatu after all! But I was now pretty certain they hadn't been here for more than a century. Erana knew this place as well as anyone, and her green-fingered father had clearly taught her to know and appreciate food-giving plants. If Rua had brought feijoas to Maungapōhatu – and they'd survived a few decades of isolation – I felt sure she would have remembered them.

———

We farewelled Erana, and drove out into the dusky damp forest. The evening light infused everything with a weird green glow. I thought of all the things that colonisation has brought to this remote valley – the influenza, fruit trees, horses and cattle, potatoes, religion, policemen, possums. Some newcomers to be survived, others embraced.

In one of Binney's books, I'd read of a lament by an unknown Māori composer:

Wai te mea ka rukupopo,
Ka whakamate ki tona whenua, i.

There is no-one more melancholy
Than he who yearns for his own native land.[228]

Feijoas originally captured my interest because of the emotions – the beautiful melancholy – they could trigger in homesick New Zealanders. But the land-yearning of Pākehā expatriates like me, people who had chosen to live outside of their homeland for a while, pales in comparison with that of Tūhoe and other Māori whose ancestral land was forcibly taken from them. In the face of this weight of history, and the contemporary struggles the people I'd met were working so hard to address, I worried my mission to find feijoas in Maungapōhatu was frivolous, lightweight, even somehow offensive.

And yet, Joe, Tahae, Brenda and Nana Erana had welcomed me into Te Urewera. They made time for me and my project amidst everything else, and I felt moved and grateful that they were somewhat invested in my strange feijoa quest. There's something people seem to relate to in my obsession, even if they find it kind of ridiculous. They get enthusiastic. Joe was totally in this now.

'Nana was stoked,' he said with satisfaction when he pulled over to show me one of his favourite native plants. 'Really stoked.' As the light faded, he yanked a small branch from a nearby bush, covered in bright green, red-speckled leaves. 'This is humenemene, the elder brother to the horopito, and it's an alpine plant. The leaves are white underneath.'

'Like a feijoa,' I said.

'She's obsessed with her feijoas!' he said, hassling me. But then he added – 'I'm so stoked we found your tree at Maungapōhatu, actually growing.'

What did it mean, to find feijoas in the heart of Te Urewera? They might not have been an early arrival, but they are here now, and that is remarkable enough. This small plant has journeyed from one set of remote, misty highlands to another, the two places separated by a continent, the Andes, and the entire Pacific Ocean. Once feijoas did arrive, though, I think they were always going to be embraced by Tūhoe – fruit-loving people who so value autonomy and abundance, and are quick to adopt any new plant or animal that has something to offer them.

When we got back to Ruatāhuna, Joe's phone was still sitting there on the fence post, right where I'd left it.

―

The next day, as I emerged from Te Urewera's rugged forests into the Waikato's paddocks and pine forests, and my own phone began pinging with messages – I hadn't had cellphone signal for the entire time I'd been in Tūhoe country – it suddenly occurred to me that I'd never seen feijoas growing wild in the New Zealand bush. Or on forest edges, or in a paddock, or along a highway. Why not? Why had feijoas *not* become a weed, when they have been thriving all over the country for a century (at least) and produce such abundant amounts of fruit, and therefore seeds?

New Zealand has a serious problem with weeds. In 1835, Charles Darwin spent nine days in Northland – just long enough to make a few racist observations about Māori, conclude that the entire country was 'not a pleasant place' and make the first recorded observations of the country's incipient weed problem. A wild French leek and the English common dock, he noticed, had 'overrun whole districts', while hedges of sweetbrier – now a major weed in Otago and Canterbury – lined the streets of Paihia.[229]

Those invaders must have made an impression on the young naturalist. A quarter-century later, in On the Origin of Species, Darwin predicted – with uncomfortably eugenic overtones – that 'if all the animals and plants of Great Britain were set free in New Zealand, that in the course of time a multitude of British forms would become thoroughly naturalised there, and would exterminate many of the natives'.[230]

Two hundred years on, New Zealand's native flora has not exactly been exterminated – but it has been swamped. We have about 2300 native plant species. At least 25,000 have been introduced. Nearly 3000 have escaped our gardens, and almost 1800 of them are 'naturalised', meaning they thrive in the wild without any human help. Around 380 (that we know of) have become agricultural or environmental pests, suffocating forests or farmland. Twenty more naturalise each year.[231]

Still, it's clear from these numbers that 'exotic' or even 'naturalised' is not the same as 'weedy' – and, in fact, the vast majority of introduced plants do not (yet) present a problem. A weed is often defined as 'a plant growing in the wrong place'. But that's a very human-centric view of nature. Who decides where a plant should grow? In te ao Māori, I was learning, the distinction is less about drawing a hard line between the exotic and the native, and more about balance and respect.

Like all gardeners, early Māori had to deal with unwanted plants invading their food gardens, mainly the native bracken, aruhe. But they managed this so successfully – by burning and moving their crops every few years – that many early European botanists remarked on how clean and 'weed-free' Māori gardens were.

Anthropologist Helen Leach has written that many European words for 'weed' – '*mauvaise herbe* (French), *mala herba* (Spanish), *malebe* and *plante infestanti* (Italian), *unkraut* (German), and *onkruid* (Dutch)' – have negative connotations. 'Thus, the European concept of weed is fundamentally a "bad plant".' But Māori vocabulary, she wrote, 'scarcely acknowledged the existence of "weeds"' in this negative sense.[232] Partly, that's because even weedy plants like bracken and exotic pūhā were quickly appreciated as food sources and taonga – treasures – in their own right.

'From a Māori perspective it could be said that a weed is a plant that upsets the balance that Papatūānuku [the Earth] needs to be well', wrote Rob McGowan in a recent report for the government.[233] McGowan is Pākehā and a former Catholic priest, but he has been a respected teacher of rongoā Māori – traditional plant knowledge and medicine – for many decades.

When I returned from Te Urewera, I called him up. He was in the middle of weeding a tray of tiny tutu seedlings when he answered the phone. The mark of a weed, he told me, was a plant that negatively affects the mauri, or life force, of the landscape – something that dominates an ecosystem or disrupts the natural balance. I thought of the native tawa I'd seen in Te Urewera. When forestry companies overharvested rimu and other podocarps there in the 1950s and '60s, tawa became overabundant, and now prevent podocarp seedlings reaching the light. Brenda Tahi and others from Ruatāhuna are trying to restore balance and diversity by removing tawa trees to create light wells where they can plant young podocarps.[234]

'The measuring stick is not whether or not a plant is a native or exotic species, or whether or not it is considered a weed by people who work the land, but how it affects Papatūānuku,' McGowan said. It is a change in focus from the needs of humans to the needs of the Earth. 'Always, always the first question to ask is, What is best for the land? What helps the land to be well?'

'"Ka ora te whenua, ka ora te tangata: when the Earth is well, people are well".'[235]

What about the feijoa – is there a botanical reason for its relative benevolence? I wrote to feijoa expert Grant Thorp, who in 2023 had just returned to New Zealand after nine years living in Australia. He'd been wondering the same thing. Several of the feijoa's close relatives are weedy, he told me. The Cattley guava, *Psidium cattleyanum*, is self-seeding and occurs in plague proportions on Réunion Island in the Indian Ocean. The common guava, *Psidium guajava*, can form dense thickets in Queensland, and the Chilean guava, *Ugni molinae*, is taking over New Zealand's Chatham Islands.[236] 'So why not feijoa?' Grant asked.

Feijoa seeds germinate easily in the laboratory on moist absorbent blotting paper, he said. And yet, in all his travels observing and collecting feijoa around the world, only once did he see feijoa seedings germinating in situ beneath a parent tree (at Caçapava do Sul in the extreme south of Brazil, not far from the border with Uruguay). Perhaps parent plants somehow prevent their offspring from germinating too close to home, relying on dispersing animals to carry them to virgin soil. Does New Zealand lack the right animals to do that?

Grant doesn't think so. Rats eat feijoas, and we have no shortage of those pests. Pūkeko steal the fruit from my trees. And then there are the humans. 'With the number of trees and fruit in home gardens, the number of fruit being thrown out from under motor mowers and the number of overripe fruit ending up in people's compost bins, I would not think dispersal away from the parent tree would be a problem,' he said.

The truth is, we don't yet know the answer. No-one has studied this in a New Zealand context. It might be that a unique combination of genetics, environment and geology determines if and when a species becomes invasive. New Zealand soils are less acidic than those where the feijoa evolved – perhaps germination requires high levels of acidity, or an association with acid-loving fungi, as Grant himself mused back in 1988 on his own feijoa trip to Brazil. Or maybe there are pathogens in our native soils which prevent seed germination. 'Luckily in New Zealand, the feijoa genetics we have here and our mix of soils and climate have meant feijoas have not become invasive,' he said.

When I'd asked Joe how feijoas would be treated in the Māori worldview, he said they have a genealogy and life force like any other plant. 'All plants have a whakapapa and all plants have a mauri. We have a saying: if it casts a shadow, it has a mauri.' The important thing, he said, was that New Zealanders don't try to claim it as a native plant when it's a recent arrival. 'It's endemic to South America, nowhere else – and we need to honour that.'

I met another Māori elder, the Ngātiwai kaumātua Hone Martin, on Aotea Great Barrier Island, while reporting a story on an invasive seaweed, *Caulerpa brachypus*, that was taking over the island's bays. The island's iwi considered the algae a tauiwi kino, a bad visitor. 'But not everything is an enemy,' Matua Hone said, when I asked him how to think about feijoas within te ao Māori.

'People learn to get on with other people, no matter what their whakapapa is. But there are certainly a lot that don't. It's the same with our taiao, our environment. Anything that comes here that starts taking over – well, they're not family orientated, they're selfish.' Feijoas might be exotic, but they aren't weeds. Perhaps we could say that, unlike *Caulerpa*, they're not selfish.

By the time I got home from Te Urewera, I felt I'd answered my question of how the feijoa had gotten to New Zealand, and something of its history here. Now, I wanted to try to glimpse its future.

CHAPTER 19
The Feijoa of the Future

I drove over the Tākaka Hill into Golden Bay at the golden hour, the sun sliding through the clouds after days of heavy rain. The Southern Alps rose damp and rumpled into the evening, and the flat pastures of the valley floor were illuminated an unreal, neon green. Nigel Ritson's place was ten minutes out of town, down a road that passed donkeys and alpacas on the way to the coast. A tiny, mouldering sign on the gate read 'Ritson', but once I made my way up the driveway, it was the scent that told me for sure that I was in the right place. As soon as I opened the car door, I could smell the thick, pungent odour of rotting feijoas. Leaves and moss carpeted the driveway, and the house was small and unfinished. Nigel clearly had other priorities.

The first I saw of him was his gumboots, as the green garage door gradually retracted to reveal them. Then the bucket in his hands, the leather waist pouch stuffed with tools, and finally his reserved but smiling face. He handed me a spoon and a sharp knife sheathed in a plastic protector, and I followed him into the orchard. Nigel Ritson is a self-taught feijoa breeder who works almost entirely alone. His great dream is to find the more perfect feijoa he believes is hiding within the plant's genetics, the cultivar that will transform the New Zealand feijoa industry and improve the health of millions. He just might do it, too.

Nigel's feijoa story started when his life fell apart. His wife left and he became the full-time parent of two little boys. One day, he was trying to drown his grief by building a canoe, and to keep his young sons busy he filled a bucket with the feijoas that had fallen on the lawn. Five minutes later, the boys had eaten the lot. 'That really tells you something, doesn't it? Could you eat a bucket of apples? A bucket of bananas? I thought, "This is quite something."' Nigel sold the Wellington house he couldn't afford, quit his job as a telephone technician and moved with the kids to a caravan on a cheap block of land near Tākaka, near the north-western tip of the South Island. It was overrun with thorny weeds – blackberry, gorse and thistles – and the terrain was pākihi, a type of heathland unique to this part of New Zealand, characterised by infertile, waterlogged and acidic soil.

Nigel had enough money to put in a driveway, some water tanks and a power cable. Not enough for a house, but there was NZ$1000 left over to buy fruit trees. One night, while his sons slept beside him in the caravan, Nigel – a Christian man – prayed to the Lord. He asked for a life less ordinary, for a meaningful challenge. A few days later, an agricultural adviser came to look at the land, and told Nigel that only feijoas or apricots were worth growing. Remembering his boys with the bucket, Nigel chose feijoas.

The adviser suggesting calling Roy Hart from the Department of Scientific and Industrial Research (DSIR) over the Tākaka Hill at Riwaka: 'They're tearing the feijoas out over there. You might be able to get some from him.' And there it was: that was the start of Nigel's great challenge.

Starting with Hayward Wright in the 1930s, New Zealand put more effort into breeding feijoas than any other country (though that isn't saying much). Independent breeder and feijoa enthusiast Dennis Barton spotted 'Unique' in a Tauranga orchard and released it commercially in 1982: one of the few fully self-fertile cultivars, it is still widely grown today. In the 1980s, a state-funded programme at the DSIR at Mount Albert in Auckland identified several new cultivars, including Apollo, Gemini and Opal Star.

One of the researchers involved was Grant Thorp, who became the country's foremost feijoa expert, and is the co-author of the only other book about feijoas.[237] Back then, his job involved taste-testing buckets of feijoas a day, but he never got sick of them. 'Whereas with the kiwifruit breeding programme you could taste about six fruit before the enzyme in the kiwifruit started eating away at your lips,' he told me. The problem with feijoas, he said, was that they hadn't found the perfect cultivar – the way Hayward Wright had stumbled on the perfect kiwifruit, and 'Hass' was the perfect avocado.

Grant theorised that all the feijoas in New Zealand were descended from a limited genetic base – the handful of individual Uruguayan trees collected by André and a few others. So, he decided to go to South America to collect feijoa seed from as wide a range of locations as possible, in order to inject a smorgasbord of new genetics, representing the feijoa's full gene pool, into the New Zealand breeding programme.

In March 1988 he set off for southern Brazil, thirty-one years to the day before I followed in his footsteps on my own feijoa adventure. Grant travelled around the countryside, meeting with local botanists, and collecting feijoas from forty-two separate locations across Rio Grande do Sul, Santa Catarina, Paraná and Uruguay. He covered 9000 kilometres over five weeks, most of it by bus. 'Every weekend I'd come back with all these bags of fruit to the not-at-all fancy Hotel Ritz in Porto Alegre and shut myself up in the room and extract the seeds.' That was when he noticed that the feijoas from the populations in the very south of Brazil and Uruguay had small seeds (2-3 mm), while some of those from the northern population – the Brazilian type – had much larger seeds (5-9 mm). To Grant, that suggested there were very few Brazilian genes present in the feijoas grown everywhere else. 'I've seen feijoas in practically all the continents, and they've all got small seeds.'

Grant gave feijoa seeds from all forty-two locations to Brazilian and Uruguayan botanists so that they could set up or diversify their own germplasm banks (I visited one with Nodari in São Joaquim in Santa Catarina). And he brought the rest of the seeds home to New Zealand, planting them out at some of the DSIR's research stations.

Sadly, nothing ever came of it. The DSIR's budget got slashed, and there was no more money for research into 'minor fruit' like feijoas. Grant's experimental feijoas were bulldozed, including all the seedlings he'd painstakingly collected in South America. Grant has since moved on to almonds, avocados, macadamias and kiwifruit. He's sanguine about the missed opportunities: 'I have always said that feijoas will never go away – they will have their time as a major crop. I just hope I am around to see it.'

Roy Hart carried the torch next. When I visited him at his home in Motueka, he was eighty-eight years old, with curly white hair, sideburns and a moustache. Roy immigrated to New Zealand from England in his twenties, after he finished his military service. He worked in a nursery, as a gardener, and then got a labouring job at the DSIR. After getting a lucky break and discovering a new kind of aphid, he worked his way up to become a technician at the institute's Riwaka research station near Nelson. 'Most of the big jobs were all taken by scientists, but they let me do all the other weird and wonderful things, and one of them turned out to be feijoas.' In around 1989, Roy put ads in the paper asking for people to write in if they thought they had a decent feijoa tree. Mostly, Roy says, they weren't decent, but a handful were reasonable.

Identifying a promising seedling in the wild or in an open pollinated orchard is one thing, but real plant breeding involves selecting two specific parents in order to influence the traits of the offspring. Breeders make these crosses by fixing bags around the flower buds to prevent any contamination from unwanted plants. When the flower opens, they collect pollen from the desired parent and brush it onto the target bloom, replacing the bag until the fruit is set. When ripe, the breeder extracts the seeds – and knows they will all be the offspring of the chosen parents.

Roy made various crosses between the existing varieties like Apollo, Gemini and Triumph, and the reasonable local selections. From the offspring, in 1992 he identified two more cultivars he named Kakapo and Pounamu after two green-hued New Zealand icons: the fat, fragrant and highly endangered night parrot the kākāpō; and pounamu, the Māori word for greenstone, or jade, a taonga collected from the white-water rivers of the South Island's West Coast and traditionally traded throughout the archipelago.

Then, like Grant, Roy was told to stop work on feijoas. 'There was no more money for the weird and wonderful crops.' Around the same time, Nigel Ritson phoned him up. Roy had 600 young feijoas that the DSIR wanted to get rid of, and nowhere to put them. Nigel had land, so they formed an alliance. Nigel dug 600 holes in the rocky ground with a pick and shovel, and planted out the seedlings.

That was more than thirty years ago. After working together for about a decade, Roy and Nigel fell out and went their separate ways. Roy enlisted some strong young men to help him dig up the three feijoa trees Nigel would allow him to take, which became

Roy's bestselling cultivars: Kaiteri, Kakariki and Anatoki. He is still actively breeding, aiming to find a longer-storing, earlier-fruiting variety that would extend the season.

And Nigel, independently, is going for it all – size, sweetness, productivity, pharmacological usefulness, disease resistance and shelf life – trying to get as close as he can to that perfect feijoa cultivar.

The lowering sun glowed through the shelter belt as Nigel led me across the rugged open ground from one isolated tree to another. Not long ago, there were 3000 feijoas growing here in the orchard, but Nigel had recently felled most of them. 'Most have been culled because they have yucky flavours on them. I mean, seriously yucky flavours. Absolutely shocking.' It seems brutal, but culling is an essential part of any breeding programme, he explained. The vast majority of seedlings won't be any improvement on their parents; to find the elusive gold you have to be ruthless. Nigel keeps only the best of the best, so he has room to plant the next generation of hopefuls.

But feijoas are so darn hardy that some of the trees refused to die. Nigel tried cutting them down and painting the stumps with glyphosate. They kept sprouting back. Then he took to hooking a chain around the stump, connecting it to his tractor, and charging down the hill in second gear in an attempt to wrench the roots out. 'The whole tractor would jerk, and I nearly smashed my teeth on the steering wheel.' Deciding that was too dangerous a task at his age – late sixties – he resorted to a more poisonous herbicide, metsulfuron. It was sucked up into the roots of nearby feijoa trees he actually wanted to keep, and some of them died. 'That turned out to be a terrible mistake.' Eventually, Nigel went back to the glyphosate, drilling up to five finger-sized holes into the stump and squirting the concentrated poison inside. Sometimes he even has to repeat the procedure. 'It takes a lot to kill a feijoa.'

Though he knows it's necessary, at times the culling breaks his heart. 'There was a lovely one called 10-14 ... It had a beautiful flavour, but it only had about ten fruit on it each year. There's no way a grower can make a living off that, and who would want it in their home garden either?' 'Waingaro', on the other hand, one of his home-garden varieties, produces 35 kilograms of fruit in a season. 'You can pick up two buckets off the ground every day.' Others he culled because they were too inconsistent. 'You might hit one tree where nine out of ten fruit are absolutely delicious, but then you get another from the same tree, and it's ghastly.' In Nigel's orchard, perfection is always just out of reach.

I looked around the mostly-bare orchard. Of the few trees left standing, one was variegated – the foliage striped yellow, green and white – and others had the large, dark, shiny leaves I had seen on some of the wild feijoas in Brazil. This is actually Nigel's second major round of culling. Of Roy's original 600 seedlings, Nigel kept only Waingaro. But then Roy brought something new over the hill. A few years earlier he had got hold of some Brazilian feijoa seed. When the seedlings started fruiting, they had strong and strange flavours. 'A lot of them were just absolutely awful,' Roy said, 'but it looked as though they could be earlier flowering. They were a tougher sort of fruit, and I thought they might store better.' (They didn't.) He chose the one that tasted the least terrible, and crossed it with Apollo and Pounamu.

Descendants of those crosses were the next 600 seedlings Nigel planted out at Tākaka. 'They were awesome plants,' he said. 'Hugely fast growth rates, some with huge round fruit, incredibly complex flavours I had never experienced before.' It might not have been the full genetic smorgasbord that Grant had hoped to bring to New Zealand, but the Brazilian genes were making an impact.

Nigel showed me 'Takaka', one of his commercially available cultivars, and I squawked in astonishment when I saw the fruit. 'Look at the size of them!' They were absolutely enormous, larger than my hand, more avocado than feijoa. 'They get up to 300 grams,' Nigel said.

Finally, we came to one large tree with a beautiful round shape, standing alone. This was 'Waitui', Nigel said. 'I reckon it's a masterpiece.' Waitui is the closest he's got so far to a truly great cultivar. It has a complex flavour, has uniform fruit size, and is very early fruiting – the second-earliest out of the 600 plants, earlier than Unique. It is also one of the highest-yielding feijoas he's found, producing around 50 kilograms of fruit a season. 'I think it was a gift from God.'

Because it's so special, and to try to gain some 'muscle in the marketplace' in terms of getting the fruit into supermarkets, Nigel will only sell the rights to Waitui to large commercial operations who are willing to license at least 2000 trees (so far, only one grower has taken him up on it). Waitui, Takaka and Nigel's other commercial cultivar, Kawatiri, are the only individuals left from the original Brazilian crosses. Nigel culled the rest. 'They were generally pretty awful. That culling and selecting process took me about six years, but I must have done a good job – Kawatiri and Waitui are consistently good through to delicious year after year.' (Being a lover of wild places, Nigel named his varieties after nearby rivers: 'Not just any river, but the clean wild ones.' Kawatiri is the original Māori name for the powerful, fast-flowing Buller River which carves through the Southern Alps to the West Coast.)

As we talked, night fell. The fruit was falling too, making sporadic thuds in the darkness – a heavy, solid sound I'd never heard from feijoas before. These were no longer the little green Easter eggs I grew up with. These were more like kiwi eggs, like baseballs, like rocks the size of my fist.

When Nigel had invited me to visit during April to taste the results of his decades of effort, he promised I would taste feijoa flavours that would be completely new to me. Before coming, I'd been kind of sceptical. I had by now eaten feijoas on multiple continents, and hadn't thought there was all that much variation between them. I also worried that my love of feijoas might be too indiscriminate – that they would all taste similarly yummy to me, and I wouldn't be able to give him any useful feedback. But now, in the orchard, as Nigel cut fruit after massive fruit open with his knife and handed the halves to me, I realised he was right: these *were* new flavours, and the variety was astounding.

One as-yet-unnamed feijoa had a creamy, substantial, almost meaty texture – like a meal in itself. 'I love this one!' I kept saying to him. 'That's good,' he said. 'It's really long-storing, too.' But then I discovered another I loved at least as much, or more: a bell-shaped fruit that tasted completely different: fresh and tangy, with large, jelly-like locules and a thin surrounding pericarp, so that I could scrape out the insides almost all the way to the skin.

When I scooped my spoon into a Waitui fruit, I realised Nigel was peering at me, trying to read my expression. 'You haven't broken into a smile yet,' he said. It was true; I wanted to love Waitui, and I certainly liked it, but it didn't blow my mind. (Nigel maintained it tastes best four or five days after falling, and also that the heavy rain of the previous few days had brought down the Brix – a measure of sweetness – so I hadn't tasted it at its best.) For now, though, my favourite was a round, apple-sized fruit from another unnamed tree: a smooth-skinned, lemony-sweet ball of deliciousness. Even the skin was tasty. 'You said the right thing,' Nigel said. 'I was saving that one for you.'

Quick flavour impressions in the field are one thing, but Nigel is more scientific than that. During March, April and May, he spends up to ten hours a day rigorously tasting and scoring feijoas. I returned to his house the following morning to join him.

When I arrived, he was all set up at the kitchen sink. There was a hand-operated juicer on the bench, a device for measuring pH, and a small electronic Brix reader for quantifying the sweetness. Renaissance harpsichord music played on the stereo. 'Isn't it beautiful?' Nigel asked. On the wall above the sink was a calendar with different parts of the world to pray for each day, and a printout of a poem attributed to Mother Teresa: 'Give the world the best you can, and it may never be enough; Give the world the best you've got anyway.'

On the kitchen table were several dozen feijoas in cardboard trays, each labelled in ballpoint pen with an identifying number. Nigel picked up a small yellowish one he said was from the variegated tree we'd seen the previous evening and cut it in half. First, he weighed it, and wrote the number by hand onto a paper scoresheet clipped to a board. He gave it an external appearance score: 2 out of 5. Then the inside: 'I'm going to give it a 2, it's pale, it's a bit soft, it hasn't got very well-defined locules, it's not very pretty.' He dropped one half of the fruit into the juicer, hand-pressed the liquid into a tiny cup, and placed the pH instrument inside for a few minutes. Then he let three drops of juice fall onto the Brix reader: '13.4 – that's good. The average is about 10.' Finally, we tasted it. He cut the remaining half into two pieces and we each put a teaspoonful thoughtfully into our mouths.

Nigel has also devised a five-point scoring system for flavour. A zero: 'Disgusting. We'd be spitting it out and washing our mouths out numerous times.' One: 'Bad, you can hold it in your mouth, but there's no way you'd want to eat it.' Two: 'Edible, but like white bread with no jam or peanut butter. An average-bloke score that covers a huge range of things.' Three: 'Good – I've tightened up, what used to be a very good is probably in the average range now, because the whole orchard has improved with the culling.' Four: 'Very good.' Five: 'Delicious.'

I've tasted a lot of feijoas in my life, but I had never given them quite such focused attention. This one was pretty sweet and tasty, I thought, though the texture was kind of smushy. 'Well, it's eleven days old,' Nigel said. The fruit had been sitting out on the bench for a week and a half, and was still decent, an indication of how Nigel has improved the storing quality – if I left any of my homegrown feijoas out for that long, they'd be no good at all. I gave it a 3, and Nigel agreed, writing it down on the scoresheet. 'I've gotten really really fussy. I've tasted tens of thousands of them, literally.'

Later, he would enter the data into his master spreadsheet on the computer, a 40,000-line masterpiece all of its own that required Nigel to learn Boolean algebra and devise formulas where the external score and the inside score, the Brix, the average fruit weight, the seasonal yield, the storage time, the acidity, the consistency and the square of the taste score all combine to help him decide which plants live and which plants die.

It's a ridiculous amount of work, and sometimes he despairs.

'Last month I was holding these pages of scoresheets in front of me – there were three or four days where they were nearly all culls, and the flavours were horrible. I felt like a real failure, miserable, that I was just wasting my time.' But then there are the days when he tastes his usual quarter-teaspoon, then finds himself eating the entire thing. 'I've tasted fruit that you'd just think were made in heaven: 5 after 5, top scores, just beyond description,' he said. 'It's like the world turns over.'

―――

It's not all about the eating experience. Walking along the rows of trees in the orchard a few years ago, Nigel had an intuition. There was one particular tree, with fruit that had a 'barely tolerable' flavour, that he sensed was potent. 'Don't ask me how. I just knew. You know when you talk to yourself because you're on your own too much? I'd walk past this plant and say to myself, "This is a mean jungle plant."'

He got in touch with Rob Keyzers, a natural products chemist at Victoria University of Wellington Te Herenga Waka, asking if he would be interested in testing the antifungal and antibacterial properties of feijoas. Rob's research focuses on finding molecules in nature that could be useful, and though he personally hates the taste of feijoas, he thought the peels could be worth investigating – with the added potential benefit of using up a waste product from the juicing industry. One of his PhD students, Mona Mokhtari, got to work on them along with Andrew Munkacsi, a chemical geneticist.

The team tested feijoa fruit from sixteen cultivars: a handful of the most popular commercial varieties and some of Nigel's personal favourites, including FFF6, one he had used in a lot of his crosses, and FFF5, the horrible-tasting 'mean jungle plant'.

The scientists found feijoa peels did indeed have antifungal powers, but that there was huge variation between the individual varieties.[238] 'There were three or four that were streets ahead more bioactive, more antifungal, than the others,' Rob told me. The most potent of all? FFF6 and FFF5 – Nigel's part-Brazilian picks, the legacy of Roy's secretive seeds. Fruits from those trees both inhibited fungal growth by more than 80 per cent, compared with around 20 per cent for the common cultivar Unique. They also contained large amounts of a compound called 4-cyclopentene-1,3-dione, which can kill *Candida* species – the fungi responsible for thrush and athlete's foot – without damaging human cells or helpful gut bacteria. The compound, however, was already known to science, meaning the university's lawyer determined it couldn't be patented, so there was no money in it for either the researchers or Nigel.

Scientists have so far identified four methods for attacking fungi that don't have negative side effects, and researchers are on the hunt for a new mechanism. The 4-cyclopentene-1,3-dione compound kills fungi using one of the known methods. 'The next billion-dollar thing has to work by a new mechanism, because the fungi are already evolving ways to overcome that mechanism,' said Rob. 'You need to hit them with a new mechanism that they haven't seen before.'

Rob's team also found anti-cancer properties in the feijoa skins, but that's not quite as exciting as it sounds. 'I've discovered a lot of things that kill cancer cells, brand new to science, and not one of them would ever be considered as worth investing further in.' To be useful, Rob said, a compound needs to only kill the cancer, not healthy cells – 'hydrochloric acid is great at killing cancer cells, but it wouldn't make a very good drug' – and it needs to be able to get to the part of the body where it's needed without being destroyed on the way.

Even if they can't cure cancer, feijoas have a reputation as a superfood. On my travels, I heard claims that they were tremendously high in antioxidants, vitamin C and iodine – to the point where Colombians were marketing them as the 'fruit of eternal youth'. But is any of that really true? Richard Mithen – a professor of nutrition at the Liggins Institute at the University of Auckland and the chief scientist for the New Zealand High-Value Nutrition National Science Challenge – offered to review the scientific literature on the health benefits of feijoas for me. He had once worked as a plant explorer in South Africa, knew all about Friedrich Sellow, and had only recently arrived in New Zealand from Britain, so I felt I could count on him to be impartial.

I really wanted feijoas to be special, but Richard had

disappointing news. 'There does not seem to be anything particularly remarkable about feijoa on the basis of the analyses of known nutrients and phytochemicals,' he said. Sorry. Like most fruits and vegetables, feijoas are a source of dietary fibre. They contain a reasonable amount of vitamin C – 30 milligrams per 100 grams, though that pales in comparison with the 88 milligrams in green kiwifruit, 161 milligrams in gold kiwifruit, or the standout 222 milligrams in blackcurrants. Their iodine content is 'insignificant', Richard said – a finding confirmed by Plant & Food Research scientist Carolyn Lister in lab studies in 2022. It is unsurprising, she told me, as few fruits contain much of the stuff.[239] (Seafood and iodised salt are both much better sources.)

There is, however, some interesting emerging research on anti-inflammatory activity. University of Auckland chemists analysed feijoa fruit from the Apollo, Unique, Wiki Tu and Opal Star cultivars, and identified fifteen separate phenolic compounds – plant-derived chemicals that act as antioxidants and have been found to have anti-inflammatory effects for humans.[240] (Richard reminded me that inflammation is not necessarily bad; it helps our bodies to fight infections. Problems arise when it persists, and chronic inflammation underlies cardiovascular disease, type 2 diabetes and inflammatory bowel disease.) In a separate study, the same Auckland researchers applied feijoa extracts to human cells, and found that they acted to suppress TLR2, a protein that increases inflammation. The feijoa extracts had such a strong effect that they were superior to the well-known anti-inflammatory drug ibuprofen, the researchers said.[241]

That doesn't necessarily mean you can eat a few feijoas instead of swilling a couple of Nurofen tablets. Applying a fruit extract to human cells in a Petri dish isn't quite the same thing as absorbing a fruit through the processes of digestion. Finding out more will require more research, and clinical trials – which may be on the cards in New Zealand shortly. In summary, Richard said: 'Including feijoa in one's diet would be beneficial, and it may have some specific beneficial effects regarding anti-inflammatory activity and improvements to metabolic health.' For now, that's about all we can say.

Still, as Rob Keyzers' team found, the chemical make-up of the fruits can vary considerably between individual feijoa trees. The other nutritional studies have mostly used the traditional New Zealand cultivars that descend from Uruguayan trees. But Nigel suspects that the most useful pharmacological chemicals find their strongest concentration in the fruits that taste terrible – in particular, in the trees with some Brazilian genes. This causes him some agony when he thinks of all the trees he's culled. 'There must have been some amazing chemicals in there that could have been really important for humanity. I still don't feel good about it, but at the end of the day, if people are going to eat fruit, it has to taste good.'

Scientific in his approach, but led by his passion, his intuition and his Christian faith, Nigel Ritson is hard to categorise. He sees feijoa breeding almost as a divine mission, a beautiful legacy to leave the world. After the taste-testing, he let me outside to show me the thousands of tiny seedlings he had deliberately sowed into soggy, poor-quality soil. 'The idea was they would be very prone to getting fungus attack in their roots, and sure enough they did. Plants have been dying all over the place, but some of them survived, and they're some of the best-looking plants I've ever seen,' he said. 'I'm trying to force plants through a bottleneck. There's no point in doing ten years' work on a plant if it's going to be wiped out by fungus attack.' And anyway, there's no room in the orchard for 1000 new plants, or time in the day to assess them all. In those seedling trays, it's survival of the fittest.

'You're very Darwinian for a man of faith,' I observed. Nigel was quiet for a minute. Then he said, 'I'm tempted to tell you something you might think is strange. But it's the truth.' The previous summer, after cross-pollinating around 100 different combinations of feijoas – such as Waitui by Opal Star, or Round Apple by Sweet Sixteen 4 – he had carefully collected the fruit from the small bags hanging on the mother trees and extracted their seeds. Each cross, represented by hundreds or thousands of tiny seeds, was laid on a separate piece of paper to dry out, and the floor of the spare room was entirely covered with them. There were perhaps 50,000 seeds in that one room, the result of months and months of careful work.

One day, Nigel was sitting on the floor, tipping the seeds into envelopes and writing labels on them, when he heard a voice speak in his mind. The voice told him that one of these myriad seeds would become an important cultivar that would be widely planted throughout New Zealand. He felt elated. 'I looked at them and thought, "I'm going to plant every single one of these."' Talking about it now made him tear up, the emotion wobbling his voice. 'Because while I'm sure I heard the Lord speak – that's my understanding of what happened – I didn't know which one He was referring to. So, I sowed the whole lot.'

The seedlings were now more than a year old and a metre high. The individuals that survived his disease-induced bottleneck would soon be planted out into the spaces in the orchard. When they begin fruiting, Nigel will start the tasting, rating and culling process all over again, hoping God will guide him to find that one superlative individual, the needle in the haystack that will justify all his labour, his sacrifice and his hope. 'I mean I could be a fool, but I'm acting on faith,' he said.

Nigel had asked the Lord for a challenge, and the feijoas had certainly provided it. Inconsistent and capricious, they are also difficult to propagate: in this case, the process of making clones of a given cultivar to sell. This can be done by grafting – which takes more than a year to produce a plantable tree – or by taking cuttings of the parent tree and encouraging the twigs to root. New Zealand feijoa retailers Waimea Nurseries told me that where other plants have a 90 per cent success rate, feijoa cuttings hover at best around 50 per cent, and can sometimes fail entirely. (This was also a significant problem for the Brazilian breeders I spoke to in Santa Catarina, and for Mark Albert in California: feijoas seem to be harder to propagate than many other plants.)

Thirty years of incremental progress, failures and frustration have also taught Nigel humility. The feijoas have made him more realistic and grounded, he believes: a better and more loving person than he once was. 'With the feijoa, you're kind of standing in front of the incomprehensible,' he said, as we walked among the thousand seedlings, these living incarnations of possibility. A pīwakawaka hopped around us, and the clouds hung low on the mountains, dark wisps reaching into the distant forests.

Nigel believes we can only ever glimpse the profound mystery hidden inside this small green fruit. 'To try to reach our minds into it, it's unfathomable – just to discover these little things about it is exciting. There are so few plants we eat, and if they were to have terrible fungal attacks or get wiped out by climate change, we'd be gone pretty fast. That's why plant breeding is so important. It's an honour and a privilege to be in a place where I've got this genetic material to work with, and I'll do my very best to make good use of my time here on Earth.' Amen to that.

CHAPTER 20

The Taste of Home

One autumn morning in 2015, my partner Sam and I left the tacky high-rises and messy surf of Coolum Beach, on Queensland's Sunshine Coast in Australia, and drove into the gentler country of the Hinterland. I was five months pregnant with Amalia, my belly just beginning to show. We wove among green hills, narrow creeks and white-skinned gum trees until we reached a place of pilgrimage: Sally Hookey and Peter Heineger's feijoa farm.

The orchard overlooked a grassy valley. A string of dams lined the creekbed, full to the brim after the latest tropical cyclone had dumped more than 300 millimetres of rain in a couple of days. The rows of feijoa trees were covered in fine netting to keep off the Queensland fruit fly, a devastating pest that burrows into and destroys the fruit. The netting spawns a whole ecosystem: insects get caught in the nets, attracting frogs, which in turn attract snakes. The week before, Sally had discovered the shed skin of a deadly 3-metre-long brown snake sloughed off between the feijoa trees and the packing shed, a shocking tale for visitors from serpent-free New Zealand!

Sally – then in her fifties with dark hair and bright eyes – greeted me with a box of feijoas in her arms, before whirling off to deliver it to a guest. The lawn and driveway were already bustling with families. Children patted ponies and climbed on a tractor. Their parents drank tea, tasted feijoa ice cream and browsed the jars of preserved feijoas, feijoa jam, feijoa chutney and feijoa balsamic vinegar. Really, though, all these pilgrims were here for just one thing: to buy fresh feijoas by the boxful. They were almost all New Zealanders – Māori, Pākehā, Asian – who had settled in Brisbane and on the Gold Coast. Most had driven more than two hours to collect their box of green treasure, booked months in advance and anticipated even longer.[242]

Commercially, it would have made sense to ship bulk orders to supermarkets, but Sally and Peter preferred to spread the word on social media and sell their produce at the farm gate.[243] That approach fit better with their Slow Food farming philosophy, rooted in a desire to connect consumers with the people who grow their food. Some years, they sold their entire annual crop of around 6 tonnes this way: 3000 visitors, 500 kilograms a day. It also meant that each autumn weekend, Sally had a front-row seat from which to observe what feijoas mean to New Zealanders, especially to those living away from home. When her customers came to collect their boxes, she said, they usually couldn't wait to eat one. She provided spoons so they could dig in straight away. After that first bite, some hugged her. Others were so overcome with emotion that they burst into tears.

Sam and I talked to dozens of people on that sunny Saturday, and we heard the same stories over and over. 'It just tastes like home.' 'It takes you right back to childhood.' 'They remind me of sitting under the trees with a spoon as a child.' 'You just can't describe the flavour.' 'Australians don't understand.'

One woman said she travelled to Hinterland Feijoas every autumn as a way to maintain her connection to New Zealand and to ward off homesickness. Another said her father refused to come because he thought the nostalgia would be too much. One young man, Benjamin Tan, now living on the Sunshine Coast, told me the trip the farm was part of an annual ritual of remembering his grandmother. The feijoa season coincides with the anniversary of her death, Benjamin said. 'So, when the feijoas ripen, it reminds us of her.' The family planned to take their box of feijoas to her grave and eat them there. Another guest, Margaret Hobbs, had 'feijoa day' marked on a calendar, and had looked forward to it for weeks. 'Sometimes it's those little things – like feijoas – that make you feel at home.'

―――

How did feijoas come to have this alchemical effect for New Zealanders? Why did the feijoa become the taste of home in a way that kiwifruit, strawberries, or native kahikatea fruits have not? To try to figure it out, I spoke with Carolyn Morris, an anthropologist specialising in food and agriculture at New Zealand's Massey University. Morris isn't a feijoa expert, and doesn't even particularly like them; she's much more passionate about passionfruit. But she is an authority on the meanings we attach to food, and has even written an academic paper about the changing significance of tinned pineapple in New Zealand culture.[244] I thought that she, of all people, might understand my quest to understand what our national obsession with the feijoa says about it – and us.

At first, I was a bit offended on the feijoa's behalf. Carolyn reckoned that, objectively, feijoas aren't all that great. 'Their texture's kind of a bit weird – gloopy plus grainy – and they're not a gorgeous colour,' she said. But that almost doesn't matter, she added. We know humans are predisposed to liking sugar, but that doesn't tell you why we have particular preferences for feijoas, passionfruit, pineapple or any other kind of sweet fruit. Not only is flavour largely determined by smell – our taste buds just tell us if something is sweet or salty, bitter or sour – studies have repeatedly found that our sense of taste is largely social and cultural; what we like to eat is determined by the positive or negative associations a certain food has for us. Feijoas are becoming a 'culture food' in New Zealand, Carolyn proposed, meaning their flavour is less important than their meaning. But what do feijoas mean, and where does this meaning come from?[245]

The feijoa's significance in New Zealand derives from the plant's particular constellation of biological traits, we decided: attributes that evolved thousands of kilometres away and millions of years ago in the South American forest. The basics first: the species thrives here. Feijoa trees are hardy and survive with very little care in most New Zealand climates. Some varieties are even known to produce in the Southland region – at a latitude comparable to the southern tip of Tasmania, or to Northern Italy or Lake Michigan in the northern hemisphere – and are easily pollinated by the ubiquitous Eurasian blackbirds, thrushes and native silvereyes. Grant Thorp told me he thinks they grow better in New Zealand than they do anywhere else, including their native Brazil and Uruguay, where the soils are generally poorer and less fertile than they are in this young, volcanic country.

The ease of cultivation – that rugged tolerance – makes feijoas egalitarian. You don't have to have specialist gardening knowledge or time on your hands to look after them. All you need is a patch of soil behind the washing line, or to live near a suburb where they're planted as street trees. In New Zealand, then, the feijoa is no longer considered exotic, and having one doesn't exactly convey status. 'It's not fancy at all,' said Carolyn. 'It's very much a home fruit.' It makes sense that New Zealanders would identify with an egalitarian sort of fruit, she said: that's one of the national myths we like to believe about ourselves, even as inequality soars, home ownership is at its lowest point since the 1950s, and fewer of those homes have space for a tree.

And yet, part of feijoas' special meaning in New Zealand

derives from the fact that they are not found in every supermarket the world over, like strawberries or kiwifruit. When we travel, people in other countries frequently don't know what we're talking about when we wax lyrical about feijoas. That distinctiveness makes them a kind of national symbol, Carolyn said. 'Your enjoyment of them is a thing you can use to mark yourself out, like insider knowledge. It becomes a kind of identity marker: "the feijoa eaters".'

———

Then there's what Carolyn called 'the glut': the spectacular abundance for just a few short months at the bittersweet end of summer. That intense seasonality is a key part of the feijoa's magic. All at once, the trees throw their plentiful fruit at our feet, onto driveways, under lawnmowers.

Feijoas might be abundant, but they are also perishable: despite the efforts of breeders and agricultural scientists, the fruit still don't keep especially well. Whereas a kiwifruit can last for up to six months in cool storage, allowing it to be shipped anywhere in the world and taste great when it gets there, feijoas are best eaten straight from the ground and last just a few days in the fruit bowl. Even when properly refrigerated, they generally keep for weeks, not months. If you can't keep up with the amount of fruit a tree's producing, and you can't store them for later, what do you do? You give them away so they don't go to waste. If feijoas were less perishable, we might keep them for ourselves. Instead, we share them at our workplace or put a box out on the street.

'They are a part of the New Zealand food commons,' said Carolyn. If feijoas fall on a neighbour's driveway or the footpath, it's okay to help yourself. 'No-one's going to come out and shout at you, because there are millions on their own side of the fence. People are like, "Take them away, they're just wasp factories out the front of my property." Whereas with other things, it's like, "'Touch my passionfruit and I'll set the dog on you.'"

For many New Zealanders, it's anathema to buy a feijoa – you expect to get them for free. And when you receive an object as a gift, as Robin Wall Kimmerer writes in *Braiding Sweetgrass*, its entire meaning changes. Kimmerer gives the example of a pair of woollen socks: if you buy them from a store, you might feel some gratitude for the sheep that grew the wool and the worker that made them, but after you pay your money, your obligations end. You buy the socks and they become your property. If, however, the socks were knitted especially for you by your grandmother, it's a completely different story. That 'changes everything', Kimmerer writes. 'A gift creates ongoing relationship . . . The more something is shared, the greater its value becomes.' She quotes the scholar Lewis Hyde: '"It is the cardinal difference between gift and commodity exchange that a gift establishes a feeling-bond between two people."'[246]

Reading this reminded me of something Carolyn had said. When your friend gives you a bag of feijoas, or you scrump one from under a tree in the park, *it actually tastes better* than one you've bought at the shop. 'They taste of more than their objective taste,' she said. 'They taste of your friend's love and care, of your social networks – and those meanings make them taste good.'

The perfect counter-example? Kiwifruit. The kiwifruit industry is a global fruit juggernaut. In 2020, New Zealand's 2800 kiwifruit growers exported 552,800 tonnes of kiwifruit to 51 countries, generating NZ$2.5 billion and making up 38 per cent of New Zealand's total horticultural exports. In the same year, the country's 200 commercial feijoa growers made just NZ$100,000 in export dollars, though they earned NZ$3.4 million on the domestic market.[247]

On the face of it, then, kiwifruit have been vastly more successful than the humble feijoa. But I don't think it's a coincidence that kiwifruit are not really beloved by New Zealanders in the way that feijoas are. Barely anyone has a backyard kiwifruit. While every garden centre will sell you a feijoa cultivar, it's very rare to find one selling kiwifruit plants, partly because of restrictions imposed to prevent the spread of Psa, a damaging bacterial disease that wiped out the first gold kiwifruit cultivar, and partly because Zespri won't licence the new Psa-resistant gold cultivar to home gardeners.[248]

Therefore, if you want a kiwifruit, you have to buy one: kiwifruit are utterly embedded in the market economy. Feijoas, on the other hand, belong at least partially to the gift economy, explaining why they've been nicknamed 'the People's Fruit', or, as one viral article put it, 'New Zealand's most socialist fruit'.[249] (The piece was accompanied by a cartoon image of a feijoa wearing a Che Guevara beret and smoking a Cuban cigar.)

There are plenty of people who would like to see feijoas achieve greater commercial and export success. In 2019, New Zealand's then Minister for Agriculture Damien O'Connor called feijoas a 'fruit of the future' with 'huge potential' and said they could become 'another amazing export fruit' – though, so far, the government hasn't taken any action on that front. But if feijoas were ever 'kiwifruited' – if the storage problem was solved, and feijoas did manage to achieve global recognition and year-round ubiquity – they might actually lose some of their significance for New Zealanders, Carolyn said.

It is not just people who give feijoas to each other. The trees gift them to us, too. They scatter them at our feet. In a world where almost everything is a commodity, where food is wrapped in plastic and disconnected from its origins by convoluted supply chains, a feijoa in the garden is a reminder of the munificence of the earth. Those freely given green gifts connect communities, enhance neighbourliness and quietly subvert the capitalist economy. Writing about wild strawberries – the plants that introduced her to 'a world full of gifts' – Kimmerer contrasts the 'story' of the market economy with that of the gift economy so common in Indigenous cultures. 'One of these stories opens the way to living in gratitude and amazement at the richness and generosity of the world. One of these stories asks us to bestow our own gifts in kind, to celebrate our kinship with the world. We can choose. If all the world is a commodity, how poor we grow. When all the world is a gift in motion, how wealthy we become.'[250]

———

Hardy, abundant, niche, a gift. But perhaps the feijoa's most important attribute of all is its heady fragrance. As Édouard André noticed more than a century ago, ripe feijoas left out in a bowl on the bench will perfume an entire room. Why does this happen, and what exactly do we smell when we cut open a ripe feijoa?

In 1970, the first scientists to ask that question identified two dominant volatile compounds responsible for the feijoa's aroma: methyl benzoate and ethyl benzoate.[251] A recent Italian study found that ethyl benzoate is found in higher proportions as a feijoa ripens.[252] Methyl benzoate, on the other hand, gives the fruit its distinctive, sweet, 'feijoa-like' smell, and has been identified in feijoa flesh, skin, juice and essential oil. This specific arrangement of carbon, hydrogen and oxygen molecules – $C_6H_5CO_2CH_3$ – is only found in such high concentrations in feijoas, but it is also produced by guavas, mangos, a type of freshwater fern and a certain Brazilian orchid.

Remember how Brazil nut trees can only thrive in intact Amazon rainforest, because the tree's main pollinator – the euglossine bee – needs the presence of particular orchids for its life cycle? While the female bees pollinate Brazil nut flowers, male bees collect a bouquet of perfume compounds from a dozen kinds of orchid, pollinating them in the process. The well-groomed males store their orchid cologne in special organs on their legs, and release the fragrance later in a choreographed display as they attempt to impress a potential mate. One of those orchid species, *Catasetum gnomus*, the 'gnome-like *Catasetum*', produces feijoa-scented methyl benzoate – meaning male euglossine bees fly through the Amazon rainforest wafting a trail of feijoa perfume. Scientists studying the bees have even used the compound as a bait to attract male bees to study.[253]

Airport sniffer dogs are also reportedly trained to react to methyl benzoate: not to apprehend illicit feijoa smugglers, but to locate drug traffickers. In certain moist conditions, the water in the air can react with scent-free cocaine powder (a hydrochloride) to produce strong-smelling methyl benzoate – so maybe think twice before filling your luggage with feijoas on an overseas trip![254]

Really, though, the true fragrance of a feijoa is more than just methyl benzoate – it's a complex combination of all the aroma compounds given off by the ripe fruit. Scientists in New Zealand recently identified twenty-five different aroma active compounds in feijoa juice that give it its specific fruity and herbal smell. They found eleven esters, including methyl benzoate, ethyl benzoate and the 'apple-peel like' ethyl hexanoate. There were also ten terpenes – mostly herbal flavours, and one each with mushroom-like, honey-like and metallic scents. Two alcohols – one 'grassy' and one 'floral' and two ketones – one lemon-like, one mushroom-like – rounded out the full feijoa pot-pourri.[255]

More than anything else, it is this penetrating, distinctive scent that gives feijoas their emotional power – their ability to make a homesick New Zealander cry. As the American journalist Tom Wolfe said, 'There's no sense that reaches more deeply and suddenly into our emotional centre – right into the solar plexus – than the sense of smell.'[256]

Science and literature have both explored the phenomenon of scent or flavour triggering a sudden, involuntary rush of memory, nostalgia and emotion. Psychologists call it 'autobiographical odour memory', but it's more commonly known as the 'Proust effect'. In Marcel Proust's epic seven-volume novel *In Search of Lost Time*, begun in 1909, the narrator picks up a madeleine cake – a tiny scallop-shaped sponge cake from France's Lorraine region – and dunks it into a cup of lime-blossom tea.[257]

'[A]t the very instant when the mouthful of tea mixed with cake-crumbs touched my palate, I quivered, attentive to the extraordinary thing that was happening in me', Proust wrote. 'A delicious pleasure had invaded me, isolated me, without my having any notion as to its cause. It had immediately made the vicissitudes of life unimportant to me, its disasters innocuous, its brevity illusory... Where could it have come from – this powerful joy? I sensed that it was connected to the taste of the tea and the cake, but it went infinitely far beyond it'.

The narrator – who is also called Marcel and is thought to represent Proust himself – doesn't at first recognise why he is having this experience. He senses something stirring within himself, 'something that seems to have been unanchored at a great depth', but it takes a while for the recollection to take shape. The emotion comes first – then, moments later, the memory appears. The taste reminds him of visiting his Aunt Léonie in the village of Combray when he was a child. On Sunday mornings, when he went into her room to say good morning, she would dip little pieces of madeleine cake into her lime-blossom tea and give it to him. That specific flavour-and-scent combination, experienced years later, then unleashes a flood of long-forgotten childhood memories that go on for the rest of the epic novel's 3000 pages.

'The sight of the little madeleine had not recalled anything to me before I tasted it', Proust pointed out, 'perhaps because I had often seen them since, without eating them, on the pastry-cooks' shelves.' The intense, emotional experience only happened when he tasted – and smelled – the cake.[258]

Nearly a century later, neuroscientists began looking into the phenomenon Proust described, and they found much that was scientifically accurate in his evocative description of what involuntary odour memory feels like. It turns out that human brains process odours quite differently than cues from our other senses. Aromatic compounds – like the methyl benzoate wafting off a feijoa – float up our nostrils and come into contact with the sensory neurons in a little mucous membrane at the top of our nose. (These are the only sensory neurons in our body that are directly exposed to the environment – one reason why it's quite common for people to lose their sense of smell as a result of exposure to toxins, smoke or pollution.)

How the message gets from there to the olfactory bulbs – two matchstick-shaped structures located just behind the eyes – is still a matter of scientific debate. The leading theory is that each volatile chemical activates a specific pattern of neurons in a particular sequence, and that this code is picked up by the olfactory bulbs and passed along to the brain's olfactory cortex. Unlike other sense centres, the scent cortex is comprised of the amygdala and the hippocampus: the same parts of the brain also responsible for processing memory and emotion.

This proximity seems to make a difference. Experiments have shown that smell and taste are not only more effective at reminding us of the past than other senses are, but the memories they summon have a different quality: spontaneously felt rather than actively remembered. They are also intensely emotional. Just as Proust recounted, the feelings often come first – it can take a few moments to attach the emotion to a particular place, person or time.

'It is a very primal, visceral sensation,' said Rachel Herz, a Canadian-American psychologist and neuroscientist specialising in olfaction, who has been researching autobiographic odour memory since the 1990s.[259] Compared with verbal or visual memories they have to think about, she told me, people tend to find these involuntary memories more meaningful. 'Memories that are triggered by scent can have this very special autobiographical, distinctive and emotional quality to them, and bring us back in time and place like no other sensory experience.'

They're also more likely to come from our earliest years. One study found that memories triggered by visual and verbal cues tend to come from the teens and twenties, while odours bring back recollections from the first decade of life, peaking at age five. Even if the study's participants had smelled a particular scent on later occasions, they thought of their earliest experiences of it.

Autobiographical memories are often clustered in childhood, Rachel said, because that's when the whole world is a wonderland: we're encountering all sorts of things for the first time. But scent-evoked memories are even *more* likely to come from childhood, because of another quirk in the way our olfactory memory works: the first association that we make to a scent imprints on our brain, and doesn't tend to get replaced by subsequent experiences. 'It's actually very hard to undo that first association,' Rachel said. Verbal and visual memories, on the other hand, are constantly being overwritten. When you get a new telephone number, she pointed out, you quickly learn the new set of digits, and before long, you forget your old number. 'But with olfaction, it's like the old telephone number is constantly there, and you can't learn your new one.'

Rachel had never personally tasted a feijoa, but when I described the fruit's characteristics for her, she said the emotive reaction of Sally Hookey's customers made total sense. Strongly and uniquely scented, highly seasonal, with a short shelf life, feijoas seem perfectly designed to set off a Proust effect, especially in those who haven't tasted one in years.

First, that distinctive fragrance – the constellation of methyl benzoate and all the other aromatic compounds that only occurs when you cut open a feijoa – makes it unlikely our earliest memories of it will be overwritten by later encounters, Rachel said. 'It's really specifically tied to that one experience.' Then, due to feijoas' ubiquity in New Zealand, most people there encounter them for the first time as a child. Because of the particular way olfactory memories work, the scent of feijoas then becomes a lifelong tag for that early experience – capturing the feeling of eating them with family or friends in a familiar neighbourhood or a childhood home.

The feijoa's intense seasonality is a part of it, too. The way the fruit comes on through the autumn equinox, that time of year when every day is a few minutes shorter than the last. 'It's the memory of summer turning into autumn,' New Zealand chef Peter Gordon told me. When he thought of feijoas, he pictured eating them in the sunshine in his swimming togs – and then, as a cool wind came up, having to put his trousers on.

This seasonality makes the scent of a feijoa 'temporally tied', Rachel said, which increases its potency: 'The way the Christmas meal is different from the meals that you have every other day of the year – it triggers a special kind of nostalgia.' Although it may contain notes of sadness, nostalgia actually makes us feel good, she said. Studies have shown that experiencing nostalgia can reduce our perception of pain; increase self-esteem, creativity, optimism and connectedness; and even guide us back to our authentic selves.[260]

For me, this helps to explain why people love these fruits so much, and why I found feijoa obsession in so many remote corners of the world. When a feijoa's fragrant esters trigger our nostalgia, they produce, like Proust's madeleine, a kind of 'powerful joy'. The feijoa's 'superfruit' status might be in doubt, but in some ways it truly is the 'fruit of eternal youth': a portal into lost time; an evocative enkindling of childhood, wellbeing and home.

RECIPE
Joe's Wild Mushroom and Feijoa, Manawa Tāwari Honey and Foraged Greens Venison Pōneke in Pastry
Pōneke Pāhi Tia, Pōkai Feijoa me te Harore Kīnaki Huawhenua
Contributed by Hamuera Orupe (Joe) McLeod

INGREDIENTS:
1 sheet puff pastry
270 g butter
12 large dandelion leaves
8 large nasturtium leaves
10 g garlic powder
80 g red onion
200 g button mushrooms
120 g peeled feijoas (one or two)
80 ml Cointreau
100 g Manawa Tāwari Honey (or other honey)
500 g venison fillet
smoked paprika
salt and pepper
80 ml oil
140 ml jus or gravy
80 g chicken liver pâté
large handful wild mushrooms or punnet of shitake, chopped

INSTRUCTIONS:
Brush puff-pastry sheet with melted butter and leave aside.

Cook dandelion and nasturtium leaves in a little butter seasoned with a little garlic powder. Spread out across a piece of greaseproof paper and leave aside.

Finely dice the red onions, button mushrooms and the feijoa, and cook together in a little butter with the garlic powder, 60 ml of the Cointreau and 80 g of the Tāwari Honey. Cook the mixture until it is quite dry and spreadable, stirring all the time to stop it sticking to the pan.

Season the venison with the paprika, salt and pepper. In a hot pan, add the oil and seal the venison quickly, leaving it quite rare, and set aside.

In a small pot, mix the jus and the remaining Cointreau and honey. Bring to the boil and cook until reduced by a third. Leave aside until the pastry is ready to serve.

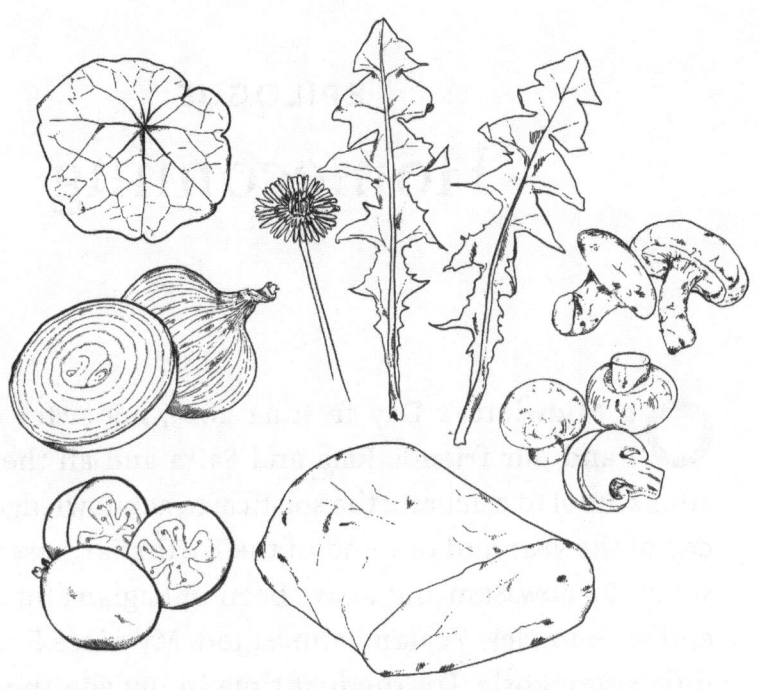

PUTTING IT ALL TOGETHER:
Spread a thin layer of pâté across the pastry, all the way to the ends.
　　Lay the dandelion and nasturtium leaves across the pâté, and spread the feijoa and button mushroom mixture on top of the leaves. Add the chopped wild mushrooms. Place the venison on top.
　　Carefully wrap the pastry around the venison, enclosing it entirely, and pinch the ends to form a parcel. Prick the top of the pastry with a fork – that will let a little of the air out during cooking – then lightly brush with butter.
　　Bake in the oven at 180°C until the pastry is cooked, remove and leave to rest for a few minutes. Serve with sautéed potato and vegetables or salad, and with the jus to accompany the venison.

EPILOGUE

Homecoming

On Midwinter's Day in June 2023, my sister Monica and I and our friends Rata and Saira and all the kids gather after school to celebrate the solstice: to acknowledge the darkest day of the year and our end of the Earth's farthest tilt from the sun.[261] By now, Sam and I have been in Raglan almost five years, and back in New Zealand almost ten. My niece Skye now has a little sister, Rosie. For the first time in my adulthood, I am not scanning the horizon for my next move.

The day is overcast and wet, but next door, in Monica and Manu's warm kitchen, we dip wicks into fragrant beeswax to make slender, knobbly candles. When the rain eases, we venture out into the garden to collect botanical treasures and notice how the plants and animals are responding to the season's change. To me, celebrating these waypoints feels like a prompt to pay more attention to both the minute and the massive - to the subtle changes taking place at the level of a single plant, and to the fact we're all riding on a slanted spinning rock hurtling through the enormity of space.

We garner the apple tree's fallen golden leaves, the last red crab apples, undersized mandarins that Rata's daughter Ursie calls 'dolls' pumpkins', and the bright orange fruits of the native coprosma, karamū. We ate the last of the feijoas weeks ago, but the lemon trees are bowed with waxy yellow fruit. In Raglan's mild midwinter, there's still plenty of floral colour, too - the tiny violet pansies called Johnny jump-ups, porcelain-like lilies, and the nīkau's fountain of cream and lilac flower heads. On the feijoa trees, I'm surprised to already find a few pale sprays of fresh new leaves.

The rain starts again in earnest. Under an umbrella, Amalia is making her own leaf arrangement on the driveway. Inside, the younger kids weave the fruits, flowers and leaves into the dry willow wreath we made in the spring for another festivity. We talk about the winter season, sing a song, light our homemade candles and blow them out together.

Afterwards, the clouds clear right on dusk to reveal a slender crescent moon cupping bright Venus, and blackbirds and silvereyes sing into the gathering dark. In three weeks' time, Matariki – the Pleiades or Seven Sisters constellation – will peer over the horizon, signalling the beginning of the Māori New Year, and celebrated, for the second time ever, with a national holiday.[262] In a few months more, the pīpīwharauroa – the shining cuckoo – will return, and I'll listen for its high, piercing glissando from the eucalypts ringing the paddock.

A while after that, the feijoas will flower. Come autumn, I will again sit under a tree with a spoon and a knife, and eat a bucketful of feijoas in one sitting with my rascal daughters and nieces – their small tanned bodies sticky with juice, the tiny seeds caught between our teeth, the fragrant scent permeating our brains and entwining with synapses in our amygdalas, becoming the taste of home.

What does it mean for me, a Pākehā, to call this place home? In New Zealand, it's becoming common to say a pepeha as an introduction in formal settings: a way to put oneself in context and to make connections. Māori typically introduce themselves by explaining their whakapapa – their ancestry and lines of descent – and speaking of the rivers and mountains of their ancestral lands. Other New Zealanders are learning their pepeha, too. In their classes at school, our children have been encouraged to name the mountain, Karioi, and the harbour, Whāingaroa, that enfold our small community of Raglan between them. But some Māori consider it presumptive to claim a deep connection with a place after only being there a few years, even a few generations, and I can understand that. Living in the shadow of a mountain or beside a river is not the same as viewing it as an ancestor.

My own forebears first arrived in New Zealand within a few years of the feijoa, in the early twentieth century. They came from the four corners of the British Isles – the Welsh borders, tiny Scottish islands, smallholder farms in southern England, a town in western Ireland. The great-great-grandmother I'm named after was born in London and lived for a time on the Indian Ocean island of Mauritius before moving to Queensland. I've barely visited any of these places, and while I'm curious about them, none are anchored in my soul. These Pacific islands are the only real home I've ever known. If I am to belong anywhere, it is here.

And yet Pākehā identity and land connection isn't straightforward. Myself and my ancestors are relative newcomers who have benefitted from the historical and continuing marginalisation of Māori. I can't belong to this land in the same way that Joe McLeod does. Māori have tūrangawaewae – a 'place to stand', a deep affiliation to a place or marae based on their genealogical links and continued presence: Joe doesn't live in Maungapōhatu, but it's the home of his tūpuna, and he returns often to show his face and contribute to important events, like the reopening of the meeting house.[263] Pākehā tūrangawaewae, on the other hand, writes University of Auckland English professor Alex Calder, is an oxymoron – 'the sort of belonging you have when you don't have tūrangawaewae. We Pākehā are at home here, we identify as New Zealanders, this is our place, we belong – and yet, without denying any of those things, there is another degree of belonging that we do not have that is available to Māori.'[264]

In *Braiding Sweetgrass*, Robin Wall Kimmerer wonders whether non-Indigenous Americans can ever become 'indigenous to place', as a way to ground themselves in the landscape, forge a healthier relationship with nature, and make a true home where they live.[265] Ultimately, though, she realises that settlers cannot, by definition, be Indigenous.

> Indigenous is a birth-right word. No amount of time or caring changes history or substitutes for soul-deep fusion with the land ... But if people do not feel 'indigenous', can they nevertheless enter into the deep reciprocity that renews the world? Is this something that can be learned?[266]

I want to hope so. Plants are our oldest teachers, Kimmerer reminds us. She decides instead that the settler's task is to become 'naturalised to place', as some plants do: 'to live as if your children's future matters, to take care of the land as if our lives and the lives of all our relatives depend on it. Because they do.'[267]

Does the feijoa have anything to teach me, and other Pākehā New Zealanders, about belonging? After a century in our gardens, it does belong here. It is unselfish, a good visitor, and has not tried to dominate native ecosystems. It is a part of our nation's story. And yet it does not belong here as deeply or in the same way as the kauri tree and the harakeke, the pōhutukawa and the tōī. It does not belong here the way it belongs to South America. The metaphor, perhaps, only stretches so far – plants, for all their agency, are not the same as people.

What it means to belong to Aotearoa as a Pākehā is something I and others will continue to wrestle with. But while tūrangawaewae might not be mine to claim, perhaps – as an Evans – I can aspire to a somewhat similar concept from Wales and the Welsh language, another 'untranslatable' word: cynefin.

I first heard of cynefin – pronounced kuh-neh-vin – on the British podcast Folk on Foot.[268] It originally referred to the habitual tracks worn by sheep and cattle into the hillsides, and is sometimes translated as 'habitat'. But according to the Welsh folk musician Owen Shiers, the word evokes much more: 'a very personal sense of place, belonging and familiarity' encompassing both the cultural and natural landscape.[269] A relationship of love, habit and close attention to a place, though not necessarily indigeneity.

For Shiers, cynefin is a conscious practice, an 'invitation to habituate ourselves with a place ... wherever we might happen to find ourselves. I see it as a skill to labour at, with as much dedication and commitment as we might as with a relationship or a job. Perhaps it's a vocation given to all of us, whether we realise it or not.'[270] Shiers' writings led me to another British writer and storyteller, Martin Shaw, who talks about trading the 'scatterling' culture of the everywhere person to instead find the place that has claimed you – learning to be *of* a place rather than simply *from* it.[271]

I'm starting to realise that this is going to be a lifelong project. For now, I'm working on noticing and nourishing my cynefin. It's composed of many things – the smell of native bush after rain, the way the evening light falls on Mount Karioi or the islands off Leigh, and the whirring of a kererū's wings in the pūriri tree near the deck. The daily cycles of the tides in the harbour and at the surf beach, and the longer cycles of the godwits and cuckoos returning and departing. The high voices of our growing children, and the even faster growth of the kauri and kahikatea trees planted above their respective placentas in Raglan and in

Leigh. The feeling of bare feet in wet grass. And the taste of a ripe feijoa on the first cool morning of autumn.

In paying this kind of deep attention to the feijoa tree out my window, I've been honing my sense of home. But at the same time, my plant-based investigations have brought the wide world closer. Every day, the sight of that tree gives my heart a barely perceptible jolt, a reminder of the invisible tangle of roots connecting the plant in our garden to the farthest-flung corners of the Earth, to powerful historical forces, to people I have loved meeting but may never see again. I think of the epic journey it took to get here – the choices that shaped it, the chances, the coincidences. 'When you gaze deep enough into the local, you find the nomad', writes Shaw.

It reminds me of a song by the Uruguayan musician Jorge Drexler, 'Movimiento'.[272] None of us are really completely from one place, and all of us are a little bit from everywhere, he sings:

> Nunca estamos quietos
> Somos trashumantes, somos
> Padres, hijos, nietos y bisnietos de inmigrantes'
>
> We are never still
> We are nomads ... we are
> Parents, children, grandchildren and great-grandchildren of immigrants.

All of us have an ancestor that once left a homeland and moved somewhere else. The human story is one of migration, and it's also one of deep attachment to place. Scatterlings and homecomings. Everywhere and somewhere. The minute and the massive. The hearth *and* the wild.

I'm learning that I don't have to choose one or the other; that

I can remain in motion while also being anchored to place. To deeply love this land, to make a home in this one specific corner of the world, while still remaining in conversation – in cross-pollination – with the vastness and beauty of the whole.

―

The feijoa had one last surprise in store for us. As I pored over genetics and taxonomy papers, checking I'd correctly understand the feijoa's evolution, a word jumped out at me that I'd missed the first time. It was a familiar one: Zealandia.

From my previous science reporting, I knew that Zealandia was an ancient landmass that once stretched all the way to New Caledonia from what is now New Zealand. It was recently recognised as the Earth's eighth continent, even though most of it is currently underwater. The feijoa's whānau, the dozens of South American fruiting Myrtaceae species – the juicy red pitanga that grew in Laura's Uruguayan orchard, the bright yellow uvaia Juan and Lido shook down from the tree for me, the jaboticaba with the funny black fruits protruding from its trunk – they all descend from a common ancestor that lived around 40 million years ago and independently evolved the ability to make fleshy, delicious fruits.

When botanists lined up the fossil, genetic and biogeographic evidence, the answer was clear: that ancient feijoa ancestor originated in Zealandia, before spreading across the Gondwanan supercontinent and into South America, where it diverged over millions of years into the myriad forms seen today.

Just like us, the feijoa has always been on the move. And if you trace its whakapapa way, way back – 40 million years or so, around the time the first canines and whales evolved,[273] and monkeys colonised South America – you could say it comes from New Zealand after all.

Endnotes

1. 'Fruits of the Future', *Hastings Standard*, 6 May 1912.
2. Michael Pollan, *The Botany of Desire: A Plant's-eye View of the World* (Bloomsbury, London, 2003), p. xx.
3. Raglan's original Māori name was Whāingaroa village, referring to the adjacent harbour. That name means 'the long pursuit' and refers to the lengthy search of the *Tainui* waka (canoe) for a place to call home. In 1858 it was renamed after Field Marshal FitzRoy James Henry Somerset, 1st Baron Raglan – a British commander in the Crimean War, who never visited. Locals are increasingly calling the town Whāingaroa, but it's so widely known as Raglan that, for now, I'll use that name.
4. John Mulgan, *Report on Experience* (first published 1947; Blackwood & Janet Paul Ltd, Auckland, 1967), pp. 3-4 (https://teara.govt.nz/en/kiwis-overseas/page-1).
5. This line is frequently misquoted on the internet as: 'When one tugs at a single thing in nature, he finds it attached to the rest of the world.' Muir never said that! The original version as given here comes from his book *My First Summer in the Sierra* (Houghton Mifflin, Boston and New York, 1911), p. 211.
6. My sister Monica has told the amazing story of this cabin in a beautiful essay in *North & South* magazine: Monica Evans, 'Follow Her Home', *North & South*, January 2023 (https://northandsouth.co.nz/2023/04/30/follow-her-home/).
7. The terms 'anywhere person' and 'somewhere person' were coined by the British journalist David Goodhart who uses them to describe a political divide between conservative small-town Brexit-voting 'Somewheres' and footloose urban 'Anywheres' – but I think the words can be separated from that specific political context. David Goodhart, *Road to Somewhere: The Populist Revolt and the Future of Politics*, Hurst Publishers (2017). Another term I love is Martin Shaw's 'scattering culture' for the globalised: Martin Shaw, *Scatterlings: Getting Claimed in the Age of Amnesia* (White Cloud Press, Ashland, OR, 2016). More on that in the epilogue.
8. Edward S. Casey, 'How to Get from Space to Place in a Fairly Short Stretch of Time: Phenomenological Prolegomena', in Steven Feld and Keith H. Basso (eds), *Senses of Place* (School of American Research Press, Santa Fe, NM; distributed by the University of Washington Press, 1996), pp. 13-52, at pp. 33-34.

9 I'm very grateful to Eve Lucas from Kew Gardens in London for her patience in explaining the evolution and taxonomy of the Myrtaceae, or myrtle family. See Thais Vasconcelos, Carolyn E. B. Proença, Berhaman Ahmad, Daniel S. Aguilar, Reinaldo Aguilar, Bruno S. Amorim, Keron Campbell, et al., 'Myrteae phylogeny, calibration, biogeography and diversification patterns: Increased understanding in the most species rich tribe of Myrtaceae', *Molecular Phylogenetics and Evolution* 109 (2017): 113-137 (https://doi.org/10.1016/j.ympev.2017.01.002).

10 Herculano M. F. Alvarenga and Elizabeth Höfling, 'Systematic revision of the Phorusrhacidae (Aves: Ralliformes)', *Papéis Avulsos de Zoologia* 43, no. 4 (2003): 55-91 (https://doi.org/doi:10.1590/S0031-10492003000400001).

11 You might know the feijoa as *Acca sellowiana* – and yes, that was its official Latin name from 1941 to 2019. Before then, as Chapter 9 explains, it was called *Feijoa sellowiana*. But during World War Two, German botanist Max Burret decided that the similarities between the flowers and leaves of the feijoa and those of *Acca lanuginosa* – a rare shrub from the Peruvian Andes – meant that they belonged in the same genus. Because *Acca* was the older name, this meant *Feijoa* had to go. However, years of analysis of the Myrtaceae group of plants by Eve Lucas and other botanists at Kew Gardens has unravelled the family tree. Their genetic results showed that *Acca lanuginosa* and another more recently discovered Andean species, *Acca macrostema*, were not as closely related to the feijoa as Burret had thought. That led the Kew team in 2019 to reclassify the feijoa. Its official scientific name is now, again, *Feijoa sellowiana* – the only species in its genus. I like to think that makes it extra special. See Eve J. Lucas, Bruce Holst, Marcos Sobral, Fiorella F. Mazine, Eimear M. Nic Lughadha, Carolyn E. Barnes Proença, Itayguara Ribeiro da Costa and Thais N. C. Vasconcelos, 'A New Subtribal Classification of Tribe Myrteae (Myrtaceae)', *Systematic Botany* 44, no. 3 (2019): 560-569 (https://doi.org/10.1600/036364419X15620113920608).

12 Ed Biffin, Eve J. Lucas, Lyn A. Craven, Itayguara Ribeiro da Costa, Mark G. Harrington and Michael D. Crisp, 'Evolution of exceptional species richness among lineages of fleshy-fruited Myrtaceae', *Annals of Botany* 106, no. 1 (2010): 79-93 (https://doi.org/10.1093/aob/mcq088).

13 Mauro Galetti, Roger Guevara, Marina C. Côrtes, Rodrigo Fadini, Sandro Von Matter, Abraão B. Leite, Fábio Labecca et al., 'Functional Extinction of Birds Drives Rapid Evolutionary Changes in Seed Size', *Science* 340, no. 6136 (2013): 1086-1090 (https://doi.org/10.1126/science.1233774).

14 Juliano André Bogoni, Maurício Eduardo Graipel and Nivaldo Peroni, 'The ecological footprint of *Acca sellowiana* domestication maintains the residual vertebrate diversity in threatened highlands of Atlantic Forest', *PLOS ONE* 13, no. 4 (2018): e0195199 (https://doi.org/10.1371/journal.pone.0195199).

15 Paul Knuth, Hermann Müller and James Richard Ainsworth Davis, *Handbook of Flower Pollination Based upon Hermann Müller's Work 'The Fertilisation of Flowers by Insects'* (Clarendon Press, Oxford, 1906), p. 74 (https://archive.org/details/handbookofflower01knutuoft).

16 Fritz Müller, 'Feijoa, ein Baum, der Vögeln seine Blumenblätter als Lockspeise bietet (Feijoa, a tree that offers its petals as bait for birds)', *Kosmos* 18–19 (1886): 7

17 For the feijoa rat study, see Carlos A. Matallana-Puerto and João Custódio Fernandes Cardoso, 'Ratatouille of flowers! Rats as potential pollinators of a petal-rewarding plant in the urban area', *Ecology* 103, no. 9 (2022). The idea of rats acting as pollinators at all was considered so unusual that the study made the *New York Times* – although in 2011, New Zealand researchers had already found that rats here have taken over the job of pollinating pōhutukawa, rewarewa and hebe from locally extinct birds, bats and geckos: David E. Pattemore and David S. Wilcove, 'Invasive rats and recent colonist birds partially compensate for the loss of endemic New Zealand pollinators', *Proceedings of the Royal Society B: Biological Sciences* 279, no. 1733 (2011): 1597–1605 (https://doi.org/10.1098/rspb.2011.2036).

18 Brazil nut trees also rely on another forest-dweller, a large rodent called the agouti, to crack open their heavy seed pods and disperse the seeds within. See 'No Rainforest, No Brazil Nuts', *Encyclopaedia Britannica*, n.d. (https://www.britannica.com/topic/mutualism-1673060).

19 For more information on the animals involved in feijoa pollination in different places, see Fernando Ramírez and Jose Kallarackal, 'Feijoa [*Acca sellowiana* (O. Berg) Burret] pollination: A review', *Scientia Horticulturae* 226 (2017): 333–341 (https://doi.org/10.1016/j.scienta.2017.08.054); J. P. H. J. Ducroquet and E. R. Hickel, 'Birds as pollinators of feijoa (*Acca sellowiana* Berg)', *Acta Horticulturae* 452 (1997): 37–40 (https://doi.org/10.17660/ActaHortic.1997.452.5); R. H. Sharpe, W. B. Sherman and E. P. Miller, 'Feijoa History and Improvement', *Proceedings of Florida State Horticulture Society* 106 (1993): 134–139. Nodari's student Fernando Sánchez Mora sent me a photograph of a toucan perched on a flowering feijoa.

20 J. E. Taylor, FLS and FGS, 'NOTES ON POPULAR SCIENCE', *The Australasian*, 24 July 1886 (http://nla.gov.au/nla.news-article142435344).

21 Anne Margaret Stewart, 'Reproductive biology and pollination ecology of Feijoa Sellowiana' (PhD thesis, University of Auckland, 1987) (https://researchspace.auckland.ac.nz/handle/2292/1728).

22 María Gabriela Nadra, Norberto Pedro Giannini, Juan Manuel Acosta and Lone Aagesen, 'Evolution of pollination by frugivorous birds in Neotropical Myrtaceae', *PeerJ* 6 (2018): e5426 (https://doi.org/10.7717/peerj.5426).

23 For the full story of the Atlantic Forest's origins and destruction, see Warren Dean's wonderful environmental history *With Broadax and Firebrand: The Destruction of the Brazilian Atlantic Forest* (University of California Press, Berkeley, 1997).

24 I wrote more about this amazing family of plants here: Kate Evans, 'Araucariaceae: The ancient giants that are the world's rarest trees', *Landscape News*, 2 July 2020 (https://news.globallandscapesforum.org/45489/araucariaceae-the-ancient-giants-that-are-the-worlds-rarest-trees/).

25 In one sauropod bone-bed in Wyoming, palaeontologists unearthed a large number of araucaria fossils – they were the most common plant found there: Nicole Klein, Kristian Remes, Carole T. Gee and P. Martin Sander (eds), *Biology of the Sauropod Dinosaurs: Understanding the Life of Giants* (Indiana University Press, Bloomington, IN, 2011). Scientists also tested the nutritional quality of ancient plant types and mimicked how long they would take to pass through a dinosaur's gut: Jürgen Hummel, Carole T. Gee, Karl-Heinz Südekum, P. Martin Sander, Gunther Nogge and Marcus Clauss, '*In vitro* digestibility of fern and gymnosperm foliage: Implications for sauropod feeding ecology and diet selection', *Proceedings of the Royal Society B: Biological Sciences* 275, no. 1638 (2008): 1015–1021 (https://royalsocietypublishing.org/doi/abs/10.1098/rspb.2007.1728). For more on South America's giant 70-tonne sauropods, see José L. Carballido, Diego Pol, Alejandro Otero, Ignacio A. Cerda, Leonardo Salgado, Alberto C. Garrido, Jahandar Ramezani, Néstor R. Cúneo and Javier M. Krause, 'A new giant titanosaur sheds light on body mass evolution among sauropod dinosaurs', *Proceedings of the Royal Society B: Biological Sciences* 284, no. 1860 (2017): 20171219 (https://doi.org/10.1098/rspb.2017.1219).

26 Michael P. Branch (ed.), *John Muir's Last Journey: South to the Amazon and East to Africa* (Island Press, Washington, DC, 2001), p. 83; Donald Worster, *A Passion for Nature: The Life of John Muir* (Oxford University Press, New York, 2008), p. 88.

27 Eunice Sueli Nodari, Miguel Mundstock Xavier de Carvalho and Paulo Afonso Zarth, *Fronteiras Fluidas: Florestas Com Araucárias Na América Meridional* (Oikos, São Leopoldo, 2018).

28 Oliver J. Wilson, Richard J. Walters, Francis E. Mayle, Débora V. Lingner and Alexander C. Vibrans, 'Cold spot microrefugia hold the key to survival for Brazil's Critically Endangered Araucaria Tree', *Global Change Biology* 25, no. 12 (2019): 4339–4351 (https://doi.org/10.1111/gcb.14755).

29 The Covid-19 pandemic would problematise this long-held custom. In 2020, government vehicles fitted with loudspeakers exhorted Uruguayans to stop sharing mate, in a bid to reduce the spread of the virus. See Lola Mendez, 'How Coronavirus Is Changing Mateando Culture in the Southern Cone', *Culture Trip*, 19 May 2020 (https://theculturetrip.com/theculturetrip.com/south-america/uruguay/articles/how-coronavirus-is-changing-mateando-culture-in-the-southern-cone/).

30 For more on the Southern Proto-Jê, see José Iriarte, Paulo DeBlasis, Jonas Gregorio De Souza and Rafael Corteletti, 'Emergent Complexity, Changing Landscapes, and Spheres of Interaction in Southeastern South America During the Middle and Late Holocene', *Journal of Archaeological Research* 25, no. 3 (2017): 251–313 (https://doi.org/10.1007/s10814-016-9100-0); Jonas Gregorio De Souza, 'Linguistics, archaeology, and the histories of language spread: the case of the Southern Jê languages, Brazil', *Cadernos de Etnolingüística* 3, no. 2 (2011): 1–16; Philip Riris and Rafael Corteletti, 'A New Record of Pre-Columbian Engravings

in Urubici (SC), Brazil using Polynomial Texture Mapping', *Internet Archaeology*, no. 38 (2015) (https://doi.org/10.11141/ia.38.7). On the pit houses, see Jonas Gregorio de Souza, Mark Robinson, Rafael Corteletti, Macarena Lucia Cárdenas, Sidnei Wolf, José Iriarte, Francis Mayle and Paulo DeBlasis, 'Understanding the Chronology and Occupation Dynamics of Oversized Pit Houses in the Southern Brazilian Highlands', *PLOS ONE* 11, no. 7 (2016): e0158127 (https://doi.org/10.1371/journal.pone.0158127). On this particular archaeological site, see Pedro Ignácio Schmitz, Jairo Henrique Rogge, Raul Novasco, Natália Machado Mergen and Suliano Ferrasso, 'Rincão dos Albinos − Um grande sítio Jê Meridional', *Pesquisas Antropologia* 70 (2013): 65–131 (https://www.researchgate.net/publication/312557873_Rincao_dos_Albinos_-_Um_grande_sitio_Je_Meridional).

31 Mark Robinson, José Iriarte, Jonas Gregorio De Souza, Oscar Marozzi and Rita Scheel-Ybert, 'Moiety specific wood selection in funerary ritual for the southern proto-Jê', *Journal of Archaeological Science: Reports* 11 (2017): 237–244 (https://doi.org/10.1016/j.jasrep.2016.11.047).

32 For more on this ritual, see Robert R. Crépeau, 'Exchange, Reciprocity and Social Dualism according to the Kaingang of Southern Brazil', *Cosmos* 26 (2010): 103–126.

33 Robinson et al., 'Moiety specific wood selection in funerary ritual for the southern proto-Jê'.

34 This bizarre botanical habit is known as 'cauliflory', meaning stem-flowers. Cauliflowers, however, are not cauliflorous!

35 S. Yoshi Maezumi, Daiana Alves, Mark Robinson, Jonas Gregorio de Souza, Carolina Levis, Robert L. Barnett, Edemar Almeida de Oliveira, Dunia Urrego, Denise Schaan and José Iriarte, 'The legacy of 4,500 years of polyculture agroforestry in the eastern Amazon', *Nature Plants* 4, no. 8 (2018): 540–547 (https://doi.org/10.1038/s41477-018-0205-y). Learning this got me obsessed with Amazon archaeology and I went on to write a bunch of articles about it.

36 Mark Robinson, Jonas Gregorio De Souza, S. Yoshi Maezumi, Macarena Cárdenas, Luiz Pessenda, Keith Prufer, Rafael Corteletti et al., 'Uncoupling human and climate drivers of late Holocene vegetation change in southern Brazil', *Scientific Reports* 8, no. 1 (2018): 7800 (https://doi.org/10.1038/s41598-018-24429-5).

37 This history is drawn from Warren Dean, *With Broadax and Firebrand*, pp. 41–45. Only 7 per cent of the Atlantic Forest remains, and brazilwood is now so rare it is protected by the Convention on International Trade in Endangered Species of Wild Fauna and Flora (CITES), though illegal logging still takes place.

38 CARTA RÉGIA DE 5 DE NOVEMBRO DE 1808 Coleção de Leis do Império do Brasil: 1808, vol. 1, p. 156.

39 This Kaingang history is drawn from Ricardo Cid Fernandes and Paulo Roberto Homem de Góes, 'Kaingang ethnic territories', *Vibrant − Virtual Brazilian Anthropology* 15, no. 2 (2018) (http://www.scielo.br/scielo.php?script=sci_arttext&pid=S1809-43412018000200407).

40 This information is drawn from Lido's thesis (in Portuguese): Lido José Borsuk, 'Avaliação da diversidade genética e morfológica da goiabeira-serrana (Acca sellowiana (O. Berg) Burret) em terras indígenas, áreas quilombolas e em unidades de conservação no sul do Brasil e acesso ao conhecimento tradicional associado ao uso e manejo da espécie' (Universidade Federal de Santa Catarina, 2018).
41 Jeremy Warne helped me to translate my tape of the conversations in Portuguese at the quilombo.
42 Tom Phillips, 'Brazilian slave port ruins unearthed in Rio's Olympic facelift', *The Guardian*, 4 March 2011 (https://www.theguardian.com/world/2011/mar/04/archaeologists-find-slave-port).
43 Matthias Röhrig Assunção, *Capoeira: The History of an Afro-Brazilian Martial Art* (Routledge, London, 2005), especially Chapter 2.
44 R. K. Kent, 'Palmares: An African State in Brazil', *The Journal of African History* 6, no. 2 (1965): 161–175.
45 Some of the history of the quilombo is told (in Portuguese) in Lidiane Taffarel, *Invernada dos Negros: História e Luta de Uma Comunidade Negra Rural* (UFFS Editora, Brasil, 2022).
46 According to Lido's thesis (see note 40 above), in communities where domestic animals grazed under the fruit trees, only 3.9 per cent reported fruit-fly problems, while in other areas it was more than 20 per cent.
47 Lai Yeap Foo and Ronald Ross Watson (inventors), US Patent for Feijoa fruit extract (Patent # 11,065,292), filed 1 November 2018, issued 20 July 2021 (https://patents.justia.com/patent/11065292).
48 Danielle Silva, 'Biopiracy: The largely lawless plundering of Earth's genetic wealth', *Landscape News*, 15 December 2020 (https://news.globallandscapesforum.org/48905/biopiracy-the-largely-lawless-plundering-of-earths-genetic-wealth/).
49 Queensland Government, 'Traditional knowledge and biodiscovery', updated 30 September 2022 (https://environment.des.qld.gov.au/licences-permits/plants-animals/biodiscovery/traditional-knowledge).
50 Grant Thorp, 'DSIR's feijoa breeding programme goes to South America', *The Orchardist of New Zealand* 61, no. 7 (1988): 213–215.
51 My mother has independently discovered that cows love feijoas. She tries to control the fruit pest guava moth by feeding all the fallen fruit to her herd—something the cows are very happy about!
52 Friedrich Sellow's expedition report 10, 24 March 1828. Transcribed by Ulrich Moritz and Carsten Eckert, and translated from the German by Veronika Meduna.
53 Peter Hein searched a botanical database for me and found 465 plant species with names like sellowianum, sellowii, and sellowiana, as well as three genera: Selloa, Sellocharis, and Sellowia. Lotte Burkhardt, *Verzeichnis eponymischer Pflanzennamen [Index of Eponymic Plant Names]*, Berlin: Botanic Garden and Botanical Museum Berlin (2016) http://dx.doi.org/10.3372/epolist2016
54 Sellow's story from Potsdam to Brazil is mainly drawn from Sabine Hackethal's writings (in German), especially Sabine Hackethal and

Frank Tillack, 'Im Auftrag Preußens: Friedrich Sellow in Brasilien (1814-1831)', in A. Kwet and M. Niekisch (eds), *Amphibien und Reptilien der Neotropis: Entdeckungen deutschsprachiger Forscher in Mittel- und Südamerika - Mertensiella* 23 (2016): 64-79; and Hans Zischler, Sabine Hackethal and Carsten Eckert (eds), *Die Erkundung Brasiliens: Friedrich Sellows unvollendete Reise* (Galliani, Berlin, 2013).

55 Sabine Hackethal, 'Wenn er seine Reise hätte vollenden können', in Hans Zischler, Sabine Hackethal and Carsten Eckert (eds), *Die Erkundung Brasiliens* (2013): 216

56 Humboldt's story is drawn from Andrea Wulf, *The Invention of Nature: The Adventures of Alexander von Humboldt, the Lost Hero of Science* (John Murray, London, 2015).

57 Pedro Moraes, 'The Brazilian herbarium of Maximilian, Prince of Wied', *Neodiversity* 4 (2009): 16-51 (http://neodiversity.org/showarticle/17).

58 Paulo E. Vanzolini and Charles W. Myers, 'The Herpetological Collection of Maximilian, Prince of Wied (1782-1867), With Special Reference To Brazilian Materials', *Bulletin of the American Museum of Natural History* 395 (2015) p. 8-9. (https://doi.org/10.1206/910.1)

59 Except where indicated otherwise, Wied's journey is drawn from his diaries: Prince Maximilian Neuwied, *Travels in Brazil in the Years 1815, 1816, 1817* (Printed for Sir Richard Phillipps, and Co., Bride Court, Bridge Street, London, 1820), p. 10.

60 Ibid.

61 Moraes, 'The Brazilian herbarium of Maximilian, Prince of Wied'.

62 Myrian Sepúlveda dos Santos, 'Naturalists in Nineteenth-Century Brazil', *Archiv Weltmuseum Wien* 63-64 (2013-2014): 38-59.

63 Neuwied, *Travels in Brazil in the Years 1815, 1816, 1817*, p. 20.

64 Hackethal and Tillack, 'Im Auftrag Preußens: Friedrich Sellow in Brasilien (1814-1831)' (2016). Translated by Veronika Meduna.

65 Details about Sellow's Uruguayan expeditions come from Nelson Papavero, *Essays on the history of Neotropical Dipterology: with special reference to collectors (1750-1905)*, vol. I (Museu de Zoologia, Universidade de São Paulo, 1971) (https://www.biodiversitylibrary.org/bibliography/101715).

66 H. Walter Lack, 'Sellow und die Brasilianische Guave', in Hans Zischler, Sabine Hackethal and Carsten Eckert (eds), *Die Erkundung Brasiliens: Friedrich Sellows unvollendete Reise* (Galliani, Berlin, 2013), pp. 144-49.

67 Pedro Escobar García, Astrid Hille, Eve Lucas and Heimo Rainer, 'The Otto C. Berg Types at the Natural History Museum, Vienna', *Phytotaxa* 228, no. 1 (2015): 1-66 (https://doi.org/10.11646/phytotaxa.228.1.1).

68 Berg was Prussian, too, and was born in Stettin in 1815, the same year Sellow set off on his Brazilian expedition.

69 Joseph Dalton Hooker, 'FEIJOA Sellowiana, Berg. Native of S. Brasil and Uruguay', *Curtis's Botanical Magazine* 124 (1898) (https://www.biodiversitylibrary.org/item/14252).

70 David Notton and Christopher Stringer, *Who is the type of Homo sapiens?*: International Commission on Zoological Nomenclature (2010).

71. E. D. Merrill, 'Destruction of the Berlin Herbarium', *Science* 98, no. 2553 (1943): 490-491, at p. 490. (https://doi.org/10.1126/science.98.2553.490).
72. It already has: in 2016, India's National Museum of Natural History was destroyed in a fire; and in 2018, Rio de Janeiro's National Museum burned to the ground, obliterating 20 million artefacts, including some of Sellow's collections.
73. K. J. Willis, *State of the World's Plants 2017* (Royal Botanic Gardens, Kew, 2017).
74. Friedrich Sellow's expedition report 4, 1-11 January 1826, Rio Grande do Sul. Transcribed by Ulrich Moritz and Carsten Eckert, and translated from the German by Anke Richter.
75. Friedrich Sellow's expedition report 2, 30 September to 29 October 1825, Rio Grande do Sul; Friedrich Sellow's expedition report 4. Transcribed by Ulrich Moritz and Carsten Eckert, and translated from the German by Veronika Meduna and Anke Richter.
76. Eleanor Byrne, 'The Globalised Garden: Jamaica Kincaid's Postcolonial Gothic', *Wagadu: A Journal of Transnational Women's and Gender Studies* 19 (2018): 77-90, at p. 83.
77. Ibid., p. 84.
78. Jamaica Kincaid, 'The Disturbances of the Garden', *The New Yorker*, 31 August 2020 (https://www.newyorker.com/magazine/2020/09/07/the-disturbances-of-the-garden).
79. Frederic Rosengarten, Jr, *Wilson Popenoe: Agricultural Explorer, Educator and Friend of Latin America* (National Tropical Botanical Garden, Lanai, 1991), p. 10.
80. Alex Fox, 'Sierra Club Grapples With Founder John Muir's Racism', *Smithsonian Magazine*, 24 July 2020 (https://www.smithsonianmag.com/smart-news/sierra-club-grapples-founder-john-muirs-racism-180975404/).
81. Charles Darwin, *The Voyage of the Beagle* (first published 1909; Cosimo, New York, 2008), pp. 218 and 234. See also 'Savages and Cannibals: Revisiting Charles Darwin's Voyage of the Beagle', *Emerge*, 27 May 2021 (http://www.whatisemerging.com/opinions/savages-and-cannibals).
82. Charlie Mitchell, 'Our Truth, Tā Mātou Pono: The New Zealanders and the genocide', *Stuff*, 13 February 2021 (https://www.stuff.co.nz/pou-tiaki/our-truth/300208816/our-truth-t-mtou-pono-the-new-zealanders-and-the-genocide).
83. Agustín Fuentes, '"The Descent of Man," 150 years on', *Science* 372, no. 6554 (2021): 769 (https://www.science.org/doi/abs/10.1126/science.abj4606).
84. Professor Alexandre Antonelli, 'It's time to re-examine the history of botanical collections', Royal Botanic Gardens, Kew, 25 June 2020 (https://www.kew.org/read-and-watch/time-to-re-examine-the-history-of-botanical-collections).
85. Ros Gray and Shela Sheikh, 'The coloniality of planting: Legacies of racism and slavery in the practice of botany', *The Architectural Review*, 27 January 2021 (https://www.architectural-review.com/essays/the-coloniality-of-planting).

86 I wrote about this proposal for *Scientific American*: Kate Evans, 'Change Species Names to Honor Indigenous Peoples, Not Colonizers, Researchers Say', *Scientific American*, 3 November 2020 (https://www.scientificamerican.com/article/change-species-names-to-honor-indigenous-peoples-not-colonizers-researchers-say/).

87 Sellow's day with the Charrúa is drawn directly from his diary, which is transcribed and appears verbatim in Sabine Hackethal's book (in German) about him. I used DeepL (an AI translator) to translate roughly to English. Veronika Meduna then corrected the translation of the parts I was most interested in. This is the technique I used for all German sources. Friedrich Sellow, 'Aus Friedrich Sellows Tagebüchern: Ein Tag bei den Charrúa', Hans Zischler, Sabine Hackethal and Carsten Eckert (eds), *Die Erkundung Brasiliens: Friedrich Sellows unvollendete Reise* (Galliani, Berlin, 2013), pp. 186-97.

88 Sellow used the Spanish word cabras. A footnote in Sellow (2013), p. 194 (in German) explains this was a nineteenth-century derogatory term for people of African and Indigenous origin.

89 For details about Sellow's death (in German), see Hackethal and Tillack, 'Im Auftrag Preußens: Friedrich Sellow in Brasilien (1814-1831)'.

90 Mario Campaña, 'La guerra de los charrúas', *Guaraguao* 8, no. 19 (2004): 141-164.

91 Stephanie Nolen, '"We are still here": The fight to be recognized as Indigenous in Uruguay', *The Globe and Mail*, 21 April 2018 (https://www.theglobeandmail.com/world/article-in-uruguay-indigenous-people-are-fighting-to-prove-they-exist/).

92 Alan Erbig Jeffrey, Jr, *Where Caciques and Mapmakers Met: Border Making in Eighteenth-Century South America* (University of North Carolina Press, Chapel Hill, 2020), p 161.

93 Their names have been spelled variously but I have followed Gustavo Verdesio, 'Un fantasma recorre el Uruguay: la reemergencia Charrúa en un "país sin indios" / A Spectre Is Haunting Uruguay: The Charrua Reemergence in "a Country without Indians"', *Cuadernos de Literatura* 18, no. 36 (2014): 86-107.

94 There is a wonderful line drawing of them here: Paul Rivet, 'Les Dernier Charruas', *Revista de la Sociedad 'Amigos de la Arqueologia'* (1930): 5-117.

95 David Christison, 'XXIII. A Journey in 1867 from Monte Video to San Jorge, in the Centre of Uruguay, with Remarks on the Vegetation of the Country', *Transactions of the Botanical Society of Edinburgh* 13, nos 1-4 (1879): 242-273 (https://doi.org/10.1080/03746607909468776).

96 The friend was Kristie Robinson, and I'm very glad she connected me with Laura! Chacra is a term from the Andes widely used in South America, it is a loanword from the Quechua chakra: 'farm, agricultural field, or land sown with seed.'

97 All three - the pitanga, arazá and guaviyú - are members of the Myrtaceae family of plants, just like the feijoa.

98 Laura Rosano, *Recetario de Frutos Nativos Del Uruguay* (MEC, Uruguay, 2012).

99 I am also deeply grateful to the Uruguayan feijoa researchers Danilo

Cabrera and Beatriz Vignale, feijoa grower Juan Carlos Burgogna, and farmer and 'New Zealand-o-phile' Julio Taborda, who all met with me that week in 2014, showed me plantations, and talked to me of feijoas in Uruguay.

100 For more on these global issues, see J. Bélanger and D. Pilling (eds), *The State of the World's Biodiversity for Food and Agriculture* (FAO Commission on Genetic Resources for Food and Agriculture Assessments, Rome, Italy, 2019), p. 114 (http://www.fao.org/3/CA3129EN/CA3129EN.pdf) and Bioversity International, *Mainstreaming Agrobiodiversity in Sustainable Food Systems: Scientific Foundations for an Agrobiodiversity Index* (Bioversity International, Rome, Italy, 2017).

101 Mónica's story is drawn from our interview and her thesis (in Spanish): Mónica Michelena, 'Mujeres Charrúas: Rearmando el Gran Quillapí de la Memoria en Uruguay' (Universidad Indígena Intercultural, Cartagena de Indias, Colombia, 2011).

102 This practice has become so common that in some New Zealand hospitals midwives give new mothers an ipu whenua, a special basket woven from harakeke (flax) leaves to take their placenta home in. Many non-Māori New Zealanders are adopting the practice, too. Sam and I, joined by my parents, buried our Amalia's placenta in Leigh under a kauri seedling, and Indigo's in Raglan under a kahikatea.

103 A much more detailed dictionary exists of a related language, Chaná, and – since their ancestors' original tongue seems truly lost – some Charrúa are trying to learn Chaná.

104 Uruguay's academics refused to take them seriously until Mónica herself became an anthropology student – now, one young Charrúa, Martín Delgado, has become the first Charrúa anthropologist.

105 Michelena, 'Mujeres Charrúas: Rearmando el Gran Quillapí de la Memoria en Uruguay', p. 45.

106 Robin Wall Kimmerer, *Gathering Moss: A Natural and Cultural History of Mosses* (Oregon State University Press, 2003), p. 13.

107 Marcos Nuñez, who carried out ethnobotanical research on the feijoa in that area in 2011, told me this in 2021. Other Argentinians confirmed it.

108 See note 11. Lucas, Holst, Sobral, Mazine, Nic Lughadha, Barnes Proença, Ribeiro da Costa and Vasconcelos, 'A New Subtribal Classification of Tribe Myrteae (Myrtaceae)'.

109 All information on Feijó comes from Magnus Roberto de Mello Pereira, translated by Ana Maria Rufino Gillies with assistance from Ian Robert Gillies, 'João da Silva Feijó (1760-1824): Brazilian Scientist in the Portuguese Overseas Empire', Chapter 11 in Karen Racine and Beatriz G. Mamigonian (eds), *The Human Tradition in the Atlantic World, 1500-1850* (Rowman & Littlefield Publishers, Inc., Lanham, MD, 2010), pp. 151-68.

110 Ibid., p. 152.

111 Information on Feijoó comes from 'An Essay on Woman, or, Physiological and Historical Defense of the Fair Sex', in Encyclopedia.com (https://www.encyclopedia.com/arts/culture-magazines/essay-woman-or-physiological-and-historical-defense-fair-sex).

112 Benito Jerónimo Feijoó y Montenegro, *An Essay on the Learning, Genius, and Abilities, of the Fair-Sex* (Printed for D. Steel, London, 1774) (https://archive.org/details/anessayonlearnioofeijgoog/page/n6/mode/2up). The following quotes are drawn from the Internet Archive source.

113 André's story is drawn from interviews with his great-granddaughter Florence André; as well as Edouard André, *L'Amérique equinoxiale: Colombie, Equateur, Pérou : 1875-1876* (Connaissance et Mémoires Européennes, Luxembourg, 1999) and Stéphanie de Courtois and Florence André, 'Édouard André (1840-1911): Cultural and botanical exchange between Europe and South America', *Studies in the History of Gardens & Designed Landscapes* 39, no. 3 (2019): 178-198 (https://doi.org/10.1080/14601176.2018.1494368).

114 In 1889, they were collected in a book in French, *L'Amérique equinoxiale: Colombie, Equateur, Pérou: 1875-1876* – his great-granddaughter Florence André gave me a copy.

115 André, *L'Amérique equinoxiale*, p. 342 (translated with Google Translate and DeepL, and checked by Salomé Serieys).

116 André was writing in the botanical magazine *Revue Horticole* which he edited, quoted in Courtois and André, 'Édouard André (1840-1911)', p 190.

117 Working out historic values is difficult and beset with inaccuracies, but a rough calculation can be made by converting to 1880s $US rates – both currencies were pegged to gold at the time – and then adjusting for inflation (https://ask.metafilter.com/275442/Historical-Value-of-French-Franc-in-comparison-to-US-dollar).

118 Courtois and André, 'Édouard André (1840-1911)', p. 196.

119 Ibid.

120 Michel Racine, Ernest J.-P. Boursier-Mougenot and Françoise Binet, *The Gardens of Provence and the French Riviera* (MIT Press, Cambridge, MA, 1987), p. 90 (http://archive.org/details/gardensofprovencooooraci).

121 Ibid., pp. 82, 92.

122 Guy de Maupassant, in ibid., p. 94.

123 Prosper Mérimée, in ibid., p. 92.

124 Tania Woloshyn, 'Zone of Transition: Visual Culture and National Regeneration on the French Riviera, c 1860-1900', in Tricia Cusack (ed.), *Art and Identity at the Water's Edge* (Routledge, UK, 2012), pp. 161-76.

125 K. A. Simpson, 'Hooker, Joseph Dalton', *Dictionary of New Zealand Biography*, first published in 1990, in Te Ara – the Encyclopedia of New Zealand (https://teara.govt.nz/en/biographies/1h33/hooker-joseph-dalton).

126 This was partly because of an error in the description of the feijoa's seeds in 1859's *Flora Brasiliensis*, which led Hooker to believe the plant wasn't a Myrtaceae. Joseph Dalton Hooker, 'FEIJOA Sellowiana, Berg. Native of S. Brasil and Uruguay', *Curtis's Botanical Magazine* 124 (1898) (https://www.biodiversitylibrary.org/item/14252).

127 Édouard André, 'Un Nouvel Arbre Frutier: Feijoa Sellowiana', *Revue Horticole* 70 (1898): 264-265. Translation of André's original article is from Anon., 'A New Fruiting Tree', *Sydney Mail and New South Wales Advertiser*, 22 October 1898.

128 Quoted in F. W. Popenoe, 'Feijoa Sellowiana; Its History, Culture and Varieties', *Pomona College Journal of Economic Botany* 2, no. 1 (1912): 217-242, at p. 238.
129 *The Gardeners' Chronicle* in *Scientific American Supplement*, 'Another New Fruit', no. 1205, 4 February 1899.
130 Grant Thorp and Rod Bieleski, *Feijoas: Origins, Cultivation and Uses* (HortResearch/David Bateman, Auckland, 2002).
131 Édouard André, 'Fructification du Feijoa Sellowiana', *Revue Horticole* (1905): 431.
132 Salomé Serieys translated my tape of the French conversations in André's garden between Florence, Brice and I.
133 Byrne, 'The Globalised Garden, p. 82.
134 Florence André-Olivier, 'Edouard André, créateur de jardins en Europe' (2008), p. 11. https://archives.touraine.fr/document/l-esprit-des-jardins
135 Racine, Boursier-Mougenot and Binet, *The Gardens of Provence and the French Riviera* p. 11 (http://archive.org/details/gardensofprovenc0000raci).
136 In a wonderful coincidence, the symbol of Occitania is a four-fold cross with dots around it: I think it looks just like a cut-open feijoa!
137 The term was coined by the French landscape gardener Gilles Clément. 'Plants and animals meet in new and unforeseen circumstances, not permitted spontaneously by geography. Butterflies, wind, seeds, people – everything communicates. The horizon is no longer the limit of our landscape,' he wrote in 2021. 'Nature is not at the service of man: we exist within her, submerged in her, intimately associated with her ... The ultimate goal of the planetary garden is to exploit diversity without destroying it, perpetuating the "planetary machine" and ensuring the existence of the garden – and hence the gardener.' Gilles Clément, 'In practice: Gilles Clément on the planetary garden', *The Architectural Review*, 16 February 2021 (https://www.architectural-review.com/essays/in-practice/in-practice-gilles-clement-on-the-planetary-garden).
138 I verified and added to the story Carolyn told me about Thomas Hanbury with the information I found here: Anita McConnell, 'Hanbury, Sir Thomas (1832-1907)', *Oxford Dictionary of National Biography*, published online 21 May 2009 (https://doi.org/10.1093/ref:odnb/54055).
139 Friedrich August Flückiger and Thomas Hanbury. *La Mortola: A Short Description of the Garden of Thomas Hanbury, Esq.* (privately printed, 1885) (http://archive.org/details/lamortolashortdeooflrich).
140 Cited in Elena Zappa and Mauro Mariotti, ALWIN BERGER, CURATOR OF THE HANBURY BOTANICAL GARDENS AT LA MORTOLA, Bollettino dei Musei e degli Istituti Biologici dell' Universitá de Genoa, v. 79, 2017, 53.
141 Alwin Berger, *Hortus Mortolensis: Enumeratio Plantarum in Horto Mortolensi Cultarum. Alphabetical Catalogue of Plants Growing in the Garden of the Late Sir Thomas Hanbury ... at La Mortola, Ventimiglia, Italy* (West, Newman & Co., London, 1912).

142 For the kiwifruit story, see John Merriman, 'Mother Gooseberry', *Orange Coast Magazine*, March 1995; for the avocado, Olga Khazan, 'The Selling of the Avocado: How the "alligator pear" went from obscure delicacy to America's favorite fruit', *The Atlantic*, 31 January 2015 (https://www.theatlantic.com/health/archive/2015/01/the-selling-of-the-avocado/385047/).
143 Frederick Wilson Popenoe, 'Dr. Fenzi's Contributions to American Horticulture: The Work of a Pioneer Plantsman in California', *Journal of Heredity* 13, no. 5 (1922): 215–220, at p. 215.
144 Frederick Wilson Popenoe, 'Doctor Franceschi on the Avocado', *California Avocado Society*, Yearbook 27 (1943): 64–66, at p. 64.
145 Four years earlier, Franceschi wrote to a contact that he had planted 150 fruit trees, with 'room…reserved for more.' Francesco Franceschi, 'To Miss Kate B Smith', 20 September 1904, 1/2, The Bancroft Library, UC Berkeley.
146 Susan Chamberlin writes that it is a myth that 'the property that became Montarioso was barren and arid before [Franceschi] arrived. This reflects the attitudes of East Coast and European observers who tended to view the winter-wet, summer-dry coastal California landscape as deficient and desert-like (not to mention lacking in fall color.)' Susan Chamberlin, 'The Life of Dr Franceschi and his Park', *Pacific Horticulture*, Winter 2002 (https://pacifichorticulture.org/articles/dr-francesco-franceschi-and-his-park/).
147 Popenoe, 'Dr. Fenzi's Contributions to American Horticulture', p. 215.
148 Ibid., p 217.
149 Francesco Franceschi, 'To Mr O. W. Barrett', 24 October 1905, 1/6, The Bancroft Library, UC Berkeley.
150 Francesco Franceschi, 'To Mr E. W. Scripps', 30 September 1904, 1/2, The Bancroft Library, UC Berkeley.
151 Thomas Jefferson, 'Summary of Public Service', Papers of Thomas Jefferson, after 2 September 1800, 124:32.
152 Francesco Franceschi, 'To Gen H. Strong', 20 January 1906, 1/8, The Bancroft Library, UC Berkeley.
153 Francesco Franceschi, 'To Sig. Domingo Basso', 17 April 1906, 1/9, The Bancroft Library, UC Berkeley.
154 Francesco Franceschi, 'Feijoa Sellowiana (Pineapple Guava)' (Montarioso Nursery, Santa Barbara, 1913).
155 Scott Way, 'Your Letter of Inquiry about My Feijoa…', 14 November 1905, Box 19, The Bancroft Library, UC Berkeley.
156 Thomas Morris Carnegie, 'To Dr F. Franceschi', 18 January 1908, Box 7, The Bancroft Library, UC Berkeley.
157 Popenoe's early life is drawn from his biography: Frederic Rosengarten, Jr, *Wilson Popenoe: Agricultural Explorer, Educator and Friend of Latin America* (National Tropical Botanical Garden, Lanai, 1991), p. 10.
158 Ibid., p. 11.
159 'Knowles A. Ryerson: Agriculture: Berkeley', University of California: In Memoriam, 1991, Online Archive of California,

UC History Digital Archives, pp. 179-182 (http://texts.cdlib.org/view?docId=hb4t1nb2bd&doc.view=frames&chunk.id=div00059&toc.depth=1&toc.id=).

160 Knowles A. Ryerson, 'Avocado Reminiscences: SOME EGOTISTICAL NOTES BY A TROPICAL TRAMP', *California Avocado Society*, Yearbook 27 (1943): 71-75, at p. 71.
161 Ibid.
162 Frederick Wilson Popenoe, 'Dr F. Franceschi', 11 October 1909, 70/11, The Bancroft Library, UC Berkeley.
163 Spanish-speakers today often use aguacate for avocado, but the word derives from the Nahuatl word ahuacatl, meaning testicle...for obvious reasons.
164 Frederick Wilson Popenoe, 'Dear Cam', 16 November 1911, Box 15, The Bancroft Library, UC Berkeley.
165 Frederick Wilson Popenoe, 'To Camillo Franceschi', 8 December 1911, Box 15, The Bancroft Library, UC Berkeley.
166 Ryerson, 'Avocado Reminiscences: SOME EGOTISTICAL NOTES BY A TROPICAL TRAMP', p. 71.
167 Frederick Wilson Popenoe, 'From Wilson Popenoe to Camillo Franceschi', 4 May 1911, Box 15, The Bancroft Library, UC Berkeley.
168 The images of Paul Popenoe and details of his visit to France are also from his brother's paper: F. W. Popenoe, 'Feijoa Sellowiana; Its History, Culture and Varieties', *Pomona College Journal of Economic Botany* 2, no. 1 (1912): 217-242.
169 Ibid., pp. 235, 222. Feijoa itself is Latin, a dead language that no-one's really sure how to pronounce. As explained in Chapter 9, the genus was named after the Portuguese naturalist Feijó, implying the Portuguese pronunciation 'fay-zho-a', as Popenoe says. However, Portuguese speakers have a different name for the fruit, and Feijó named himself after the Spanish monk Feijóo, which is pronounced 'Fay-ho-o'. So, I think you can pronounce it however you like!
170 Ibid., pp. 217, 223.
171 While making the final edits to this book in 2023, I learned Mark Albert had sadly passed away.
172 Jared Diamond, 'Evolution, consequences and future of plant and animal domestication', *Nature* 418, no. 6898 (2002): 700-707 (https://doi.org/10.1038/nature01019).
173 Glen Woodmansee has done a lot of work to trace the feijoa's early history in California, and I gratefully rely on his efforts throughout this section on Coolidge, in particular. Glen Woodmansee, 'Feijoa: The Beginning', *The Fruit Gardener: California Rate Fruit Growers*, June 2019.
174 Anon., 'Douglas William Coolidge', *California Avocado Society*, Yearbook 13 (1928): 94-95.
175 D. W. Coolidge, 'AVOCADO AND FEIJOA', *Pacific Rural Press*, 4 December 1909, California Digital Newspaper Collection (https://cdnc.ucr.edu/?a=d&d=PRP19091204.2.5.1&srpos=12&dliv=none&e=-------en--20-PRP-1--txt-txIN-feijoa-------1).

176   *Coolidge Rare Plant Gardens Catalogue* (Coolidge Rare Plant Gardens Inc., Pasadena, CA, 1914), pp. 3-4.
177   Woodmansee, 'Feijoa: The Beginning', p. 11.
178   George C. Roeding, *Roeding's Fruit Grower's Guide* (Geo. C. Roeding, Fresno, California, 1919), p. 76.
179   Woodmansee, 'Feijoa: The Beginning', pp. 9-10.
180   For the story of Dorothy's death, see Rosengarten, *Wilson Popenoe: Agricultural Explorer, Educator and Friend of Latin America*, p 109. For more on ackee poisoning, see John Rashford, 'Ackee Poisoning and the Evolutionary Biology of Jamaica's Ackee Motif', *Proceedings of the Caribbean Food Crops Society*, no. 32 (1996): 185-192.
181   Frederick Wilson Popenoe, *Manual of Tropical and Subtropical Fruits* (The Macmillan Co., New York, 1920).
182   Knowles Ryerson, 'That Popular Fruiting Ornamental, the Feijoa', *Los Angeles Times*, 6 April 1924 (Farm and Tractor Section).
183   Julia F. Morton, *Fruits of Warm Climates* (Florida Flair Books, Miami, FL, 1987), p. 367.
184   R.H. Sharpe, W.B. Sherman, and E.P. Miller, 'Feijoa History and Improvement', *Proceedings of Florida State Horticulture Society* 106 (1993): 134-39.
185   Interview with Geoff Ross, 15 October 2021
186   Still, along the state's coast, the feijoa is a favourite in the fruit-tree club Glen Woodmansee belongs to. He and his friends wanted to try growing the modern New Zealand varieties, so Glen travelled down under and attempted to bring some back in his luggage. The U.S. Department of Agriculture confiscated them all. The next year, he went to New Zealand again, and again brought back fifty feijoa plants. This time he washed every leaf and bagged them up separately, and they were allowed in. Glen gave them to the Huntington Arboretum, which created a special feijoa grove for them. The feijoa has come full circle across the Pacific, he told me - 'once developed by Coolidge and others, then improved by a hundred years of selection in New Zealand, now back to California to be enjoyed as a backyard tree'.
187   Thanks to Angela Alvarez on Instagram (@angela_alvarez_v) for this 'Colombianism'!
188   Letter from Frederick Wilson Popenoe to David Fairchild, Bogotá, 21 August 1920, p. 3 (of the letter). Digitised by the Hunt Institute for Botanical Documentation, Carnegie Mellon University, Pittsburgh, PA http://huntbot.org/findingaids/0204/204_Popenoe_Bx7FF93r.pdf
189   Most of this history is drawn from Wade Davis, *Magdalena: River of Dreams - A Story of Colombia* (The Bodley Head, London, 2020).
190   Gerhard Fischer, 'Ecofisiología, Crecimiento y Desarollo de la Feijoa', in Gerhard Fischer, Diego Miranda Lasprilla, Gerardo Cayón Salinas and Manuel Mazorra Agudelo (eds), *Cultivo, Poscosecha y Exportación de La Feijoa (Acca sellowiana Berg)* (Universidad Nacional de Colombia, Bogotá, 2003), p. 11.
191   Over Quintero Castillo, 'Selección de Cultivares, Manejo del Cultivo y Regulación de Cosechas de Feijoa', in Gerhard Fischer, Diego Miranda

Lasprilla, Gerardo Cayón Salinas and Manuel Mazorra Agudelo (eds), *Cultivo, Poscosecha y Exportación de La Feijoa (Acca sellowiana Berg)* (Universidad Nacional de Colombia, Bogotá, 2003), p. 50.

192 Gerhard Fischer and Alfonso Parra-Coronado, 'Influence of some environmental factors on the feijoa (Acca sellowiana [Berg] Burret): A review', *Agronomia Colombiana* 38, no. 3 (2020): 388-397 (https://doi.org/10.15446/agron.colomb.v38n3.88982).

193 DANE, *Encuesta Nacional Agropecuaria (ENA): Caracterización del productor, comercialización y riego* (Boletín Técnico, Encuesta Nacional Agropecuaria (ENA), Primer semestre 2019, Bogotá, 11 May 2020) (https://www.dane.gov.co/files/investigaciones/agropecuario/enda/ena/2019/boletin_ena_2019-I-caracterizacion.pdf).

194 Steven Grattan, 'Colombia's ex-FARC leaders admit kidnapping and other crimes', *Al Jazeera*, 30 April 2021 (https://www.aljazeera.com/news/2021/4/30/colombias-ex-farc-leaders-admit-kidnapping-and-other-crimes).

195 Frank Bajak, 'Kidnapped American Had Long Marches', *AP NEWS*, 9 August 1998, sec. Archive (https://apnews.com/article/d5958e2ab6adeffeabc76b9fe7c01043).

196 Newspaper articles claim this represented 'the first matriarchy in Latin America' and credited the mayoresses with making Tibasosa into one of the most beautiful towns in the country. But María Fernanda pointed out that they weren't elected to the position, they were appointed by Boyacá's (male) governors, perhaps even as a deliberate gimmick. As soon as Colombia switched to direct elections for mayors in the late 1980s, the Tibasosa electorate voted in a man. Finally, in 2007, a woman was elected, and another in 2019, shortly after my visit.

197 I found lots of great information about Colombian folk music to back up what Javier told me in Andrés Ramón, 'Colombian Folk Music in an International Context: An Overview' (Master of Arts in Musical Composition, Iceland Academy of the Arts, 2010), pp. 80-106 (https://skemman.is/bitstream/1946/5914/3/Lokarigerd.pdf).

198 John Dawson, 'Conifer-Broadleaf Forests - Loss of Conifer-Broadleaf Forests', in Te Ara - the Encyclopedia of New Zealand (https://teara.govt.nz/en/interactive/11674/deforestation-of-new-zealand).

199 Allan Ross Ferguson, 'Hayward Reginald Wright: Nurseryman, the Importer and Raiser of New Fruits', *Annual Journal (Royal New Zealand Institute of Horticulture)* 11 (1983): 36-56.

200 Anon., 'The Garden: The Late Mr Alexander Allison', *Manawatu Standard*, 23 September 1932, p. 4. Another later source also says Allison was the first to grow the feijoa: Anon., 'Letters from a Self-Made Nurseryman to His Son: Some Facts about Feijoas', *New Zealand Gardener*, 1946.

201 J. W. Whelan, 'Feijoa-Culture', *The Guide/Horticultural Division, NZ Dept Agriculture*, 1934.

202 Frank Bailey, 'Culture of Feijoa Trees', *New Zealand Journal of Agriculture* 84, no. 4 (1952): 291.

203 F. Sydenham, 'Culture of the Feijoa', *New Zealand Journal of Agriculture* 73, no. 5 (1946): 465.

204 K. J. Nobbs, *New Zealand's Greatest Plantsman: Hayward Reginald Wright* (K. J. Nobbs, Te Kauwhata, 1985).
205 Except where indicated otherwise, all Hayward Wright information is drawn from Allan Ross Ferguson, 'Hayward Reginald Wright: Nurseryman, the Importer and Raiser of New Fruits'.
206 'The Solomon Islands Murders', *Mercury* (Hobart), 13 November 1896, p. 4.
207 'Cosmopolitan Fruits', *Mercury* (Hobart), 12 August 1932, p. 6.
208 C. P. Gibson, 'Feijoa, or Pineapple Guava', *The Guide/Horticultural Division, NZ Dept Agriculture* 2, no. 1 (1932): 2.
209 Hayward Wright, 'Valuable Fruit: Feijoa Sellowiana', *New Zealand Herald*, 12 May 1934, p. 23.
210 Todd Niall, 'Auckland losing 1000 trees a week, properties "worth more if you bulldoze"', *Stuff*, 4 August 2021 (https://www.stuff.co.nz/environment/125949157/auckland-losing-1000-trees-a-week-properties-worth-more-if-you-bulldoze).
211 I'm grateful to Robin Bremer who showed me the former Wright property in 2018 – it had been in her family for sixty years until they had had to sell, and she was devastated at the immediate loss of so many of Hayward Wright's historic trees.
212 L. Paynter, 'Feijoa Trees', *The Guide/Horticultural Division, NZ Dept Agriculture*, 1937, p. 279.
213 Anon., 'Information Exchanged', *New Zealand Herald*, 14 May 1937, p. 4.
214 C. P. Gibson, 'Feijoa Trees', *The Guide/Horticultural Division, NZ Dept Agriculture*, 1937.
215 *Horowhenua Chronicle*, 31 July 1939, p. 6.
216 'Fruit Hedges', *Auckland Star*, 11 June 1941, p. 10.
217 FEIJOA DUMPLINGS – 6 servings
   8 oz. short pastry
   6 large feijoas
   6 dessert spoons sugar
   3/4 cup water
   ½ cup sugar
   1 oz butter
   1. Slit each feijoa lengthwise, drop in 1 dessert-spoon of sugar.
   2. Make pastry as for Apple Pie; roll into 6 ovals, place a feijoa on each, roll up, seal, place in buttered baking dish.
   3. Boil water, sugar and butter; pour while boiling over dumplings. Bake in moderate oven 350 degrees F for ¾–1 hour.
   Variation: Replace sugar in syrup with ½ cup golden syrup and add dash of cinnamon.
   From Otago University Association of Home Science Alumnae, *New Zealand Dishes and Menus* (Price Milburn, Wellington, 1960), p. 32.
218 Judith Binney, *Encircled Lands: Te Urewera, 1820–1921* (Bridget Williams Books, Wellington, 2009), p. 8.
219 Māori wardens are volunteers who act as a bridge between their communities and the police and government.
220 'The Treaty of Waitangi is New Zealand's founding document, and takes

its name from the place in the Bay of Islands where it was first signed, on 6 February 1840. This day is now a public holiday in New Zealand. The Treaty is an agreement, in Māori and English, that was made between the British Crown and about 540 Māori rangatira (chiefs).' In 1975, a commission of inquiry called the Waitangi Tribunal was created 'to investigate alleged breaches of the Treaty by the Crown. More than 2000 claims have been lodged with the tribunal, and a number of major settlements have been reached.' 'The Treaty in brief', Ministry for Culture and Heritage, updated 17 May 2017 (https://nzhistory.govt.nz/politics/treaty/the-treaty-in-brief).

221 Binney, *Encircled Lands: Te Urewera, 1820–1921*.
222 Te Urewera Act 2014, section 3(1)–(3).
223 Ibid., section 3(10).
224 Binney, *Encircled Lands: Te Urewera, 1820–1921*, p. 160.
225 Ibid., p. 213.
226 Manawa Honey NZ (https://www.manawahoney.co.nz/worlds-best-tasting-honey/).
227 Judith Binney, Gillian Chaplin and Craig Wallace, *Mihaia: The Prophet Rua Kenana and His Community at Maungapohatu* (Bridget Williams Books, Wellington, 2019), p. 12.
228 The original appears in Apirana T. Ngata, 'Nga Moteatea', *The Journal of the Polynesian Society* 65, no. 2 (1956): 182–183 (Supplement).
229 Some of the material on weeds in this chapter first appeared in a story I wrote for *New Zealand Gardener*: Kate Evans, 'New Zealand is the weediest nation on earth, and it's about to get worse', *New Zealand Gardener*, 12 June 2022 (https://www.stuff.co.nz/life-style/homed/garden/128768309/new-zealand-is-the-weediest-nation-on-earth-and-its-about-to-get-worse).
230 Kennedy Warne tells the story of Darwin's grumpy visit wonderfully in *New Zealand Geographic*: Kennedy Warne, 'Irritable in Aotearoa; Darwin & the Barbarians', *New Zealand Geographic* 95 (January–February 2009) (https://www.nzgeo.com/stories/irritable-in-aotearoa-darwin-the-barbarians/).
231 These figures are drawn from Simon Upton, 'Space invaders: A review of how New Zealand manages weeds that threaten native ecosystems' (Parliamentary Commissioner for the Environment, Wellington, November 2021) (https://pce.parliament.nz/publications/space-invaders-managing-weeds-that-threaten-native-ecosystems).
232 Helen Leach, 'Gardens without weeds? Pre-European Maori gardens and inadvertent introductions', *New Zealand Journal of Botany* 43, no. 1 (2005): 271–284, at pp. 279 and 281.
233 Robert McGowan, for the Parliamentary Commissioner for the Environment, 'Mauri tū! Mauri ora! Māori perspectives on exotic plants in Aotearoa', 15 February 2021, p. 8 (https://pce.parliament.nz/media/qotb5d2g/mcgowan-mauri-tu-mauri-ora-ma-ori-perspectives-on-exotic-plants-in-aotearoa-pdf-13mb.pdf).
234 According to a story by my sister Monica, who also went on a reporting trip

to Te Urewera, in 2018, and happened to interview Brenda: Monica Evans, 'A Māori community leans on tradition to restore its forest', *Mongabay*, 17 December 2018 (https://news.mongabay.com/2018/12/a-maori-community-leans-on-tradition-in-regaining-custody-of-its-forest/).

235 McGowan, 'Mauri tū! Mauri ora!', p. 17.

236 'An Invasive Fungus May Be The Solution in The Campaign Against Chilean Guava in A Polynesian Archipelago', *Biológicos Latam*, 28 April 2022 (https://biologicalslatam.com/issue-05/un-invasivo-hongo-puede-ser-la-solucion-en-la-campana-contra-la-guayaba-chilena-en-un-archipielago-en-medio-de-la-polinesia/).

237 Thorp and Bieleski, *Feijoas: Origins, Cultivation and Uses*.

238 Mona Mokhtari, Michael D. Jackson, Alistair S. Brown, David F. Ackerley, Nigel Ritson, Robert A. Keyzers and Andrew B. Munkacsi, 'Bioactivity-Guided Metabolite Profiling of Feijoa (*Acca sellowiana*) Cultivars Identifies 4-cyclopentene-1,3-dione as a Potent Antifungal Inhibitor of Chitin Synthesis', *Journal of Agricultural and Food Chemistry* 66, no. 22 (2018): 5531–5539 (https://doi.org/DOI: 10.1021/acs.jafc.7b06154).

239 So why the iodine superfood claims? Carolyn traced the high-iodine references back to a Russian paper, and suggested to me that the samples might have been contaminated with something else, or that units might have translated incorrectly from Russian – milligrams rather than micrograms, an enormous difference.

240 Yaoyao Peng, Karen Suzanne Bishop and Siew Young Quek, 'Extraction Optimization, Antioxidant Capacity and Phenolic Profiling of Extracts from Flesh, Peel and Whole Fruit of New Zealand Grown Feijoa Cultivars', *Antioxidants* 8, no. 5 (2019): 141 (https://doi.org/10.3390/antiox8050141).

241 Yaoyao Peng, Karen Suzanne Bishop, Lynnette Robin Ferguson and Siew Young Quek, 'Screening of Cytotoxicity and Anti-Inflammatory Properties of Feijoa Extracts Using Genetically Modified Cell Models Targeting TLR2, TLR4 and NOD2 Pathways, and the Implication for Inflammatory Bowel Disease', *Nutrients* 10, no. 9 (2018): 1188 (https://doi.org/10.3390/nu10091188).

242 I originally wrote about this visit in the June 2016 issue of *North & South* magazine (the article is no longer online).

243 Sally and Peter have since retired, and now lease the orchard out. The fruit is available at local markets every year.

244 Carolyn M. Morris, 'Yellow Power: The Role of Pineapple in New Zealand Cuisine', *The Aristologist: An Antipodean Journal of Food History* 3 (2013): 51–72.

245 Some of this material was first published in *New Zealand Geographic* in 2020: Kate Evans, 'The People's Fruit', *New Zealand Geographic* 164 (July-August 2020) (https://www.nzgeo.com/stories/the-peoples-fruit/).

246 Robin Wall Kimmerer, *Braiding Sweetgrass: Indigenous Wisdom, Scientific Knowledge, and the Teachings of Plants* (Milkweed Editions, Minneapolis, MN, 2013), p. 26.

247 A. G. Aitken and I. G. Warrington, *Fresh Facts: New Zealand Horticulture*

2020 (New Zealand Institute for Plant and Food Research Limited, Auckland, 2020).
248 Nicky Pellegrino, 'Meet the man who saved New Zealand's billion-dollar kiwifruit industry from disease', *Stuff*, 1 February 2022 (https://www.stuff.co.nz/life-style/homed/garden/127554093/meet-the-man-who-saved-new-zealands-billiondollar-kiwifruit-industry-from-disease).
249 Greg Pritchard, 'In praise of the feijoa, New Zealand's most socialist fruit', *The Spinoff*, 4 April 2017 (https://thespinoff.co.nz/society/04-04-2017/in-praise-of-the-feijoa-new-zealands-most-socialist-fruit).
250 Kimmerer, *Braiding Sweetgrass*, p. 30.
251 P. Hardy and B. Michael, 'Volatile components of *feijoa* fruits', *Phytochemistry* 9, no. 6 (1970): 1355–1357 (https://doi.org/10.1016/S0031-9422(00)85331-5).
252 Antonella Smeriglio, Marcella Denaro, Clara De Francesco, Laura Cornara, Davide Barreca, Ersilia Bellocco, Giovanna Ginestra, Giuseppina Mandalari and Domenico Trombetta, 'Feijoa Fruit Peel: Micro-morphological Features, Evaluation of Phytochemical Profile, and Biological Properties of Its Essential Oil', *Antioxidants* 8, no. 8 (2019): 320 (https://doi.org/10.3390/antiox8080320).
253 Lucille Moore, 'Orchid Fragrance Complexity as a Mechanism for Euglossine Bee Pollinator Specialization', *Writing Excellence Award Winners* (Paper 4, University of Puget Sound, 2009).
254 Alison Frontier, 'Solvent: methyl benzoate', *Not Voodoo*, University of Rochester, 2023 (http://www.chem.rochester.edu/notvoodoo/pages/sixty_solvents.php?page=methyl_benzoate).
255 Yaoyao Peng, Karen Suzanne Bishop, Jingying Zhang, Donglin Chen and Siew Young Quek, 'Characterization of phenolic compounds and aroma active compounds in feijoa juice from four New Zealand grown cultivars by LC-MS and HS-SPME-GC-O-MS', *Food Research International* 129 (2020): 108873 (https://doi.org/10.1016/j.foodres.2019.108873).
256 Jay Fielden, 'The Proust Effect', *The New Yorker*, 15 December 1996 (https://www.newyorker.com/magazine/1996/12/23/the-proust-effect).
257 Recently discovered early drafts of the novel suggest that when Proust himself actually had this experience, it was not triggered by a madeleine cake, but by a piece of toasted bread with honey! Gayil Nalls, 'Proustian Memory: Was It Really a Madeleine Tea Cake? Emblem of Olfactory Memory Called into Question', *Psychology Today*, 15 April 2016 (https://www.psychologytoday.com/nz/blog/sensoria/201604/proustian-memory-was-it-really-madeleine-tea-cake).
258 Marcel Proust, *In Search of Lost Time, Volume 1, The Way by Swann's*, Penguin Classics (2003) pp. 47-49.
259 The science of the Proust effect is drawn from my interview with Rachel Herz, as well as Rachel S. Herz, *The Scent of Desire: Discovering Our Enigmatic Sense of Smell* (HarperCollins, New York, 2008); Rachel S. Herz, 'The Role of Odor-Evoked Memory in Psychological and Physiological Health', *Brain Sciences* 6, no. 3 (2016): 22 (https://doi.org/10.3390/brainsci6030022).

260 Links to all these studies can be found in: Oliver Campbell, 'Feeling nostalgic? Your brain is hardwired to crave it', *National Geographic*, 23 July 2023, https://www.nationalgeographic.com/science/article/nostalgia-brain-science-memories

261 We were inspired by New Zealander Juliet Batten's books on celebrating seasonal rituals: Juliet Batten, *Sun, Moon, and Stars: Seasonal celebrations for children and families, tamariki and whānau* (Ishtar Books, New Zealand, 2020) and *Celebrating the Southern Seasons: Rituals for Aotearoa* (2nd edn, Random House, Auckland, 2005).

262 Tūhoe professor Rangi Matāmua (a cousin of Joe McLeod's) was instrumental in campaigning for the holiday – the first time an Indigenous celebration has been put back on the national calendar in any colonised country. Nic Low, 'Matariki Rising', *New Zealand Geographic* 176 (July-August 2022) (https://www.nzgeo.com/stories/matariki-rising/).

263 Ngāi Tahu writer Nic Low explains the concept of tūrangawaewae beautifully here: Nic Low, 'A Place to Stand', *New Zealand Geographic* 181 (May-June 2023) (https://www.nzgeo.com/stories/a-place-to-stand/).

264 Alex Calder, *The Settler's Plot: How Stories Take Place in New Zealand* (Auckland University Press, Auckland, 2011), p. 5.

265 Kimmerer, *Braiding Sweetgrass*, p. 207.

266 Ibid., p 213.

267 Ibid., p. 215.

268 Folk on Foot is the creation of British broadcaster Matthew Bannister. It is very restful, and was the only thing I could cope with listening to when bedridden with Covid-19 in 2022 (https://www.folkonfoot.com/).

269 'CYNEFIN' (https://cynefinmusic.wales/en/about).

270 Owen Shiers, 'Welsh Keywords: Cynefin', *Planet* 249 (2023) (https://www.planetmagazine.org.uk/planet-online/249/owen-shiers).

271 Martin Shaw, *Scatterlings: Getting Claimed in the Age of Amnesia* (White Cloud Press, Ashland, OR, 2016).

272 MOVIMIENTO
Composed by JORGE ABNER DREXLER
© 2017 WARNER CHAPPELL MUSIC SPAIN S A (SGAE)
All Rights on behalf of WARNER CHAPPELL MUSIC SPAIN SA
   Administered by WC MUSIC CORP.
All Rights Reserved
Used by Permission of ALFRED MUSIC
I'm grateful to Juan Otálora Villamil, the feijoa scientist from Brazil who took me to the Carnaval party, who first shared this song with me.

273 Whales became fully aquatic around 40 million years ago, and *Hesperocyon*, the first common ancestor of the canids – dogs, foxes and wolves – also appeared around 40 million years ago. Bob Strauss, '40 Million Years of Dog Evolution', *ThoughtCo*, 17 August 2019 (thoughtco.com/prehistoric-dogs-1093301); Michael Marshall, 'Timeline: The evolution of life', *New Scientist*, 14 July 2009 (https://www.newscientist.com/article/dn17453-timeline-the-evolution-of-life/).

Acknowledgements

So many people helped this book to grow from the tiniest seedling of an idea into the bushy, branching tree it has become. Dozens of feijoa-lovers all around the world took me into their homes and lives, endured my many questions and generously shared their obsessions with me. Scientists patiently explained all sorts of niche things to me. My life is richer for knowing them all, and their names and stories fill the pages of this book.

Creative New Zealand and the Winston Churchill Memorial Trust both backed this idea long before I had a publisher, and their grants covered my research trips to Brazil, Colombia, France and Germany and a little of the writing time. This book would not have happened without them. Thanks also to Akatea Hill near Raglan for the writing solitude.

From the publishing industry – a whole new confusing world – Robbie Burton and Jeremy Sherlock gave me crucial initial encouragement. Editors Kimberley Davis in New Zealand and Amber Dance in the United States provided valuable early feedback and developmental advice. In the United Kingdom, Beth Kempton and the other writers who took her masterclass with me helped to shape my book proposal.

I did not choose my literary agent, Kate Evans from Peters Fraser + Dunlop, because we have the exact same name – yes, I know, it's wild – but for her editorial insights and her passion for the book and my work. I look forward to drinking feijoa cocktails together one day.

Kate Stephenson from Hachette Aotearoa never wavered in her commitment to *Feijoa*. She made it better, and I'm absolutely thrilled the book found a home at Moa Press. It's been a joy working with Kate, Dom Visini and the rest of the team at Moa Press to bring it to life.

My Patreon patrons gave me income, accountability and encouragement at critical moments during the writing: especially Roger Matthews (the president of the NZ Feijoa Growers Association), Stephen FitzHerbert (who introduced me to both 8Wired's epic feijoa sour ale and Carolyn Morris), my sister-outlaw Anna Marshall and my cousin Taimus Werner-Gibbings, Beth Colbert Moline and Perry Webb in Oregon, Andrew McKenzie, Tania O'Brien, Natalie Reeve, Shane Bilish, Sariah Wilson, Suz Burgess, Janine Ryan, Joan Valentine, Peter Bell, Tony Meyer, Sophie Gladwell, Vivienne Nunis, Meredith Youngson, Latesha Randall, Kelly Paddison, Sarah-Jane O'Connor, Anke Richter, Naomi Arnold, Kirsty Johnston, Mark Crysell and Briar McCormack, Tureya Healey-Diaz and Xavia Healey-Diaz, Allison Bodznick, Althea Willans, the de Jong family at Southern Belle Orchard and my treasured friend Ruby Watson, who also contributed the stunning feijoa illustrations that have made this book even more beautiful.

Peter Gordon has supported this book in numerous ways from the moment he heard about it. My friends Jeremy, Anke, Veronika and Salomé helped with translations from Portuguese, German and French. New Zealand Geographic friends and colleagues Rebekah White and Nic Low provided invaluable feedback on various chapters and drafts, as did my sisters Monica and Tessa – two of my favourite people on this Earth.

Thank you to Manu, for sharing my love of fruit trees while also actually knowing how to plant and take care of them, and to Aran Taylor, my high-school history and classics teacher who ignited my love of long-ago worlds and first introduced me to the story of Rua Kenana – via spirited classroom re-enactments of his trial.

For moral support, thanks to the friends I've known since Mr Taylor's history classes – Sophie, Ruby, Kelly and Xavia – for sharing the obsession and the bottles of feijoa wine. To my Raglan crew, particularly Rata, Belinda, and my ~~food~~ book club. And to my Raft of Bitches – Anke, Michelle, Kirsty and Naomi – writers all, and the best damn group chat I can imagine.

Three beloved and influential women in my life died before I'd quite reached the finish line: my grandmother Marie Gibbings, my ABC boss and mentor Patricia Barraclough and my Italian host mother Carla Ricci. I'll always hold you in my heart. And for nearly a decade, I enjoyed corresponding with Californian feijoa expert Mark Albert over our shared obsession. I'm saddened he never got a chance to see this book, but I hope I've captured something of his spirit.

My amazing outlaws, Jen and Dave, have been ardent supporters of this book from the beginning. They contributed in so many ways, including introducing me to many inspiring works of nature writing that helped me see what form *Feijoa* might take.

To my parents, Susan and Jo, thank you for planting that feijoa hedge, for fostering the wide-ranging curiosity that led to this book, and for providing a warm and loving home I feel connected to wherever I am in the world – while also encouraging my independence and wanderlust. We don't say this often, but I love you very much.

Finally, thank you to my beloved kids, Amalia and Indigo, for sharing my love of both feijoas and stories, and to Sam, my love, my partner in everything, who took care of the hearth while I went out into the wild, and who knew long before I did that I could pull this whole thing off.